SIT
STAY
HEAL

HOW AN UNDERACHIEVING LABRADOR
WON OUR HEARTS AND BROUGHT US TOGETHER

MEL C. MISKIMEN

Published by Sourcebooks, Inc.
P.O. Box 4410, Naperville, Illinois 60567-4410
(630) 961-3900
Fax: (630) 961-2168
www.sourcebooks.com

Library of Congress Cataloging-in-Publication data is on file with the publisher.

Printed and bound in the United States of America.
VP 10 9 8 7 6 5 4 3 2

For my father, Markie Good Guy,
and his lovely wife, Old What's-Her-Name.

INTRODUCTION

My father cupped his hands to his mouth and yelled, "Blow. Your. Whistle!"

Was I supposed to blow a short toot from the whistle made out of a deer antler that hung from a lanyard around my neck? Or a toot, to-ooot?

He was on the opposite side of a muddy pond. I stood on the other side and wondered if that tickling sensation coming from my leg was indeed a tick. I bent over to look and was immediately reprimanded. "Pay attention to your dog!"

My seven-year-old black Lab, Seamus, was swimming back toward me with a white rubber training dummy in his mouth. He was a high-octane kind of Lab in need of a regular outlet for his relentless retrieving urges that I had thought I'd gotten a handle on. He had ample opportunities—getting the newspaper, bringing me my shoes, finding the errant dirty sock, and stealthily removing my just-washed-and-hung-on-the-line bedding from the laundry basket one piece at a time. But, judging by the way he longingly looked at the TV dogs on Animal Planet bounding into lakes, carrying dead ducks in their mouths, I'd say I had been in denial.

I had no clue what to do with him. I didn't hunt. I really didn't care if my dog had what my father called a "hard mouth," meaning he tended to chomp and chew on the thing he had stolen from my closet, nor did I care whether or not I had lived up to his expectations of what a pack leader should be. Seamus rolled his eyes at me whenever we were around other dogs, so expectations not met.

My father cupped his hands to his mouth again and repeated the command: "Blow. Your. *Whistle!*"

I put it in my mouth and gave it what I thought was a good, loud enough toot, so Seamus would hear it and somehow know what it meant. And what did it mean again? Come back? Turn? Stop? If I didn't know, how could I expect the dog to know? Um…because don't dogs just know these things? Like how the car ride to the beach was different from the car ride to the vet?

Seamus was still on course. I was still worried about that alleged tick.

I loved the outdoors as much as my father did—well, maybe not *that* much. My definition of spending time outside with the dog involved sitting on the patio, sipping a smoothie while Seamus busied himself with a stick, gnawing it like I had done in third grade with my number-two pencil. Once the temperatures dropped to freezing, I preferred the comforts of a cabin with indoor plumbing rather than my father's choice of a tent and a sleeping bag. And I liked to start my day in dry clothes and end the day in dry clothes and not have one side soaking wet from dog shake-off spray.

My father speaks fluent retriever. His dogs win trophies, ribbons, certificates. His current dog—a fourteen-year-old springer spaniel named Mugsy, now retired—reached the pinnacle of the dog-retrieving world and earned the title of Master Hunting Dog Excellent, which in the field-trial world is kind of a big deal. So, yeah. He knows his stuff. My father is also a retired cop. He commands. He takes charge. Of course he would know how to blow a whistle.

Seamus trotted up the slippery bank with the dummy clenched in his mouth, gave me a dismissive sideways glance, and ran off with it into the high grass. My father shook his head in disgust. Why had I insisted on this Dad-and-dog-with-a-dummy-in-his-mouth bonding? Because, after my mother died…I thought it would help.

CHAPTER ONE

THE INCREDIBLE SHRINKING BRAIN

Since Labor Day, my eighty-three-year-old mother's health had been fading. Tests revealed no cancers; all systems were operating as expected for a woman of her age. Although apparently her brain was shrinking—something everyone's brains do, according to the doctor, which was comforting to me in a very uncomfortable way.

I was at that empty-nester-with-aging-parents stage in life. Both of my children—a daughter, Caitlin, and son, Angus—lived a one-and-a-half-hour bus ride away in Madison, Wisconsin. Caitlin is the oldest. She has a master's degree in journalism and is well on her way to a PhD. She is blond, witty, beautiful, and just happens to be the commissioner of her fantasy football league. Angus is four years younger and charming, handsome, thoughtful, and caring. He can't watch any movie with a dog in it unless he knows ahead of time whether or not the dog dies. As their mother, I am required to love them, but more importantly, I really, really *like* them. I am their Facebook friend with a caveat—I cannot post any comments.

The only people left rattling around in my household were myself and my patient husband, Mark, whom I met in a bar on a cold November night in the big-haired 1980s. He had the best pickup line in the history of pickup lines. I was alone. He was alone. He walked up to my bar stool and said, "Mind if I ask you a question?"

"Sure," I said.

"Um…by any chance did you go to an all-girls Catholic high school?"

I did not know how to answer this, because, yes, I had gone to an all-girls Catholic high school.

"You just have an aura," he said.

"Plaid and pleated?" I said.

Besides Mark, the only other life-form occupying our domicile after the kids left was our seven-year-old black Lab, Seamus.

Officially, he is an American Field Lab. He is stocky, built lower to the ground than other black Labs. His paws are the size of paddles. His tail can clear a coffee table set for an afternoon of football watching— bowls of chips, dips, and salsas swiped onto the carpet with one wag. He couldn't care less about the score because he's too busy licking the residue from the carpet fibers.

During the months when my mother's condition deteriorated, one of the things I needed Mark, Caitlin, and Angus for most was to vent— about my sister's lack of empathy, about the toll it was taking on my father, and about my feelings of helplessness, anger, and frustration. I wasn't looking for answers from them. Their nods, hugs, and shoulder squeezes shored up my weakening walls of courage. Seamus offered me his big, boxy head to pet, his muzzle to nuzzle, and his brown-eyed, I'm-here-for-you stare. He didn't ask me for anything in return other than food and a grassy patch to pee and poop on.

By Thanksgiving, my mother needed a cane. She couldn't remember what day it was or whether or not I had just been there to organize her knitting bag, but she could still converse about the current political climate. How was this possible?

At Christmas, she needed a walker, was a lot quieter, was more difficult to engage in conversations, and would only eat pudding. She spent her post-holiday days sitting on the sofa, staring out the picture window, waiting for the goldfinches to return to her bird feeder.

Dad had called me one day to come over and "Mom-sit." He needed to go to Sam's Club because they only had fourteen packages of toilet paper left and, after five years, had finally finished the five-gallon drum of dill pickles.

She seemed on edge.

"A bird hit the window," she said, a tinge of panic in her voice. "You know what that means?"

"Oh, yeah. That happens," I said.

"It was a goldfinch. You know how much I like my finches."

"Mom. It was just a bird. Flying into a window," I said, trying to convince myself of its insignificance.

"A cardinal hit it, and then…my sister Ellen died."

"Mom, she was ninety and had a stroke."

"Right before my sister Jane died? A robin."

"Mom, she was eighty-five and had heart failure."

She shook her head. "No. No. A goldfinch… I'm next."

I sat there with her, looking through a smudge of yellow feathers stuck on the picture window, hoping the old wives' tale had nothing to do with another aging wife.

My parents were from the generation of Tojo and Hitler. Ration books and big bands. They met when they were twelve. My father stole her mitten during a raucous game of "girl tag"—to be "safe" you had to hold on to a girl—on the frozen lagoon in Kosciuszko Park. They grew up a few blocks from each other, in the same working-class Milwaukee neighborhood. My father's family was considered

3

by my grandmother to be affluent, high-society Polish (they had a car and a telephone!). My mother's family was considered (again, just by my grandmother) to be low class, subpar, and unsuitable. They had no car. No phone. No central heat. They lived in a rented basement. The worst part? My mother was *Irish*. My parents married in 1950, and they still lived in the same house they bought back in 1955 and decorated in a midcentury interpretation of Early American—a lot of plaid upholstery, braided rugs, and knotty pine. My mother never wanted to trade up to a bigger, better house. To her, a two-bedroom, one-bathroom ranch with a rec room in the basement equaled a palatial estate.

She didn't play tennis or golf; her sports were vacuuming and folding laundry. Her biceps and triceps were developed from carrying baskets heaped full of our dirty clothes into the basement, then lifting the load of wet shirts and bedding up the steps to hang out on the wash line. She was the one who taught me how to fold a fitted sheet, that rayon is made from cellulose fibers, and how to use a press cloth to iron the pleats in my wool high school uniform skirt.

But as she got older, Dad had to assume more and more of the housekeeping duties because she couldn't manage the climb down (or back up) the steep basement stairs to do the laundry. She didn't have the arm strength to operate her Oreck. She kept forgetting about her coffee in the microwave and whether she had turned off the burner on the gas stove. I would call my dad to see if he needed any help or how that particular day had gone, and he would answer in the just-the-facts-ma'am style he picked up from his career as a cop: "Nobody fell down. Nobody threw up. Nobody crapped their pants."

In other words, a good day.

Dad had been a Milwaukee police officer for close to forty years. He'd walked a beat. Drove an ambulance back when an ambulance was pretty much two cops driving a modified station wagon with a gurney in the back. In 1958, he was young and blond, perfect for working undercover on the vice squad. Doing what, he never said. I had found out a couple of Thanksgivings ago, when he and my mother brought the dinner rolls, apple pie, and a large cardboard box full of blurry carbon copies of his police reports. The turkey was dry that year, because I was in the kitchen reading about my father as bait for hookers and perverted men in public toilets, and that left a bad taste in my mouth.

He'd had run-ins with organized crime that involved threats on his and our lives—we'd had a twenty-four-hour watch put on our house during a particularly sensitive investigation. He was made sergeant in the middle of the civil unrest of the late 1960s—it was tough on teen-aged me and my sister, when our dad was the Man. When I was in college, he was a member of the tactical unit and rode around the city in an unmarked squad that didn't fool anyone. Why else would four burly white men wearing nylon jackets be in a black sedan with no hubcaps? His final stint was as the firearms instructor for the police academy— the only time in his forty years he had a regular nine-to-five shift with weekends off, and the only time my mother got a good night's sleep.

Retirement had given him the time to spend doing what he loved—hunting and fishing—with the two loves of his life, his dog and my mother. He had started deer hunting when he was a smart-alecky youth back in the early 1940s. I have a favorite picture of him taken on his first hunting excursion. If I had to pick one, out of the hundreds of photos stashed in boxes, books, and drawers, that defines who my father is, I would choose this one. Another would be the one taken of him on his beat, in uniform, smiling with a bunch of *West Side Story* Jets and Sharks types.

The farm scene is of the dusty backyard of a farmhouse right out of *The Grapes of Wrath*. A ten-point buck is strung up on the windmill, another draped over the hood of a 1939 Ford. There are four men in plaid mackinaws with Stormy Kromer caps, the kind that Elmer Fudd wore when he went "hunting wabbits." My father is jacketless, his flannel shirt collar popped up and out of a ragged sweatshirt. His pants have holes, his blond hair sticks out from under a knit hat, his boots are caked with mud. He is copping an attitude with a rifle propped up by his side and one of the scruffy farm dogs at his heels.

Duck hunting hadn't been part of his early outdoor repertoire because for that he needed a trained dog, and he didn't have the time to train one, nor did he have the right kind of dog. Growing up, he had mostly mutts, strays that followed him home. When he was in his forties, he bought himself a springer spaniel and joined a kennel club with acres of fields and ponds, a place where he could learn all things retriever.

He didn't miss an opportunity to sit in a damp duck blind or on a cold stump waiting for that trophy buck that never crossed his crosshairs. Never. Not even when *his* mother's health was deteriorating or that time when our little nuclear family was being blown apart by my sister's second in a series of divorces.

But my mother's decline had put the brakes on Dad's dog days— his five, six hours spent walking up and down fields, a shotgun slung over his shoulder, up to his Wellingtons in muck, while his dog did what he had trained it to do, retrieve felled fowl. How long had it been since he'd been able to go out to the kennel club? Gone duck hunting? Deer hunting? A year? Two? I offered to stay with my mother for an afternoon, maybe even overnight, if he wanted to go run his dog, get some air, or shoot things. But he wouldn't. He couldn't. "What if something were to happen? I'd be hours away, and besides there's no cell phone reception in the duck blind or the deer stand."

After Easter, Mom was hospitalized because she'd become weak and dehydrated. We were under the impression that all she needed was fluids and she'd be right as rain. Wrong. Turned out that fluids were the problem. Normal pressure hydrocephalus was the diagnosis. It meant her spinal fluid was filling in the space around her shrinking brain; perhaps it was the reason for her not-Alzheimer's dementia, her incontinence, her issues with balance?

There was a solution, in the form of a surgically implanted shunt that would redirect the buildup. The doctors told us that, yes, it could help, but we shouldn't expect her to jump off the operating table and do the polka. One night over pizza, my father; my older sister, Linda; and I weighed the pros and cons of shunting.

"I don't know, Dad. She is eighty-three…but I suppose… I mean, if the doctors didn't think she was a good candidate, they wouldn't have recommended it, right?" I said.

"I want green peppers," Linda said.

"No onions for me," he said. The multiple-pierced, neck-tattooed server named "Wait Ress" scribbled our order on her curling pad of paper, then grabbed the poster-sized, laminated menus from our hands. "It'll be a coupla minutes," she said.

We sat there, silent for a while. I was thinking about what life was going to be like from here on out, wondering if my father would be able to manage. And if he wasn't, there'd have to be in-home care people or maybe a hospital bed in the living room, where the Christmas tree usually went. Either that or we'd have Christmas in the nursing home because that's where she'd be. All three scenarios sucked.

"Say we do the shunting thing," I said, "and she can't come home unless—" The waitress brought us a red plastic basket full of bread and shiny packets of butter.

"Unless what?" My father unwrapped his utensils from the paper napkin.

"You retrofit the house. You know, ramps?"

"Then I'll build a ramp!" he said.

"You will not!" my sister said. "Not with *your* knees!" Oh, *now* she was concerned about his knees? What about three weeks ago when she wanted him to install a wood floor in her kitchen?

The pat of butter he had selected was frozen. His efforts to spread it turned his bread into gaping holes held together by a crust.

"What if"—I hated to say it, but someone had to—"the shunting doesn't work? Then what?"

"Well, aren't you a vision of doom and gloom?" Linda fared better with her butter. She had taken two pats and put them down the front of her shirt to warm them.

My father sighed, shrugged his shoulders.

"If…I don't do anything"—he ripped the paper off of his straw before he took a swig of water from the red plastic tumbler—"I'll kick myself in the ass for not trying."

The pizza came, but I couldn't eat it. My father stared at the pizza covered in bubbling cheese, sausage, mushroom, green pepper, and olives. He couldn't eat either.

"I'm starved!" my sister said and lifted a big piece onto her plate. I needed Wait Ress to bring me a container for my leftovers. Seamus would be eating cold pizza tonight.

CHAPTER TWO

THE SHUNTING

Surgery was scheduled for that Sunday, a.k.a. Shuntday. I didn't go into Mom's room to see her before she was wheeled away because I felt like she and my father needed to say things to each other, personal things that would have made me feel like I was intruding. Plus, I knew she wouldn't have her teeth in, and she was very sensitive about that.

I had found out she had dentures only three years earlier, when I took her for an MRI and had to help her fill out the standard preprocedure intake treatise.

"Mom? Are you allergic to iodine?"

"Yes."

"Really?"

"Yes."

I checked the box.

"Do you have any implants?"

"Implants?"

"Yeah, you know, hips, knees—"

"Oh, I thought you meant breasts!"

"Do you?"

"No!"

I checked the box.

"No partials or bridgework or dentures, right?" She got a funny look. I'd seen it before on my son when he was nine and I'd found out he changed his religion grade from a D to a B. I had given him three chances to come clean, but he'd denied me three times.

"Mom? Dental work?"

"Um…yes."

"Like a crown? A bridge?"

"No. More like uppers and lowers."

"Dentures?!"

"Yes." She shushed me.

"When did you get dentures?"

"Oh…when…I was…twenty-one. I had such bad teeth."

"Why didn't you just get braces?"

"I couldn't afford braces! And I was getting married and wanted to look my best, so I went to the dentist and he said the only thing he could do was to pull them." Over the course of my twenty-three years living under the same one-bathroom roof, I had never seen anything that might indicate she had false teeth. No cups. No cleaners. No special toothpaste. I was as shocked as she had been the day I'd come home from grade school and told her that I had learned in history class that FDR couldn't walk. The technician came and wheeled her away for the MRI, and I thought, *What* else *don't I know about her?*

The shunting procedure would take forty-five minutes. My father, my niece Amanda—who was there as a stand-in for my sister—and I sat together in the family waiting room. My father was upbeat. "I heard of a guy whose brother had the same thing—"

"Oh?" I said.

"—and he lived another twenty years!"

Did it surprise me that my sister wasn't there? Yes. And no. She hadn't been coming around, to the house or to the hospital… I think she was mad. At Mom. For not watching any of the *Sit and Be Fit* DVDs or using the large rubber exercise bands Linda had been buying her for the past few birthdays and Christmases. My mother would open a gift from my sister and look more confused than she normally did. Linda would offer an explanation in a loud voice, like an obnoxious American in a foreign country: "They're rubber bands! FOR. YOUR. LEGS! If you don't *use* these, you will *fall* and break a hip…and WE WILL HAVE TO SHOOT YOU."

My father hastily flipped through a *Better Homes and Gardens* magazine from 1999, turning the pages with a distracted forcefulness. "By the way, where the hell is your sister?"

Amanda explained that her mother had to work, that she really had tried to take the day off but couldn't because she (Linda) was the only one who could open the theater lobby door and work the popcorn machine.

The surgeon poked his head into the room and said everything had gone "textbook." Mom would be in recovery for the next couple of hours. My father discarded the magazine he hadn't been reading and looked relieved. He said there was no reason for me to stay. I insisted. He insisted I should go. I insisted I should stay. He insisted I should go. So I left. I phoned my sister from the car.

"Hey, it's me," I said.

"Uh-oh. What?" She sounded like she was in the middle of something. I hoped it was important.

"Mom's out of surgery. It went well. Dad is still there. Amanda and I left… Oh, and one more thing—Dad thinks that you don't give a shit about Mom."

"What?!" She dropped the phone.

"He wanted to know why you haven't been to the hospital."

I heard her sigh. She knew she was in the wrong. I knew I was in the right. It felt good. On the sibling rivalry scorecard, she was the Daughter Who Didn't Love Her Mother Enough and Deserved Nothing, and I was the Daughter Who Cared.

"I-I...you know it's ha-ard!" she whined.

"I know it's hard! Man up! Get your ass over there!"

I went to the hospital the next day, hoping to see my mother sitting up, watching *Andy Griffith*. But when I walked into the hospital room, Mom was asleep. It was hard to tell where the white sheets ended and she began. I saw something small and yellow on her faintly moving chest. It was a Post-it note.

I was here. You were sleeping. L.

Six days post-shunting, she still couldn't stand or walk, but she was stable, had a better appetite, and her vitals were good. There was no reason she needed to be in the hospital. Next stop? Rehab.

She had a nice room with a window and a roommate named Helen whose son my father had worked with on the police force. A good sign. The nursing staff was caring and attentive. How long Mom would be there was up to her. Her ticket out of rehab? Standing. Not even walking. Standing. But from what I had seen, the equipment and the amount of burly staff it took to get her in and out of her bed, then into a chair, and how exhausted she looked, standing was a long way off.

Insurance would only cover a thirty-day stay, and then Medicare would kick in, but only for so long. After that, the financial burden would fall to my father, and while we hadn't come to that road, he had mentally gone ahead to scout it. How was he going to manage $700 a week on his policeman's pension?

"I'll have to sell some rifles, I guess."

He kept his Winchester twelve-gauge shotgun and the lever-action rifle and the carbine from World War II locked inside a walnut-and-glass gun cabinet. My mother had bought the cabinet for his sixtieth birthday. She chose it because of the images of springer spaniels flushing game on the sides and bottom panels. His police service revolver—a pearl-handled Smith and Wesson six-shooter that I used to watch him take apart and clean on the kitchen table—hung on a hook in the back.

The guns were supposed to be handed down to his grandsons, who didn't hunt, but they met the one important Dad criterion—they were men.

"Or maybe the boat?" Dad suggested.

No. Not the boat!

He had always wanted a boat, but every time he came close to having the money, something always came up, like braces for my teeth or sending my sister and me to an all-girl Catholic high school or the summer of 1969, when my sister got on her boyfriend's motorcycle, revved it up, and crashed through the back of the garage, ripping a large hole in the wall and her leg.

After making do with hand-me-down aluminum boats that came without motors and trailers, he finally had the boat of his dreams, a sixteen-foot fiberglass with a fifty-horsepower outboard motor, a trolling motor, a fish locator with GPS and a "man overboard" feature, a live well, padded seats with lumbar support that swiveled, and a broad, blunt, carpeted bow, so the dog wouldn't slip jumping into the lake for ducks. He had used it for almost twenty years, and it was still showroom shiny.

"I could part with a couple fishing rods. Maybe some lures. Hey, I've had some since the forties. They gotta be worth something!"

Not the rods! The reels! That would be like he was cutting off a limb.

If I were the health insurance companies, I couldn't live with myself knowing that some guy in Milwaukee was selling his prized possessions to pay for his wife's hospital and rehab stays. How can the healthcare system live with itself?

But I wouldn't be able to talk him out of it. Of course he'd sell his stuff. That's all it was to him—stuff. It was all about Mom. Marian. That's how he rolled. Standing there in front of the nurses' station, hearing him make small (to him) sacrifices for her? He went from my ordinary, everyday hero to super-duper megahero.

I knew if *she* knew that he was even *thinking* of selling his boat, guns, rods, reels, and lures, all because of her, she wouldn't have been able to live with herself.

I spent the rest of the afternoon with Mom, catching up on her progress, or lack of progress, then drove two hours from Milwaukee to Madison to pick up my son, so he could visit his grandmother the next day, eat our food, and do his laundry.

When I got home, I took off my jacket, kicked off my clogs, and had just settled in with a fish-bowl-sized glass of Pinot that my husband had waiting for me, and that's when the phone rang.

The caller ID said "Wheaton Franciscan."

Why did I have that acidic burning sensation in my stomach? It could be something. Or nothing. Or my mother. She had called me the other night.

"Hello? Who is this?" she had said.

"Mom, you called *me*."

"Oh. I must have dialed the wrong number. I meant to call my sister, Ellen."

We had a short conversation about shoes, how she wanted go shopping at Schuster's. I did not remind her that Ellen was dead or that Schuster's had gone out of business fifty years ago.

I picked up the receiver. The voice on the other end was garbled. I thought it was a butt dial. "It's—it's Mom... She's...in cardiac arrest. They're working on her. Oh God...oh *God*."

At first, I didn't recognize my father's voice; it was strained, small, strangled.

I can't remember putting on shoes. Did Seamus bring them to me? Or a jacket. I hated driving at night. Driving at night when it was raining—and when I was in a panic—was even worse. I went through a few stop signs, didn't quite wait for the red lights to turn green. I hit the curb as I made a sharp turn into the parking lot. The fire department truck was there, and knowing it was for my mother made it look bigger, the lights brighter, the motor louder.

The front doors to the rehab center were locked. Should I go to the back? Pound on them? Where was the little, gray-haired lady, with the reading glasses on a flowery chain, who always made me sign in? There was a beige phone next to an intercom. The calm recorded voice told me to push the button and dial nine and wait for someone to pick up. I pushed. I dialed. No one picked up.

"Come on! Pick up!"

I pushed the button. Again. I dialed nine. Again. No one picked up.

"Jesus Christ! My mother is *dying*!" I yelled. I heard a click.

I didn't wait for both sliding doors to open all the way. I ran through the lobby that I had just walked out of hours earlier, toward the bank of elevators, got in, pushed two, and took the world's slowest elevator up to the second floor.

He was sitting in a chair, in the dimly lit dining room, where I had sat with my mother and listened while she complained about being cold. "Eat some soup," I had said.

A paramedic was holding my dad's shaking shoulders, talking to him man-to-man, EMT to retired cop. Before now, I had only seen my father choke up one time, at the end of *Saving Private Ryan*.

What did the EMT mean, she died from cardiac arrest? So…nothing to do with the shunt?

Five hours ago, I had told her I'd see her tomorrow. That Angus would be here. She was looking forward to seeing him. I was informed by the night nurse that her last moments on earth had been with Dad, eating frozen custard while watching a Fred Astaire and Ginger Rogers movie on the portable DVD player my sister had bought her. Seemed kind of perfect.

His years on the police force taught my dad to be in control of uncontrollable situations—riots, mobs, fracases. In 1964, he worked crowd control for the Beatles, and when their limo driver turned right instead of the prearranged and barricaded left, hundreds of girls mobbed the car, and my father had to peel them off the hood, the roof, the trunk. How many people can say their father saw fear in the eyes of John Lennon? But now? He was caught unprepared, and that was a state he never ever expected to be a citizen of.

I would have bet that he'd have been the one to die first. Not her. Think of it—his job involved bad guys with guns and grudges. His recreational sporting activities involved bullets. He sometimes engaged in risky behavior with unsteady ladders, heights, tree limbs, and pissed off wildlife.

If Dad had gone first and left Linda and me to deal with Mom, it would have been easier for all of us. Sure, she'd probably become über dependent, and there would be issues about nursing homes versus assisted living, but she was trainable. Dad, on the other hand, was a stubborn old dog, set in his ways, hewn from a rough log with a dull knife. How was I going to smooth out his edges?

I stood in the hallway, getting in the way. The EMTs told me they had worked on her for ten minutes, couldn't get a pulse. They had to call it. I peeked into the room, not really wanting to go inside, and saw my sister amidst the personnel. She came out of the room and ushered me into the lobby, past my weeping father.

"Just so you know, I cut off some of her hair," she said. "I went in there. She still had the tube in her mouth—oh, and I've got her teeth." She produced Mom's smile from her pocket. Besides thinking about how my sister, who had a problem with hospital visits, did not have an issue with seeing Mom's body on the floor or about retrieving her teeth or hair, I thought, *now what?*

I had to talk to the medical examiner, who had phoned and wanted to know the cause of death. Wasn't that her job? I had the nurse call the parish priest. I thought he should be notified and would want come out to be with my father, but he felt there was no need.

"She had that all taken care of."

She had *what* all taken care of?

The undertaker materialized from a darkened hallway with a gurney. He had two black eyes and an *X* made out of bandages on his forehead, the kind of details that my mom, had she been me, would have relayed: "And the mortician had *two* black eyes!" He wanted to know if we were thinking cremation.

We weren't.

A crypt?

Hadn't thought about it.

Did we have a plot?

No, no plot. A couple of years ago, my father told my sister and I that, upon his demise, we were to have him cremated, then loaded into shotgun shells and blasted out and over the puppy pond at the kennel club. We had never discussed what to do with Mother.

"I don't want her in the ground, where dogs can pee on her," my father said in between sobs.

"I guess we're going crypt," I said.

My father's head hung low on his chest, his eyes puffy. He was a man in need of a hug, but he wasn't a hugging kind of guy and, consequently, we're not a hugging kind of family. He showed us affection with a pat on the back, a muss of the hair, a squeeze of a shoulder. Twenty-some years ago, I was going in for a lumpectomy on my left breast, and my husband and I had just been over to my parents' for dinner, and as we were leaving, my dad came outside on the back step and yelled, "Hey! Good luck with that, uh, thing!"

Of all the uncertainties that a life post-mother would be, one thing was for certain—it was going to be messy. I didn't like mess. Neither did my father. We liked our lives organized: the bath towels folded on the shelves with the folds facing out, life events color coded, the spice rack alphabetized, emotions in check.

I couldn't tell you who came to pay their respects at the funeral, if or what I ate at the luncheon afterward… I do remember coming home, weighed down with a heavy, palpable pull of sadness. I felt lost. Where was up? Which way was north? My son and daughter returned to their lives. My husband went back to work. Oh, how I envied them! How nice it must be to worry about other things, like Caitlin and her postgraduate thesis or which bike helmets my son Angus needed to reorder and restock.

Before Mom died, we all knew what our roles were. She was the able-bodied assistant who carried out my father's instructions. He was the alpha-dog pack leader. Me? Comic relief. Linda? The crazy one. What were our roles, now? Was he still capable of being the alpha dog, even if his pack was down by one? How could I become both comic relief and able-bodied assistant?

Those days after the funeral, after the out-of-town relatives left, I took to my bed. Seamus would trot upstairs and plop down next to it and wait for a clump of damp Kleenex to fall. Sometimes I would crawl out from under the covers and lay next to him on the carpet, comforted by the smell of his doggy breath. When I could talk, I would. To him. He was a very good listener.

"This sucks." I was on the dog-haired rug, lying on my side. "Somebody needs to clean this place. Seamus, go get the vacuum cleaner."

He thumped his tail and lay next to me, while I sobbed, "I miss my mother!" I rolled onto my back; he put his head on my chest. He thumped his tail again. Two thumps. I started to cry. Seamus wriggled his face closer to mine and licked the tears from my cheeks.

CHAPTER THREE

CALL WAITING

İᴛ ʜᴀᴅ ʙᴇᴇɴ ᴀ week since I had spoken to anyone other than my husband and Seamus. Should I call my father? Or should I wait until he calls me? He was never one for calling, other than to pass on head counts, ETAs, test results. Calling just to gab was my mother's MO. When I would call to talk to my mother and Dad answered, our conversation went something like:

Him:	Hello?
Me:	Hi!
Him:	Here's your mother…

She had always been a phone call or a ten-minute drive away.

"Mom? Can I use hydrogen peroxide instead of bleach in the washer?"

"Yes."

"Mom? Is it feed a fever, starve a cold, or the other way 'round?"

"Feed a cold. Starve a fever."

"How many teaspoons are in one tablespoon?"

"Three."

She was Google before there was Google. She was the sender of cards. The one who always called to thank me for the dinner, the present, or just the time spent with her. She had taught me that the red dot in the middle of Queen Anne's lace was the ruby, how to match plaids when sewing a skirt, how to worry. And I was. Worrying. About my father. What was he up to? Did he need someone to talk to? Would he sink into despair? Should I leave him alone in his corner, to lick his wounds? I couldn't *not* call, right? If he didn't want to talk, well, he'd give me some reason why. Or he wouldn't answer, and then I would be worried that he was lying on the kitchen floor, dead from a self-inflicted gunshot wound.

I phoned. One ring. Two. Three. Five. One more and it would go to his answering machine and I'd have to leave a message about… But he picked up.

"Hello?" he said.

"Hi, Dad. How's…things?"

Silence, then a sniff.

"Dad? So…how are you?"

Silence, then a blowing of his nose.

"Dad?"

"Fine. I'm…fine."

His voice was reedy. His throat crackly. All symptoms of his not-fineness.

"Do you want me to come over?" I asked, hoping he'd say no, because then I wouldn't have to put on pants.

"What for?"

"Um, to dust?"

"Nah. It'll just get dusty again."

"What about dinner?" I pushed. "Do you need anything?"

"I got plenty of cans of tomato soup."

I couldn't ask him if he needed me to take care of him, because I knew what the answer would be: No! He didn't like being taken care of. He took care *of us*, put the roof over our heads, fixed things, like the leaky plumbing and our parking tickets.

"Um, Dad? So…what are you up to?"

"Oh, just going through all the cards. There must be over a hundred here. I got cards from our old, old neighbors. My old squad partners. I got one here from my buddies at the kennel club." He blew his nose. "How are *you* doing?"

"Oh, fine. I guess."

"Liar."

He was right. I was lying. I had been having a hard time falling asleep. I would doze off, then wake up thinking that something was crawling up my leg, my arm, or across my face. I'd use the flashlight app on my iPhone to see if there was anything in the bed. Nothing. When I did fall asleep, I had dreams about my mother. Sometimes she was as frail as ever, living in an Edward Hopper painting. Or she was young, in a fifties-style dress, white, with red rickrack. I had this dream—she was in a backyard. There was a birthday cake. She was talking to me, but I couldn't hear her, like she had done in so many of our home movies, talking to the camera, waving her hand, shaking her head. If it wasn't the creepy feeling of bugs or the dreams, I was jarred awake by a primal howl. It wasn't the dog. It was me.

"I haven't been sleeping all that well," I told him.

"Yeah, me neither. Woke myself up. Yelling."

My mother used to complain about how he would yell in his sleep and kick the sheets off. She would ask him about it, and he would tell her he was chasing a guy and his gun had jammed. Now that he had the bed all to himself, he could chase all the perps down all the dark alleys of his subconscious, and when his dream gun jammed, he could bolt upright and not worry about waking her.

"I've been watching that DVD, that one you made for Mom and I."

I had taken home movies and stills and put them together on a DVD with appropriate music for their sixtieth anniversary. It took me an entire summer, and it drove me nuts getting the timing of Frank Sinatra's "I've Got a Crush On You" to track through the pictures of Mom and Dad at a picnic, then just Mom in a canoe, him and her at their high school graduation, and end on the picture of my just-married father pushing my mother on a swing.

"Mom was sure pretty." I heard him blow his nose. I was beginning to well up. Again. Where were these tears coming from? I thought I had cried enough to turn myself into a raisin. Seamus was downstairs, barking. "I hear the dog," he said.

"Yeah. Must be the mail," I said.

"You should train him to *get* the mail."

"Yeah, I should train him to do a lot of things," I admitted, sort of as a throwaway, but...it got me thinking.

"The guys at the kennel club want to do something for Mom."

"Gee, Dad, how long has it been since you went out to the kennel club?"

"I don't know. A year? Two?"

Seamus came into the room and put his fat head on my arm—his way of letting me know he needed something.

"You should take your dog, get back out there," I said.

I heard him sigh.

"Dad?"

"Yeah. I heard you," he said. "Old Mugsy isn't as spry as he used to be. His back legs go out from under him. He's got arthritis, real bad, just like me. I may have to put him down—maybe you'll have to put *me* down."

I laughed. Weakly. Because…he was kidding, right?

I decided to take a sharp conversational course correction.

"So, what are your plans for the day?" I said.

"Oh, I thought maybe I'd go visit Mom at the—cemetery."

Those two words didn't go together. Mom. Cemetery.

"Then what?" I asked.

"I don't know. Feed the dog, clean his kennel."

My father had designed and built a custom dog run out of chain-link fencing alongside his one-car garage. He kept his dogs outside, because they were "working" dogs. Don't get me wrong. Just because his dogs lived outside didn't mean they weren't comfortable. His dogs had amenities. He had built an insulated doghouse big enough for two dogs to curl up in and keep each other warm. He had made my mother sew a custom-sized dog bed that he filled with cedar chips. If the weather became too unbearable, hot or cold, he put the dogs in the basement in their own private crates.

Was this how he'd live out his days? Flushing dog urine out of the kennel and watching it run down the driveway?

He, like me, had to go through the process of grieving, and his wouldn't be the same as mine. It wouldn't look the same. Feel the same. Sound the same. Was it a comfort to see her clothes hanging in the closet? Her hair-care products still in the bathroom cabinet? Her smell on the pillow?

Seamus lifted his head, releasing my arm.

"You know she blamed me," he said, his voice wavering.

"Who blamed you, for what?"

"I was in the room when she came out of surgery and she pointed her finger at me and said, 'You did this to me!'"

"Oh, Dad. She didn't mean it!" She had known how to push my father's buttons. All she had to do was say something about how he hurt her feelings or how she thought he had taken a joke a little too far, and he would slink off into a corner with a hangdog look. She couldn't have meant it. Whatever the motive or reasons, I couldn't let him think that—it would kill him.

"She was loopy on pain meds."

"I suppose." He didn't sound convinced.

"She called me one time and asked where you were—" I said.

"When?"

"She'd had the surgery, and she called and told me she was at the airport, waiting for you." I mimicked her voice: "Tell your father I'm at the baggage claim!"

He laughed. "Yeah, I suppose it was the drugs, but still. I keep thinking about *Saving Private Ryan*—that last line? When the old guy says, 'Was I a good man?' Was I a good man?"

I had to blow my nose. I wanted to say, *Dad, you were a good man*, but I couldn't get the words out.

Seamus trotted back into the room with something in his mouth, a welcome distraction.

"Seamus has something. He won't give it to me." I put the phone down and pried open his mouth. He coughed up a fingernail clipper.

"What did he have?" my father said.

"Nail clippers."

"Where'd he get those?"

"Yesterday he had a comb; then he got into the recyclables and brought out all the yogurt containers."

"You gotta give that dog something…to…do…" His voice trailed off, like he was falling off a cliff. Sad Dad was killing me. What did

26

he have to look forward to other than the day my mother came to get him? He needed a project. Painting? No. Handyman? No. It had to be something along the lines of his preferred world of dogs and ducks.

Seamus nudged my leg, then my hand. He refused to unlock his gaze from my face. He drooled. My brain hit the rewind button and replayed the earlier snippet of the conversation, the part where I said, "I should train him to do a lot of things." Repeat. "I *should* train him to do a lot of *things*." Repeat. "I should *train him* to do a lot of things."

"Dad…you know…Seamus?"

"Yeah. Kind of an idiot, but what can you expect from a Labrador?"

I let the insult go. This little semi-dig made me think that the Dad who was quick with a quip was still in there, underneath the sadness, behind the closed doors of grief.

"I was thinking—"

"Uh. Oh."

"Maybe…Seamus needs a retrieving job. But not my underwear. Like real dog things. Maybe…you could give me some pointers?"

"Like what?"

"Water retrieves. Running in tall grass. Doing what a Labrador retriever should be doing."

He went silent. I hoped he was thinking about it. Entertaining the idea. Switching from Sad Dad to Making Plans Dad.

"He's what…seven?" I heard him take in a deep, thoughtful breath.

"Dad? What do you think? You, me, Seamus, the kennel club?"

I heard nothing. Had he hung up? Had his phone battery died?

"Dad?"

"Hmm…yeah…I guess so. Sure. Like when?"

He said *sure*. This was good! At the very least, we would both get out of our respective houses, and my antics would give him something else to talk and think about.

Mondays were bad for both of us. He said Tuesdays were bad for him. I couldn't do Fridays. Or Thursdays.

"How about Wednesday?" I offered.

"Wednesday? This Wednesday?" He sounded uncertain. Was he having second thoughts?

"Or we could make it *next* Wednesday," I said. "Come on, Dad. It will be fun!"

"No. Not fun. Work!"

"Whatever...fun...work."

"Okay. Sure. Next Wednesday. At the kennel club. Around nine?" He sounded a smidgen brighter since our phone call began.

"Sounds good," I said. Seamus let out a little yip of approval.

Dad didn't say good-bye or anything else. He just hung up.

I began to process what I had just put into motion. Me and Dad, together. What would we talk about? Would he want to talk about Mom stuff? I didn't know if I would feel comfortable talking with him about those things. Sometimes it was best to not know everything about a person—that way the larger-than-life myth that I had built up about him in my head would be intact.

Did I have the right equipment? I had a lead. I had a Frisbee, a few stiff-with-dried-dog-spit tennis balls. I had cargo shorts that I hated wearing because they made my fat thighs look fatter. The only sensible shoes I had were running shoes, if you call neon-green mesh sensible. My father was big on sensible shoes. When my sister and I were growing up, that's all we wore—brown leather lug-sole shoes. Oh, how we envied our cousins and their impractical, flimsy, yellow flip-flops!

Seamus had picked up on something. A change. A vibe. Perhaps I was giving off a more positive smell. His eyes had that *car-ride!* look in them. His tail was a metronome set to "Flight of the Bumblebee."

"Guess what?" I said to him. "We're going to the kennel club. You'll get to go swimming and run around! With Grandpa!" He barked and did a perfect downward dog. "But...it's not going to be all fun and games. You've got to do stuff. Obey. Be good. Okay?" He stood up and woofed an approving woof. He spun around twice before he jumped up and knocked the phone out of my hand.

CHAPTER FOUR

SHAMELESS

I GOT THROUGH THE first motherless Mother's Day by leaving town with my husband and Seamus. We packed the Chevy to the roof with dog accoutrements, things necessary to catch fish, binoculars, flashlights, and several suitcases full of clothing that would cover any and all weather contingencies. It was May. But it also was Wisconsin, and we weren't really out of the winter woods yet. That's where we were heading—the woods. Specifically, the northern Wisconsin woods.

We had been making the seven-hour drive (nine hours when Caitlin was four and Angus was trying to kick his way out of my uterus) once a year for close to thirty years. We had booked a long weekend *last* May for the opening of *this year's* walleye fishing season. I had thought about canceling, but I needed to get away and think, or not think, and what better place than an idyllic resort with one-hundred-year-old log cabins on a spring-fed lake? Maybe I'd be able to get some sleep if I was lulled by loons and the drone of a distant boat motor.

And I didn't have to think about cooking, because three times a day, someone rang an old-fashioned bell that summoned the guests to the lodge for pot roast and potatoes, turkey with stuffing and gravy, ribs, bacon, waffles, pies, cake, and to-die-for chocolate chip cookies—a.k.a. comfort foods that I hoped would do the job of comforting.

My plan for the four-day weekend was to spend time in the cabin by the fire or taking long walks in the woods with Seamus. I might toss a few tennis balls into the lake, so he could run into the water and grab them if I felt like it. My husband planned on fishing. He is a fanatic when it comes to fishing. He will get up before the sun, fish, fish, fish, pee in a bucket, fish, fish, fish, pee in a bucket, fish, fish, fish. He returns to shore only for number two and for dinner. He hated to fish alone, and unless it was sunny and seventy-five degrees, I hated to go with him.

"Come with me. It'll be fun." He stood on the screened-in porch, kitted out in his expensive rain gear, a minnow bucket in one hand, rod and tackle box in the other. "Please?" He did that thing with his lip, a little pout, and gave me his very best puppy-dog eyes.

"But it's raining!"

"Not that hard!"

"But…"

His definition of fun was a lot different than mine. My kind of fun did not involve being cold, getting wet, sticking my hand in a bucket of minnows, and pulling a hook out of a wriggling walleye.

"Didn't you hire a rent-a-friend?" He usually paid one of the three guides who worked at the resort to sit in the boat with him and fish, a kind of fishing whore.

"Nope. Forgot. And now, they're booked. Pleeeease?"

"But…I'm still in my flannel pajamas…and Seamus is keeping me warm—"

"We could take the dog with us!"

Take. Dog. Trigger words. Seamus jumped off the sofa and had already pushed open the screen door with his snout.

"Seamus!" I yelled.

He flew down the hill toward the lake, a furry black blur that startled an unsuspecting family of five from Illinois. I ran out of the cabin into the yard in my moccasin slippers, plaid Green Bay Packers pajama pants, and a green hooded sweatshirt that had the lodge's logo across the front. I apologized to the small, towheaded child Seamus had bowled over, then to her mother, who scolded me for not being a good dog mother and for letting my dog child run wild. He was headed to the docks full speed ahead.

"Seamus! Heel!"

I thought he would crash into the lake, but he stopped just at the edge of the dock, like a dog in a Warner Bros. cartoon, then he jumped into a boat and barked. *Come on! Let's go! Fish!*

Seamus kept on with his volley of barks. They echoed out and across the lake. I ran back inside and threw on a down-filled vest, then my waterproof jacket, with gloves still in the pockets from last year, and picked up a plastic bag for dog poop. I grabbed my wool beret and headed toward the lake. My moccasin slippers offered no traction, and I skidded on the wet wood of the dock. Seamus didn't need any down-filled this or Smartwool that. He was already insulated with his thick, water-resistant Labrador coat.

He barked. Again.

"I would be more impressed if he had jumped into the boat with our name on it," Mark said. "Well? Are you coming?"

I took my seat next to the fishing net, the tackle box, and the minnow bucket. Seamus had jumped out of the other boat and jumped in our boat. Then out. Then back in.

"Would it have killed you to wait until I put on real pants?" I directed my ire directly to Seamus. He offered a happy apology in the form of a fishy lick on my face.

"It's not raining anymore! See?" Mark unzipped his rain jacket.

"Lucky us!" I said, heavy on the sarcasm.

"Did you bring a lead?"

"Lead? I'm lucky I have a jacket on!"

Mark adjusted his gear—rain gear stowed, tackle box secured—started the motor, and we were off. Walleyes, you've been warned.

I thought Seamus would sit calmly in the bow of the boat with his head up, nose into the wind like a hood ornament, and not create havoc like a dog with ADHD. He insisted on drinking the water out of the minnow bucket—along with most of the minnows—and jumping over the seats, tipping the tackle box over with his paws. We made it across the lake, to one of the less windy bays, but there were three deer that had wandered down to have a drink and Seamus insisted on trying to join them.

"Seamus, no!" I said. I grabbed the fur on either side of his head. I pulled it, so he looked like he'd had too much work done, a bad face-lift. "No!"

He had stopped barking and leaping, probably because I had him wedged between the seat and the bow of the boat with my knees.

Mark made a nice cast out into the lake. The minnow landed in the calm water with a nice, soft plop. A signal for Seamus's energy level to spike. He managed to wriggle free of my barrier to get a better look at what had made that sound, using me as his ladder. His fish-slimy, worm-gut-y paws left marks on my down-filled chest. My husband was oblivious to my struggles. He reeled in his minnow and made another cast toward the shore as if he were alone, no worries, no cares.

Seamus was concerned. *Is this thing that is being tossed into the water something I need to retrieve?*

"I think he thinks he has to retrieve your minnow," I said.

Mark laughed his isn't-that-cute laugh, while I continued to try and get Seamus in a figure-four leg lock. Taking a page from my father's book—the page that was all about making do, using what's at hand—I fashioned a lead out of the long, yellow rope that was supposed to tie off the boat anchor. It had begun to rain again.

"I'm getting wet!" I said.

"Why didn't you bring your rain pants?"

I gave him an are-you-kidding-me look.

Mark reluctantly and begrudgingly conceded to my request of going back to the cabin to put on dry clothes—any clothes that weren't pajamas.

The rain had stopped. Mark decided to fish by himself off the docks, and I wanted to take the dog to the beach for some water retrieves. I had borrowed a training dummy from my father and figured I'd toss it into the lake and wait to see what the dog would do. Seamus's retrieving experience up to that point had been all about a red Frisbee and tennis balls that he turned into foamy sponges with his drool. I had some modicum of control, but with every toss, there was always a chance that something would go wrong, and by wrong, I meant... I didn't know what I meant, but I'd know it when I saw it.

The first time I threw the borrowed-from-my-father training dummy, I made sure it stayed on the beach side of the pier. It was a white hard-plastic thing that looked like a boat bumper. Seamus ran in from the sandy shore and, in a few seconds, brought it up on the beach, then ran around before I caught him and pulled it from his clenched jaws. He barked and I threw it. Three times. Four. Five. He'd bring it up on the shore and I'd chase him. Repeat. Then I got bored and decided to throw it in the greater part of the choppy lake. He started out fine, making a beeline to it, but he either lost sight of it or decided some other thing was more to his liking.

I'm sure, to a dog, a channel marker looks an awful lot like a retrieving dummy—white, capsule shaped, seemingly floating on water. I would have thought, once he got closer to it, that its hefty size and his inability to grab it would have made him abandon his quixotic quest to retrieve it, but it didn't—if anything, it emboldened him. But even if he could have successfully mouthed it, it was attached to a twenty-foot steel underwater cable.

I kept calling. He kept trying to pull it from its mooring. After twenty minutes, his smooth dog paddle turned into more of a flailing dog panic, and then his head went under.

Oh no!

I ran to the docks, untied a boat, climbed in, and didn't bother with the motor, because I didn't know how to start it—but I did know how to row. I put the previous year's rowing classes to use. In no time, I was up to ramming speed and pulled up alongside him, his big, boxy head bobbing out of the water just within my reach. I yanked him into the boat, almost causing it to capsize, his legs still kicking. I kept him on a leash after that, and when we'd walk near the lake, he'd cast a sideways glance at that buoy and growl. At dinner that night, Mark and I were known as the "People in the Boat with the Crazy Labrador."

Seamus was better behaved on our walks. He stayed on the private road, galloping ten or twenty feet ahead of me; then he'd stop and look back at me, for…my approval? Or was he checking to see if I was still there? When he stopped, I would pause and listen to the quiet. The only sound was Seamus sniffing a pile of frosty fallen leaves. I breathed in the woodsy smells. If the calmness I was waiting for was going to come, this would have been a nice time for it. The break from raw emotions was nice, but it was just that. A break. In a couple of days, I'd have to face the places and the faces of sorrow and grief. Couldn't we just stay here? Until the sad parts were done?

Seamus and I got to the end of the forest and walked past the fields of grass. A large herd of deer sprang up and leaped back into the pine trees, the white flags of their tails the last things I saw of them before they disappeared.

We turned around and headed back to the cabin. It was hard to imagine that all this land had one time been clear-cut by overzealous timber barons. It looked primeval, the tree trunks thick and mossy, the floor crowded with ferns and fungi. It had only taken one hundred years to remake itself. Only! I walked. Seamus sniffed. I stopped near a hollowed-out stump with toadstools growing. "That's where the fairies live!" my mother would have told six-year-old me. And six-year-old me would have believed her—so would fifty-six-year-old me.

Where was my mother? Was she here? Was that a woodpecker or her? Was she a part of the wind in the trees? Was she next to me, behind an invisible barrier, trying to get my attention, banging on it, like I had done with the sliding glass doors of the rehab place after I found out Mom had passed? During her last stay in the hospital, prior to her shunt surgery, she told me that she'd heard her mother calling her home for supper. Was that where she was? In another dimension, eating supper?

I heard the dinner bell ringing. It was Saturday. Pot roast! "No dillydallying," I said to Seamus, then caught myself because that sounded a lot like my mother talking.

The weekend in the woods had left me feeling...not rejuvenated. If anything, I felt worse. I'm like those people who never take a vacation because they'll spend it thinking about all the work piling up on their desks. What would be waiting for me? An inbox overflowing with sadness? Piles of grief I'd have to figure out where to file?

For the first time in forever, I didn't have to call my mother the minute we got in the door to tell her we had made it back. There weren't ten messages on my machine from her because she had forgotten we were going fishing. Dad was the one who had called. Dad? Calling?

"How was fishing?" He sounded a little bit more like himself. A little bit peppier. "We still on for Wednesday?"

I thought about Seamus's incident in the boat, my inability to control him, how he ran over the towheaded child and put me in the bad-dog-mother category.

"Yep."

"Okay. I got a few questions, then." A few questions meant he had been thinking about me and my dog and not dwelling on the woulda coulda shouldas. "Is your dog delivering to hand?" he said.

"Um…I don't know. Maybe?" I could have asked him what "delivering to hand" meant, but I didn't want him to know that I didn't know what it meant.

"Can he hold a sit?"

"Kind of."

"Do you have a long piece of rope?" he said.

"Uh, I have a wash line."

"Do you still have that training dummy? I think I gave you one."

"No. Seamus had it stolen from one of the other dogs in residence at the lodge."

I heard a heavy sigh.

"Do you have a whistle?"

"Um, no."

38

Another sigh. "I think I got an extra one. What about scent? Didn't I give you a bottle that one Christmas?"

By "scent," he did not mean Chanel but a bottle of liquid the color of dried blood that was extracted from somewhere inside a duck. He had gifted it to me five years ago, after Seamus and I brought disgrace upon the family at the Milwaukee Journal Sentinel Sports Show.

● ● ●

The sports show is a yearly event of all things hunting, fishing, boating, and camping that attracts large numbers of serious outdoor people, who wander up and down aisles looking for lures, rods, reels, or ShamWows.

I had seen the ad in the newspaper:

> Enter your dog! Fastest Retriever Contest! Open to
> any breed! Amateurs Only! First Prize…$500!!!

I had a dog. He was fast. I was definitely an amateur. All he had to do was run forty yards, pick up a rubber training dummy, and run back to me. How hard could it be? He was genetically programmed to retrieve. I paid the twenty-dollar entry fee, got my number, was told where and when to show up—all moot as far as I was concerned. They should have just given us the prize money.

The designated backstage area was in the parking lot outside the loading dock of the big exhibition hall. Our competition was mostly Labs who sat nicely at their owners' sides and a couple of mutts of undetermined lineage. Seamus wore his pinch collar that I clipped to a short, thick lead. I chose that collar because whenever he wore it, he tended to listen to me, and without it, he didn't.

Seamus squirmed and barked with annoying enthusiasm. He tried to retrieve a training dummy from a stranger's pocket, which aroused the ire of the no-nonsense, marine-drill-sergeant guy in charge. "Control your dog!" he said.

I pleaded with Seamus to sit. He did. For .001 of a second. Mr. No-Nonsense interrupted his rules-and-regulations monologue with a quick turn and penetrating gaze.

"I will *not* allow *any dog* on stage with *that collar!*"

I looked around to see who the idiot was who he might have been yelling at. Who? What collar? Did he mean me? My dog? This collar?

"Take it off, or he's *out!*"

My repeated questions of why I couldn't have it on my dog if there was no mention of this in the rules were ignored and only made him meaner. He was like a dog chained to a tree. Barking at anything. Anyone. Ready to attack. The kind of dog you cross the street to avoid or prepare a strategy for self-defense against. But I couldn't avoid him. I shouldn't have let him get to me. I should have stood my ground. But I was nervous. He smelled it.

"But…I don't—I didn't bring a backup!"

"I don't give a shit, lady!" He gave me an if-you-can't-take-the-heat, blah-blah-blah kind of look.

I took the collar off and made the lead into a slip collar. Seamus would have to win the contest au naturel. I could not regain my focus. I was flustered. Embarrassed. Confused. Anxious. Worried that I had already failed. I felt like I had lost whatever control I had convinced myself I had of Seamus, of the situation. When it was our cue to go onstage, Seamus stiffened at the sight of the open metal stairs. Mr. No-Nonsense (surprise, surprise, he was also the emcee!) told me through clenched teeth, "Get your dog on the stage!"

I tried to pull Seamus onto the first step, because I thought once he got going, he'd be okay. But he dug in and started scream-barking.

"Get. Your. Dog. On. The. Stage!" he said through his gritted smile.

I wanted to abort the whole thing and take him back to the car, and I was ready to leave when Mr. No-Nonsense grabbed Seamus by the scruff of his neck and yanked him onstage. Panicked screams of a dog who sounded like he was being beaten filled the arena. Oh, so a pinchy collar was totally out of the question, but this was okay?

I tried to calm the dog and myself as much as I could before Mr. No-Nonsense gave me a signal. What was I supposed to do? He kept pointing. At me. Then the other end of the stage. Was I supposed to lead the dog off the leash? Seamus was the Lab equivalent of Usain Bolt. The audience of about two hundred people—my dad and mom wedged in somewhere—oohed and aahed. He picked up the dummy.

Yes!

I called his name and clap-clap-clapped. He turned and started back to me, a black Labrador version of a nitro-fueled dragster. The only time I had seen him run this fast was when he ran after the black feral cat that had breached our yard's perimeter. He hated that cat. After they'd taken a few laps, it would sit on the other side of our fence, just out of his reach—the only thing left in Seamus's arsenal was to bark at it. The cat couldn't have cared less.

At the coveted seven-second mark, I saw him avert his eyes from mine and onto something else. I clapped. Harder. "Come on! Yoo-hoooo!" I called. I could see it in his eyes. He had lost all interest in me and the task at hand, and he'd decided to take the scenic route. He ran off the course, past the fake duck pond, around the bend, to check out the pickup truck display, and then he left a pee mail on a boat trailer—all while holding on to the dummy, which I thought should have counted for something. I clapped, jumped, and waved to get Seamus to return, which he did, a lifetime later.

I caught up with my parents in the parking lot after I had sequestered Seamus inside our car.

"Thank God you don't have the same last name as mine," my father said, distancing himself from me so the stench of shame would not rub off of me and onto the bomber jacket he'd had custom made from deer he'd shot and skinned.

I knew I had let the family down, but I felt worse because I had let Seamus down. He was a perfectly capable Labrador who I was wasting. I didn't necessarily want to win, but I didn't want to be the clown act.

"Oh, honey," my mother said, giving me a there-there pat on my cheek. "You did the best you could!"

Had I? The best I could? I could have done better. I should have practiced.

My mother grabbed my head and bent it, so she could kiss the top. "I thought you were great! I mean…you were very, um…entertaining!"

CHAPTER FIVE

FIELD TRIALS

THE SPORTS SHOW FIASCO was the last time Seamus and I had done anything close to retrieving. How would he perform now? At the kennel club? Had I opened myself up for more ridicule, only this time from my retriever-as-a-second-language father? Would he be a little harsher with Seamus because he was a Lab and my father was a springer spaniel man? In a couple of hours, I would find out.

My dad had bought his first springer, a female he named Belle, when I was fifteen. He was going to train her for duck hunting, but then he got wind of this thing called a field trial—a competition that involves a team of a dog and a handler. I knew it took place in a field, that guns and shooting were involved, but the subtleties, the rules—those I did not know. According to the official English Springer Spaniel Field Trial Association's website:

> The purpose of a spaniel field trial is to demonstrate the performance of a properly trained spaniel in the field. The performance should not differ from that in any ordinary day's shooting, except that in the trials a dog should do his work in a more nearly perfect way...the following qualities are to be emphasized: retrieving promptly to hand, hunting

and game finding, working within gun range, control, steadiness to wing and shot (the dog should "hup," or sit and hold its position, until released by the handler), and responsiveness.

The first one they entered, they won. Dad and his dog Belle were hooked.

I put on my blindingly neon-green, high-visibility running shoes. Seamus's casual, around-the-house collar was replaced with the pronged collar—the same one that had raised the hackles at the sports show. To him, the collar meant *Car ride! Fun!* He jumped and spun and flung his hard-to-wipe, stringy drool on the hallway wall.

"Will you sit down?"

He sort of sat.

"Stop wiggling!"

I had found a swivel clip from my husband's disorganized pile of hardware that he'd amassed in the basement and tied a ten-foot piece of my wash line to it with a knot I made up. Seamus stopped long enough for me to attach it to the loop on the collar.

"Now, just wait."

I had only opened the back door a crack, but it was enough of an opportunity for him to bolt outside and run into the garage. His eagerness was borderline wild frenzy that, when combined with a long rope, made it difficult for me to avoid entanglement.

For any other car ride, I wouldn't have gone through all the trouble of scraping my knuckles putting the crate in the car, but if I didn't crate the dog, it would be the first thing my father would criticize me for. "You know, that's a hazard, having him in the back, loose like that. You have an accident and he's a cannonball."

I put the crate down onto the oil-stained garage floor, then opened the back of the car. Seamus jumped in.

"Seamus! Not yet. Out!"

He was too amped up to hear me.

"Seamus. Come on! Get out!"

He licked my face.

I pulled on the rope. He got the hint and jumped out.

"Now, just sit there, and let me get this…thing…inside. Okay, now you can get in."

He would have succeeded had I opened the wire door. He banged his head and bounced off, then sat on the floor of the garage, unsure of what I wanted him to do, where he should go.

"Oops. My bad. Come on. Kennel!"

He made a half start, then stopped short.

"Kennel. Come on. Ken-nel."

He sat there. It would have been very nice if I had wanted him to sit, but I didn't. I wanted him to get his butt inside the kennel so we wouldn't be late. I found a goldfish cracker belly up under the front seat and used it as bait. I threw it into the kennel. He jumped in after it.

A flowery canvas bag that I got at a farmer's market was filled with the extra-long rope and the bottle of Chanel No. K-9. I left the Frisbee and tennis balls behind because they were not Dad-sanctioned retrieving tools.

We were to meet at 1030 hours at the kennel club—roughly one hundred acres of tall grass, rolling hills, spring-fed ponds, and marshes, a.k.a. doggy heaven. It had at one time been my father's future eternal resting place, but that was before he rescinded his prior plans of being loaded into shotgun shells and blasted out and over the puppy pond. He had made those on a day when he could afford himself the luxury of thinking of death in comedic terms, when my mother was sitting in her camping chair, laughing with all the rest of the dog people. When his day comes, we will have his coffin slid into a drawer next to her. He will be wearing his jeans, red suspenders, camo flannel shirt, and high-visibility game vest, per his instructions.

The kennel club was slowly being hemmed in and squeezed by suburban sprawl and golf courses, the reasons for the "No Firing Shot Guns before 8 a.m." sign that hung from one rusty nail on the pitted post. Who knew how long those fields, those ponds would last? Or my dad? He was eighty-three. Longer lived than his parents. They both succumbed to cancers that have since been made less frequent and not necessarily a death sentence.

I pulled into the gravel parking area that was next to the club-house, a modest and serviceable structure made out of concrete blocks. It was a no-frills place, where no one cared if you tracked mud on the floor. Dogs were welcome. Dad was sitting inside his pickup truck, his head down. Dear God...was he...crying? If he was...shouldn't I give him a minute to compose himself? But...what if he wasn't? I'd look stupid just sitting there in my car.

"Oh, you're here!" he said, startled. "Just checking my email!" He hadn't heard me drive up because he refuses to wear his hearing aids. My mother used to call me to complain: "He has that TV turned up so loud, they can hear the Hitler Channel down the street!"

"Mom, don't you mean the History channel?"

"All he watches is the World War II and Hitler stuff, so..."

Point taken.

He was unshaven. Looked a little ragged around the edges, a look I had only seen when he had gone to Wyoming to hunt for antelope and hadn't shaved in two weeks. My first thought was, *Oh shit. Has he given up? Should I be concerned? Say something? I mean, he does have a house full of loaded weapons.* My second thought was, *Maybe he feels like he doesn't have to shave because Mom's not around, just like he probably feels he doesn't have to put the toilet seat down anymore.*

I pulled up next to his truck. He rolled down his window.

"You got your dog? Follow me!"

I could see why my father loved the place. It wasn't that far a drive—twenty minutes, give or take—and it had that clean, just-rained, forest-y smell. A yellow-shafted flicker swooped past the hood of my car—a sign of good luck, according to something I read in a book somewhere. I followed the dust cloud regurgitated from my dad's Ford F-150 pickup, down steep hills, around bendy-bends, the side of my car slapped by branches. Seamus squeaked in anticipation.

"Listen," I said to him, "all I want you to do is get the dummy and bring it back to me. Easy peasy. Please, please, please, for the love of God, let's not have a repeat of the sports show!"

We parked our vehicles on the soft grass near a stand of black walnut trees. Seamus could not keep still, not even inside the kennel. His gyrations rocked it side to side.

"Get him out of the kennel," my father said.

My plan was to open the wire door gradually, then get ahold of the rope to prevent Seamus from exploding, but he shot out of there like one of those novelty snakes in a can.

"Control your dog!"

(Flashback, anyone?)

I grabbed a piece of the rope and held it high and tight, so the collar would pinch his neck, like his mother would have with her teeth had she been there, but like any son, he paid the mother-facsimile no heed.

"Tell him to heel!"

"Heel," I said.

"Are you asking him or telling him?"

"Um—"

"You've got to be more firm! Don't say it like, 'heel.'" He used an affected, over-the-top version of a female voice. "Try to sound more like a man."

I tried it again, this time from the diaphragm, to deepen my voice and make me sound more authoritative, but instead, it came out like a bad Marilyn Monroe impersonation.

My father grabbed the rope from my hands. *"Heel!"* he said in the tone he used when he meant business, when my sister and I were about to go too far with our sisterly squabbles.

She and I had shared a bedroom, which meant we each also used half of the dresser and half of the closet. She was Oscar Madison to my Felix Unger. She would convince me to clean up her side of the room by making empty promises to play a board game with me or allow me to touch her *Meet the Beatles!* album. But once I had dusted her side of the dresser and folded or rehung all the clothes scattered on the floor of her side of the room, she wasn't in the board game mood anymore.

And she chewed gum.

I am chiclephobic—I don't like gum. I cannot tolerate it. I hate the smell. I can't touch it. I go out of my way to avoid it. Wads of it on the street or under a table make me dry heave. Of course, she knew this and used it against me. She'd leave a chewed piece on my pillow. Leave open packs on my side of the dresser. And I could do nothing, because to touch it also made me dry heave. The only thing left for me to do was go passive-aggressive:

48

"I don't have any idea how that hole got in your sweater."

"Wasn't that stain on your blouse before?"

"How would I know where your *Beatles '65* album went?"

When our arguing reached a certain level, when it impinged on his episode of *Gunsmoke*, Dad would yell, "Knock it off!" And we did.

My dad's *heel* command was accompanied by a quick, firm downward jerk of the rope. It caught Seamus by surprise and lifted him off his feet for a few seconds before he got the message and sat, panting submissively at my father's wrinkled khaki pants.

"Be firm. Remember, you're the one in charge. Not him. When he's out here and has that collar on, he's got to do what you want him to do, not what he wants to do—and Jesus Christ what the hell kind of knot is this? Don't you know how to make a buntline hitch?"

He gave me back my dog, and immediately, the not heeling commenced. "Tell him—"

"Heel!" I said.

"Give him a jerk!"

I gave Seamus a jerk.

"Downward!"

I gave him a downward-ish jerk.

"Don't pull!"

"Wasn't I jerking?"

"No. It's got to be more like this." He grabbed the rope and did what I had thought I was doing, but clearly, after paying closer attention, I realized I was not.

"Is he supposed to do this heeling thing, like, all the time?" If he was, then this being in charge was very stressful, and after the past few months, I didn't need any more stress, thank you.

"He should sit at your side and wait for you to tell him what you want him to do."

"Seriously? According to who?"

"Do you want to do this or not?"

I did not know how to answer that.

"Did you bring a whistle?" he said.

"No."

"Are you planning on wearing *those* shoes?"

I looked down at my flashy, hi-vis running shoes.

"Yes?"

"Are they waterproof?"

"Uh…"

My father is a firm believer in clothing that can handle whatever nature can dish out. This is why, to this day, I have a hard time buying anything frilly and froufrou. Until Ann Taylor makes a pencil skirt that can double as a flotation device, my Eddie Bauer shirt with built-in UV protection is as froufrou as my comfort level will allow.

"Do you have a game vest?"

"A what now?"

"A vest like this, to put dead ducks and dummies in."

"Why would I?"

He went around to the back of his truck and pulled out a khaki vest with pockets concealed in the back, two on each side, plus smaller pockets within pockets. Basically, it was one giant pocket with armholes. It was also three sizes too big.

"Here, you can have this one."

"Well, with the right accessories…I *could* make this work. Maybe a belt?" I struck a cover-of-*Vogue* pose. Dad did not appreciate my fashion-based humor. He handed me a whistle that hung on the end of a cord. He had pulled it from a used ammo crate he had in the back of his truck.

"Here."

I took it from him but balked. "Has anyone used this?"

"Oh, for Chrissake! Just take it! Bring your dog to heel, then get him to the edge of the water and make him sit and wait."

The only reason I got the dog to walk close to my side was because he had coiled me up in the remaining nine and a half feet of rope. My shoes had absorbed the moisture of the muck on shore, dimming their vis.

My father pulled a canvas retrieving dummy from a dirty, blood-stained five-gallon bucket that he used for dead-bird and training-dummy transportation. "I've had this dummy for, gosh, four? No…five dogs…close to forty-five years!" He threw it almost to the other side of the pond. It landed on the water with a slap.

"Send your dog."

I did as instructed and yelled my designated "go" word: "Okay!" I said it when I wanted him to get the newspaper or the mail or chase his nemesis, the black feral cat, out of my hostas.

Seamus caught air like a Labrador on the cover of *Just Labs Magazine* and made an impressive splash.

"Pretty neat, huh?" I said.

"I don't like it when dogs do that," Dad said.

"Why? I think it looks cool!"

"You never know if there's a stick under the water. He could get impaled, and then you'd have yourself a Lab kabob."

A Lab kabob?

Seamus homed in and swam in a straight line to his canvas target.

"That's real good, real good," Dad said. Was that the rise in humidity I felt or smugness?

"Blow your whistle as soon as he gets that dummy in his mouth."

Ew. I didn't want to put a whistle in my mouth not knowing whose mouth it had been in last. Plus, it was lost inside one of the secret tunnels of pockets.

Seamus grabbed the canvas dummy in his mouth.

"Now! Blow!"

"How many times?"

"Twice. And it has to be firm. *Toot! Toot!* Loud. Don't be shy. Give it a good blast." I gagged a little bit when I put it in my mouth, but I blew it. Firmly. Loudly-ish. Seamus turned and started the long swim back to shore, barely making a wake. It was when he reached the bank that he regressed into what I call Fastest Retriever Runaround. He zigged left. I zagged right.

"Keep calling him!"

I tooted. I called. I tried to grab the dummy when he came close, but he had more moves than an NFL punt-return specialist.

"Step on the rope!"

I tried, but my non-waterproofed running shoes slipped. My father stepped in, grabbed the rope, reeled Seamus in like a rodeo calf, and pried his jaws open.

"Look at this! You've punched holes in it!" He showed Seamus his toothy handiwork before he turned and walked away from us. Were we supposed to follow? He sat on the edge of his tailgate, looking as crushed as the dripping canvas dummy he still held in his hands.

"Five dogs have carried this in their mouths. Belle. Duke. Buddy. Trooper. Mugsy. And you!" His voice cracked a teensy bit.

Great. First his wife and now his favorite training dummy were dead.

Seamus wagged his tail. His brown eyes shifted from my dad, to me, back to my dad, then back to me. *I want to go swimming and carry things!*

In his mind, the crushing blow to my father's keepsake was in the past, gone, forgotten.

"Put your dog in the kennel," he said in his I'm-very-disappointed-in-you tone, the one that was usually followed by a terse lecture about how I should be getting better grades. He and I sat on our respective tailgates.

"Well, I think I know what I'm getting you for Christmas!" I said, hoping to lighten the mood. I had no idea an old, weather-beaten dummy held such sway. Had I known, I would have suggested he use a different one, one less sacred.

He shook his head and wiped his wet hands on the legs of his pants.

"That…*dog*…has a hard mouth!"

"What do you mean, 'hard mouth'?"

"He shouldn't be biting the dummy! That's very, very bad."

"It is?"

"Yes! A judge would see that and…out!"

He didn't think I was going to be entering Seamus in a field trial, did he? Oh God.

"Dad, I wasn't thinking of—"

"Can you imagine what he'd do to a duck? He'd make a meal out of it."

I had no intention of either entering him in a field trial or taking this dog duck hunting, so I didn't understand why biting down on the dummy was a bad thing. Wasn't he just being a dog?

"And, that's another thing…he's *got* to deliver to *hand*!"

"Deliver to hand?"

"He should bring the thing to you, sit, and hold it in his mouth until you give him the command, 'give.'"

Oof. That sounded like a lot of work. *I should just quit this non-sense and go home. Life with this dog was fine yesterday.* Sure, he had some annoying habits, like bolting to the front gate every time it clinked opened and scuttling underneath the dining room table with stolen goods in his mouth, but he brought me the paper, and he could balance a dog biscuit on his nose. Did I care whether or not he was trained enough to bring me an unmolested duck? No. Should I? Yes. Because wasn't this all about my dad? Getting the dog to listen was secondary.

"Next time, we'll try something different."

"He seems kind of hopeless to me," I said.

"I wouldn't say hopeless, no. He needs work. A *lot* of work."

CHAPTER SIX

PICK OF THE LITTER

The inside of my car smelled like sweat and wet dog. I looked like I had just spent six months in the jungles of the Amazon. My father and I had agreed to try this training thing again next Wednesday, and now that I knew what I was up against, I'd be better prepared. Seamus was quiet inside his kennel, worn out from a morning of not doing what he was supposed to be doing. He was so quiet that when I pulled into the Kwik Trip for gas, I opened the back hatch to make sure he wasn't dead.

"I hope some of this sunk into your thick head," I said to him. What about my thick head? Did I remember what my father had been telling me? How he handled the rope? His whistle-blowing *toot*-elage? Um…

I had known Seamus would be rough around his retrieving edges, but I hadn't expected he'd be *this* rough. I thought spending a morning in the fields with Dad and dog would be fun. Not work. And I hated getting wet, having my socks squishing inside my shoes. A rivulet of mud mixed with pond water ran down the front of my leg, forming a puddle under the gas pedal. And how did a clump of grass get into my hair?

"Seamus." I addressed him in the same manner I had with Angus and Caitlin in minivans past, keeping an eye on the road while looking at the two of them in the rearview mirror to see if they were paying attention to me. "If your father, the field trial champion that he is, saw the way you acted today, he'd disown you!"

I turned to check my blind spot to change lanes and saw that he was sitting in the kennel with his back to me. Was he giving me the cold, wet shoulder?

"Well, I suppose it's all *my* fault you're clueless when it comes to retrieving?"

He began to bark at a mixed breed in the car next to us. I couldn't take all the blame for the dog's ineptitude. I had to put most on my husband.

• • •

When the time had come for Mark and me to consider a successor to Harvey, our twelve-year-old golden retriever with issues—liver issues, back leg issues, spine issues, hearing issues, eye issues, seizure issues—I wanted the successor to be another golden retriever. Harvey was like a seventy-two-pound cat, a.k.a. Mr. Mellow.

"I want a Labrador retriever!" Mark had said. "Ask your dad if he knows anyone who's having a litter."

Of course my father, who had over forty years' experience training dogs for field trials, knew people who had Labs. But these Labs were bred from champions. They needed to work, and by work, I meant running, jumping (correction, *bounding*) into lakes to retrieve ducks and geese, maybe some upland game birds as well. My husband was a fisher. Not a hunter.

"If I were to agree to this high-octane Lab," I said, "who would be the one to train it?"

"I'll do it!" my husband said.

Uh. Huh. Sure. He owns a production company that does

lighting, audio, and staging for corporate events, galas, and chichi weddings. He works eighty hours a week. When was he going to do this alleged training? My gut told me to hold out and not let him talk me into a purebred Lab, but...then again, maybe this was just the thing my husband needed. Maybe working with a dog, walking up and down fields, over hills, and through thickets would relieve some of the stress from running his own business. It could help lower his blood pressure. His cholesterol.

The subject of puppy procurement came up during one of our regularly scheduled Sunday family dinners. My sister was boycotting at that time. She was miffed that she had been passed over in the hosting/cooking rotation. Again. She wasn't always keen on checking expiration dates on things, and dinners at her house left one, two, sometimes all of us (except her) with a bad taste followed by cramps.

Dad had made a tenderloin tip stew with green peppers, oyster mushrooms, and pearl onions in a wine reduction. Back in the late 1950s, when he was a young cop and walked a beat, he'd duck into warm, steamy restaurant kitchens to escape the cold Milwaukee winter nights, to thaw out his frostbitten ears and toes. He'd sit in a corner and eat his complimentary fettuccine Alfredo or Wiener schnitzel or steak Diane, while he picked up tips on how to chop, sauté, and braise. I don't think my mother objected to his usurpation of her dinner cooking duties, and neither did Linda and I. We prayed that Mom's Chef Boyardee canned-spaghetti concoctions with scrambled eggs and Spam were a thing of the past. Her gastronomical niche was baking. Her flaky piecrusts were legendary. Her rich chocolate layer cakes with creamy white frosting were must-haves at any and all birthdays. The only baking my father co-opted from her were the spritz cookies at Christmastime, because making them involved wielding a gun-like cookie press, and who better than a trained marksman to shoot a sheet full of perfectly formed stars?

"We're thinking of getting a puppy," I said, shoveling a load of hot, buttery egg-noodle goodness onto my plate.

"A puppy? What kind?" my mother said on her way to the oven to retrieve the dinner rolls.

"We were thinking a Lab!" my husband said.

"Why a Lab?" my father asked.

"Yes, Mark, tell my father, why a Lab?" I was slightly sarcastic, but I truly wanted to know how he'd had made this decision. I hadn't seen him doing any research. Had he done it at work? Asked someone who had a Lab, about Labs? So, yeah. I wanted to know.

"Because, oh, I don't know, they're just so…Labby!"

Labby?

"Why not another golden? Harvey is such a good dog. His head is very convenient for me to pet," my mother said as she sat down, then got up because she had forgotten her coffee was in the microwave.

"Mel picked the last dog, and this time it's my turn! And I want a Lab!"

My father pulled the early American dinette chair closer to the table. He put both elbows on the plaid tablecloth and leaned in, over his food. He had assumed his lecturing position, the one he used when he had to give his popular speech: the Consequences of Violating Curfew.

I hoped he would be the one to talk some sense into my work-aholic husband, say something along the lines of "When the hell are you going to have time—" etc., etc., etc.

"I know a guy—" he said.

Oh no. No. No.

"—he comes to the kennel club. He has Labs. Maybe he's got a litter."

I put my head in my hands. The microwave beeped and my mother returned to the table with her third steaming cup of Sanka. She patted the top of my head. "They're going to do what they're going to do. You might as well face it." She shrugged and then said, "Who wants pie?"

If we were to get a Labrador retriever from a breeder who knew my father, wouldn't that dog be expected to accomplish something? And if it didn't? Tongues at the West Allis Training Kennel Club would wag.

"I want to go on record," I said. "If we're getting a Lab, it has to be a female. Yellow."

My father contacted his Lab guy, who happened to have a litter due in February or March. Emails were exchanged between Mark and the breeder. We made a down payment. Our names were added to the waiting list. We—Mark—had two months to prepare.

I expected to find him with his nose buried in Labrador retriever training manuals, instead of his usual James Patterson novels. Or going with my father to kennel club meetings. Becoming a member. Getting the lay of the kennel club land.

No.

Had he phoned my father? Talked to him at length about dogs? Did he have any questions? Concerns?

No.

"Work is just insane right now," he said.

Work was always insane.

"Are you sure you'll have time for this dog?" I said.

"Of course!"

"Shouldn't you be reading up—"

"Yeah, I will."

"When?"

"When I get some time."

Tick. Tick. Tick.

The puppies were born on Saint Patrick's Day 2006, a good sign, according to my Irish mother. I mean, come on...Saint Patrick's Day!

Six weeks later, Mark and I made the one-hour drive to the idyllic farm to make our choice. There were five pups: four males, all black, and one yellow female who kept getting trounced and pounced upon in the corner of the whelping box by her rambunctious brothers. She had a get-me-out-of-here look on her face, and I would have, had it not been for the red piece of yarn tied around her neck that meant she had been spoken for.

This was a crucial make-or-break moment. Years before, I hadn't really picked Harvey; he'd just happened to be the last puppy left, and I'd felt sorry for him. He was the backup puppy to our then-fourteen-year-old Labrador-collie mix we had gotten from the Humane Society back in the day when people didn't have to have background checks; she had just licked Mark's finger through the cage, and we knew she was ours.

But these Lab pups? They all looked the same. They all had equal amounts of energy, except for the well-behaved, already-promised female.

"Go ahead. You pick." My husband had deferred to me.

"Me?! I thought this was *your* pick."

"It is, but you know more about dogs than I do."

"No, I don't." Maybe I did, but I did not want the responsibility of picking this dog. What if I picked the wrong dog? When the dog didn't do something it was supposed to do or did something it shouldn't have, I wanted to be the one to say, "Well? It's your fault. You picked him!"

Mark said, "Maybe you should call your father. He'll know."

I had to step out of the barn and stand next to a fence in the back forty in order to get cell reception. A horse sidled up alongside and blew air out of its nostrils.

"Dad? How do you pick a puppy?"

"Where are you? What's that sound?"

"A horse. We're out at the breeders. Trying to pick out a puppy. Like, how do you?"

"There's no real science to it. You just stick your hand in there and grab one." That's it? There had to be more to it than that. Shouldn't I observe them? See which one settles back? Which pup is jumpy? A biter? I needed more clarification, but he had already hung up. Necessary information, dispensed.

I patted the horse's nose.

Put my phone in my jacket pocket.

Walked back into the barn.

Put my hand into the tumbling ball of paws and tails and tongues, did just as my father told me to do, and pulled out a Seamus.

CHAPTER SEVEN

SIT. STAY. HEEL.

Our next session was Wednesday. One month since the funeral. I had thought by now I would be sleeping and not tossing and getting up and then lying in bed, staring at the ceiling. I thought I would be eating more foods on the pyramid, instead of just bread and butter, crackers and butter, noodles with butter, sometimes just butter. I was making some progress. I felt like I was slowly coming out of anesthesia, still a little groggy. I wasn't quite connecting.

The idea portion of my brain had become noticeably quiet. Usually, my head was like a six-lane freeway—concepts, schemes, plots, paragraphs, characters, stories, all traveling at eighty miles an hour. I had nothing. Other than the dog-training idea. My head had become a desolate country road—no cars, no trucks, no nothing. All it needed was Cary Grant, a cornfield, and a low-flying airplane.

When I pulled into the kennel club's parking lot, my father gave me a high sign—briefly raising his hand—and left me choking on his F150 dust. I followed him down the road, trying to stay in his ruts. He had four-wheel drive. I didn't. There were several lumpy bumps that scraped the bottom of my undercarriage. The kennel slid in the back. "Hang on, Seamus!"

This field was more hidden than the first we'd gone to. More overgrown. It was a lot farther away from the two-lane highway. The rolling hills hid the nearby subdivision. He parked his truck near a picnic table that had been on the receiving end of several shotgun blasts. He got out. He looked more stooped than usual. His shirt was wrinkled, the collar frayed. There was a stain on the placket. I knew we weren't exactly going out on the town, but even when he dressed for the dogs—in faded and weathered shirts and very broken-in, worn jeans—he had that J. Crew–ish outdoorsy look. This ensemble made him look a little bit like a bum. He winced a little when he opened the back of his truck and pulled out his Wellies. He sat on the seat of the wounded picnic table and took off his shoes with a grunt.

Was this too much for him? All this walking up and down hills with hidden holes? The bending? The throwing? Was it his back? His knees? Should I ask him? I played the scene of how that would go in my mind:

Me:	Dad? Are you sure all this stuff isn't too much for you?
Him (dismissive):	Nah.
Me (unconvinced):	Because if it is—
Him (emphatic):	I *told* you, it isn't.
Me (still unconvinced):	Yeah, I know, but—
Him (terse):	I said *it isn't.*

So, no. I wouldn't ask.

"I got another sympathy card," he said.

Oh no. If I had to write another thank-you card with a picture of my just-married parents next to one of the last pictures of them together, holding hands, I'd be re-dredging my cavernous sadness. When would it end? I remembered there was a girl in my high school class whose mother died when we were sophomores, and now, I thought how lucky she was—she had already been through this. Her hurt had scabbed over. Mine was still a seeping, gaping wound. If it wasn't for this cockamamie dog-training date, I wouldn't know what day it was or have any reason to get out of bed. I would have been sitting on the shoulder of my desolate country road, waiting for a busload of happiness that never seemed to be coming.

"Oh, that reminds me," he said, tottering over a bit before he regained his balance. I bet he needed a cane and couldn't bring himself to use one. He had kept the one my mother used—or was supposed to use—propped up against his gun cabinet. I don't think I was ready to see him using a cane. Getting old. Weaker. Less Dad-like.

"Could you maybe do something with Mom's obit?"

"What do you mean?"

"Like frame it or something? I cut it out and saved it."

I had never understood the practice of clipping out of death notices. Well, until a couple of weeks earlier, when I had dealt with the moments right after my mom's death, the what-happens-now part, and the parts between the initial bad-news phone call and the funeral. Death had happened to aunts, uncles, grandparents. *Other* people handled the details. Death happened *over there*. After fifty-eight years, I was finally a member of the club.

Was he becoming one of those people who saved death notices? I used to make fun of people who did. I'm sorry. I get it now—although that blanket apology does not cover anyone who takes pictures of dead loved ones in coffins. I'm talking to you, icky Polish grandma.

Would I do something for my father like frame the obituary? Of course.

He used the edge of the picnic table as leverage to get up. He grabbed a longer rope from somewhere inside his truck and a pair of leather gloves. "You're going to use these today, so you don't get rope burn."

Well, at least he had been planning. Thinking of ways to teach my dog (and me) how to accomplish whatever we were supposed to be accomplishing.

"Wait...Dad?" I hesitated. I could have called an audible—not asked what I was going to ask and asked him something about the dog instead, but...

"So...how's...you know...things?"

He rubbed his stubble. Pinched his eyes with a ruddy hand. What if he said that he had no reason to live? Or that he was selling the house and buying a condo in Florida, next to his sister? Or that he was done with this dog-training thing, that my dog was an idiot, or I was, and that he regretted the day I talked him into doing it?

He took a deep breath and puffed out his cheeks as he exhaled. "Shitty."

I put my around his slumped shoulders.

He gave my arm a pat. "Okay, okay. That's enough. We've got work to do. Let's get this show on the road." He said it with a tenderness in his voice, a tone that he had used when I'd had a roller-skating fail and scraped a knee, or when one of my children had sustained a minor bump, a pinched finger, or a disappointment devastating to a toddler. It worked then; it worked now.

I got the dog out of the kennel and gave him a treat so he would sit while I clipped the long rope to his collar. In order to get Seamus to go into his kennel or to bring me the paper or to hurry up and pee when it was raining, I would usually bribe him with stale fries, cheese, chicken, leftovers in foam containers that had been forgotten and pushed to the back of the refrigerator, anything. Turns out that was wrong. All terribly wrong.

"What did you just do?"

"Uh, clipped the rope to—"

"No, before that."

"Gave him a little biscuit?"

"You don't reward the dog for the thing you *want* him to do. You reward him *after* he's done what you want him to do."

"Yeah, but, then how am I supposed to—wait. What?"

"If he comes to you because he smells the chicken in your hand, then he's not coming to you because he *should*. He's coming to you only because he gets chicken. Got it?"

I got it. I just didn't get what was wrong with it.

"Make your dog sit."

"Seamus. Sit." He sat on my foot.

"Stay there, and keep him at sit."

Seamus never took his eyes off my father as he walked away from us, down a stretch of rutty, rocky road, looking at the ground—and so alone. He stopped where there was a narrow clearing in the reeds that hugged the opposite shoreline and took off his Ducks Unlimited baseball hat to wipe his brow with his red bandanna handkerchief. Seamus had a bead on him as he stuffed the bandanna back into one of the pockets of his game vest. The only things moving were Seamus's black nostrils and his eyebrows. My father crouched a little bit, as much as he could with his bad back, and clapped his hands. "Seamus! Heel!"

I let go of the rope and Seamus took off toward him. Sixty pounds of solid Labrador with a long rope trailing behind him like a whip. If my father hadn't timed it right and moved out of the way just enough, Seamus would have run into him. "Heel!" Seamus's momentum carried him past my father. Dad grabbed the rope and pulled Seamus over to his side. "Sit!" And when he sat, my father cupped Seamus's big head in his hands. "Good boy! Good boy!" Seamus responded by jumping up and getting a swift knee in the chest. "That's what you've got to do. See how I used my hands? No treats!" he yelled back at me.

"O-kay," I said, forgetting that "okay" was also a go word. Seamus danced around, wondering if he was supposed to be running off somewhere, getting something.

"Not okay. You've got to do it!"

"All right. All right. I'll do it."

"If you don't—"

"What? You'll ground me?"

We did that five more times. Dad at one end of the road, me at the other, Seamus like a black Lab volleyball that we kept serving to each other. Then Dad decided to add a new wrinkle. "Let's try it with a different training dummy!"

This dummy looked like a little boat bumper, the kind tied to marine docks to prevent scratches and dents. It was white. Hard. Had little bumps on it. A short black cord attached at one end.

"Why the nubs?" I said.

"They're supposed to prevent him from chewing it."

Little nubbins? Who were the dummy designers kidding? Seamus had a lengthy record of things chewed and or destroyed, mostly household items—kitchen towels, magazines, hairbrushes—forgivable due to human error, i.e., leaving said items within a Labrador's reach. I thought I had arranged the somewhat sturdy Nativity in a safe zone—on the top of the built-in buffet in the dining room. I was wrong. We have a customized Christmas crèche now—a three-legged camel, two mauled sheep, and a king that bears no gift because he has no arms.

"Toss the dummy just a little bit ahead of you."

I tossed it, but it went straight up in the air and fell two feet away. "Whoopsie!" I said.

"Try again."

This time, it made a nice arc and landed fifteen feet away from us.

"Send him, and when he gets it in his mouth, give him a tug."

"Okay." I meant "okay" as in "okay, I'll give the dog a tug on the rope," not "okay, Seamus, go get it." I couldn't blame him for blasting off. Seamus picked up the training dummy and was heading back, no tug needed. He swung wide of us.

"Pull him in!"

I tugged on the rope, pulling, then yanking.

"No! Hand over hand! Tell him to heel!"

I was not coordinated enough to pull and speak at the same time. Seamus was as confused as I was.

My father took over the reins. "Here, like this." He tossed the training dummy. He sent the dog with a loud and excited "Okay!" and when Seamus picked it up, my father yelled, "Heel!" and commenced with a smooth, firm, yet gentle hand-over-hand motion, preventing Seamus from his usual not-a-retrieve retrieve. "Not bad! Not bad!" he said, ruffling the dog's neck fur. "That's enough for today," he said.

"Really?"

"Yep. Keep your sessions short and end on a high note."

My father gave me homework, or rather "yard work," as he called it. My first assignment? Proper heeling, i.e., not the way I had been doing it.

Whenever I took Seamus for a walk on the nature trail, having him stay at my side was optional. On the days I felt like the world was taking me for granted, I was an alpha female; the days when everything came up

Mel, I'd let him run freely without any rhyme or reason. He crisscrossed in front of me; I didn't care. I knew he was supposed to be at my side, but it was a nature trail, and he was a Labrador. Wasn't it in his DNA to romp and cavort through tall grass? He got his aromatherapy for the day, and my shoulder was still sitting in its socket. Everyone won!

Our yard work began with me getting out his pinchy collar, which got him all excited. *Are we going to the kennel club? Am I going swimming? Is there a boat?* I chose to ignore this bad, jumping-up-and-down behavior, because I read somewhere that dogs jump up so they can make eye contact with you, and if you want the behavior to stop, you should turn away. Averting my gaze only encouraged him to jump higher. On his fifth up, I timed my knee to meet his ribcage on his way down, which didn't faze him as much as it had when my father performed it. Maybe my father's success had something to do with his police training. He had attended the FBI Academy in Quantico, Virginia. His kneecaps were licensed to kill.

Finally, with Seamus collared and on a short leash to inhibit the jumping, we walked around and around and around the outside of the house. I used my best growly voice and gave a very commanding "Heel!" And to my surprise, he heeled. Sort of. He slowed down and looked up at me—and wasn't trying just as important? He did better when we were on the narrow sidewalk, or when I could push his side up against the neighbor's fence as we walked. He had nowhere to go there, couldn't do anything *but* heel.

I probably should have ended there, on a high enough note, but we had to work on our stop and sit. In order to speed things up, I went into the house and put a handful of kibble in my front pocket. I knew it was wrong, but my father wasn't there. It was the outcome, not the process, right? Dogs can smell fear and detect cancer and traces of explosives, so why I thought a thin membrane of cotton would be enough to hide the scent of ground-up lamb and rice, I don't know.

The kibble was in the pocket on my right side. He forgot all about heeling. He kept running behind me, then in front, trying to get at—in—the pocket. He pawed at my pants. Drooled down my leg. "No!" I yelled and gave him a downward jerk. I should have given him an apology for setting him up to fail. He was only doing what his nose told him to do.

"Fine!" I said. "Here!" I grabbed the contents and dumped it on the grass. I had just rewarded him for being a pest and probably erased the heeling from his Labrador hard drive.

I had to end on a high note, and this was an all-time low. He was licking up the crumbs from the grass. "Heel!" I said, and gave him a quick jerk. He heeled. We retraced our steps. On the first lap, all was lost. But the second lap was better. I only had to jerk him once on the third, and by the fourth lap, he got it back.

"Let's not tell Grandpa about the…you know." I didn't want to use the doggy *F* word (food) because the heeling part of Seamus's brain would be pushed aside by the bigger part that had to do with eating. *Food? Where? Now? Here? How much? When can I have it?*

I walked Seamus around, then stopped and told him to sit, and when he did, I gave him a scratch behind his ears and a "Whoseagooddog?" No treat. Just praise. We did another lap. He heeled. I stopped. He sat. "Good boy!" I said. Dad had been right about the reward thing. The next time, I stopped. He sat and nudged my hand with his nose, no doubt thinking, *Well? I stopped. I sat. Where's the food? What's with this "whoseagooddog" crap?* I wanted to explain to him that he'd have to go cold turkey when it came to treats, but I knew him. All he would have heard would have been "turkey."

71

CHAPTER EIGHT

MOM-ORIAL DAY

It was Sunday, May 30. It would have been my mother's eighty-fourth birthday. My father had arranged a Mass to be said in her honor. Immediate-family-member attendance mandatory.

Caitlin and Angus had bused in from Madison the night before. We walked into the back of the church. Dad was sitting way, way in the front. I hate sitting in the front. I'm a back-of-the-church person. I feel less like I'm being judged. Dad wore his blue button-down shirt and a caramel-colored corduroy sport coat that my mother would have never let him leave the house in because it was May. No tie. He hates ties. He only wears one in extreme circumstances: my wedding, my sister's weddings, and Mom's funeral. He looked like a left shoe without a right, a sock whose mate had gone MIA in the laundry. We made the long walk up the aisle, then had the awkward "after you, no, after you, no, I insist, you go first" between me, Mark, and the kids, before I slid in next to my father.

He had his handkerchief at the ready. Shouldn't my mother be there? Next to him? In her London Fog trench coat? These were the same pews where my mother had held my mittened, three-year-old hand, and when I made a fuss, she'd let me sit down on the kneeler and play with her purse. We had crowded into them as a family since 1955. Christmas.

Easter. First Holy Communions—we walked in a processional from the school building two-by-two in long lines that stretched around the block, led by nuns in long black habits with face-pinching wimples.

I hadn't sat in that particular pew since the funeral. Smelling that church-y smell of incense and Jesus triggered bits and pieces of that day—like how the casket was off to the side, near the baptismal font. How I had elected not to hang out there because I was never good with dead people. They always looked so…dead. But—and I know this sounds cliché—she looked good. Much better than the last time I had seen her, back in the rehab center, looking hollow, waxen, and shrunken. The black-eyed mortician had done a good job. Her hair was fluffed. Her face nice and full. She was dressed for a comfortable after-life, in her favorite L.L.Bean white cotton turtleneck, her cranberry-colored cardigan, and those navy-blue fleece, elastic-waisted pants she loved—"They're sooo soft and keep me sooo warm!"

I remembered how my sister had lifted Mom's stiff arms and replaced the rosary that was wound around them with a bouquet of flowers. And how my father had sobbed, "Oh, Marian! Don't leave me!" when the pallbearers wheeled the casket down the aisle.

My niece, Amanda, arrived and slid in next to her cousins. She had her multiple tattoos hidden by a long-sleeved jacket and a scarf looped around her neck. My mother didn't understand the whole ink thing. "Why would anyone want to look like a sideshow freak?" My nephew, Adam, came in from New York. He was the golden boy—the firstborn grandson, and, therefore, my mother's favorite, even though she denied having any favorites. He got the premier Lego sets, so many Matchbox cars he needed a suitcase to carry them, and when he had come *this close* to spending a weekend in the pokey because of some (a lot) of unpaid parking tickets, who paid them? Grandma.

The organist announced the entrance hymn and launched into the first bars. My father leaned over to me and whispered, "Where the hell is your sister?"

Had she forgotten? Or had she remembered and thought it best not to show up? I thought of excusing myself from the pew, walking the long walk down the aisle to the back of the church, and calling her on my phone, but then I thought, *No.* As much as it would hurt my father—and I would hate to see him hurt—it should be on her to do damage control. Not me.

I shrugged a beats-the-hell-out-of-me shrug.

The celebrants walked up the aisle. When the holy book was placed upon the lectern and opened to today's Gospel, my sister made her entrance. She is an aspiring actress who has appeared in several low, low, *low*-budget, very, very, *very* independent films, shorts, and some Internet TV. She had chosen to come as a 1940s dame from a film noir. She wore a vintage dress, a felt tilt hat with a net, and platform open-toed Mary Janes. "Well, so far, I haven't burst into flames!" she announced loud enough for the congregation to hear before taking her seat.

My father shook his head. "Well, she made it," he said.

The Mass was the same as any other Sunday, except for the part about praying for our dearly departed who have left this world and were now in the hands of the Heavenly Father. When the priest said my mother's name, it was like the first time someone calls you Mrs. So-and-So or Mommy.

My father blew his nose into his handkerchief, while the rest of us dabbed our eyes with lumpy pieces of forgotten, linty tissue pulled from our pockets. Except for Linda. She remained Jackie Kennedy stoic. "Do you need a Kleenex?" I whispered to her during the collection.

"No," she said. "I've already moved on."

How? I spent the rest of the Mass wondering if she was in denial or better adjusted than the rest of us.

Brunch was held in a restaurant of Dad's choosing. It was one of those all-you-can-eat buffet places where the pancakes are as big as hubcaps, waffles are the size of tennis rackets, and ordering an omelet made with only three eggs causes a lot of raised eyebrows.

The subject of what to do with the memorial monies people had included in their sympathy cards came up.

"How about a year's worth of fresh flowers for her crypt?" I said.

My father shook his head. "Nope. Can't. The cemetery doesn't allow it."

"What?!" we said in unison.

He explained that there were rules. No fresh floral arrangements. No stuffed animals. No cards. "What is this? A cemetery? Or Nazi Germany?" Linda was on her third Bloody Mary.

"If I want flowers, I have to buy the ones that they sell there, and those aren't even real. They're fake and they fade."

"And that is why"—Linda turned to her daughter and son—"I want to be thrown in one of those places where you are just left to decompose, and then people have to come and determine how long you've been lying there, depending upon the maggots, for, like, science."

Typical family-table talk.

"I have an idea," my daughter, Caitlin said. "Grandma loved to read to the kids at the grade school—"

"Uh-huh." The table nodded.

"—so why not take the money and maybe buy some books for their library?"

Maybe a bookcase to go with them? Perfect!

Starving college students and the one husband helped themselves to seconds. Drunken sisters to thirds. I had a hard time finishing firsts. Golden Boy and I stayed put.

"So, Grandpa," he asked, "what have you been doing with yourself?"

I wanted to hear the answer because it might shed more light on my father's stage of grieving. He wouldn't lie to his grandson. He would fess up to whatever, and if his whatever was not acceptable, Adam wouldn't let it slide. He would tell Grandpa what he should be doing, or not doing, and Grandpa would listen because Golden Boy.

"Oh, you know," he said, pouring a river of syrup over his pile of pancakes, "trying to teach an old dog new tricks. Hers." My father rolled his eyes and pointed at me with his thumb.

"How's it going?"

"Oh…as good as you'd expect."

"What's that supposed to mean?" I said, a little offended.

"Nothing! Just, well, come on. That dog? You?"

Adam wanted details. In Grandpa's version, I was really inept. Seamus was inept-er. The jury was still out on our hopelessness.

"Hey! You just wait until the next time. We've been working on our heeling," I said.

"Yeah. Uh-huh. Sure."

He either truly doubted that Seamus and I had been working on our assignment, or he was setting me up to play the part my mother had played: foil.

"What? You don't believe me?"

"Oh, I believe you. I just don't think it'll do any good."

Adam laughed.

"Oh, really? Well, game on, mister!"

My sister tink-tinked her glass of extra-bloody Bloody Mary. She stood. "I have an announcement to make!"

The table talk ceased. She had our attention as well as the rest of the brunch crowd's.

"I will be costarring in an Internet cooking show, playing the role of Cynthia, a drunken sidekick to a drag queen named Ruthie."

No one said anything. I think Linda had expected us to be more shocked, that my father would have had an outburst, but he didn't. He simply turned to me and asked, "So, are we on for Wednesday?"

CHAPTER NINE

HOW YOU SAY "GIVE"

MAY WAS IN THE books. We were into June. June might be easier to get through. There weren't any mom-centric holidays or anniversaries to contend with. Just Father's Day.

When I drove into the kennel club parking lot, I felt confident. Prepared. Ready for whatever Dad would throw at us. My father was parked in the same place he always parked, under the tree, next to the oil tank. He wore his favorite blaze-orange Purina Dog Chow baseball cap. He was clean shaven. He smiled and waved a follow-me wave.

We took the other road, the one on the other side of the parking lot, down a different hill than usual, and ended up at a different, much bigger pond. We parked in the shade, my tailgate pointing into the woods, instead of out and into the sun.

"You did the yard work, right?" he said, changing into his boots.

"We did!"

"Every day?"

"Um, yeah. Every day-ish."

My father shook his head. "Bring him out and over to the pond."

I opened the kennel door, and Seamus rocketed pond-side before I had a chance to grab the rope, his collar, his anything.

"Heel!" I called after him.

"Keep calling him!" became an all-too familiar refrain, as did "I thought you said you worked with him?!"

Seamus barreled toward the shore, full steam. I had forgotten he was attached to a twenty-foot-long rope. I remembered to step on it just before he hit the water. He jerked backward, like a bungee jumper at the end of the bungee.

"Tell him to sit and make him wait."

I did. He did. That should have been good for some praise from Dad. I—we—got nothing. My father grabbed one of several dummies from his five-gallon bucket, tossed one of the white, hard plastic ones into the pond just far enough for the rope to reach.

"Do like I showed you. Pull the rope hand over hand. Got it?"

"Got it."

I sent the dog. He went in, swam a short swim, got the dummy in his mouth, and when he turned, I began my hand-over-hand pulling. When he got up on the shore, he tried his evasive maneuvers.

"Keep pulling him toward you!" my father shouted.

"I am!"

"Now, reach down and say, 'give'!"

"Give!" I said.

"No! GI-*VE*!" he said.

"GIVE!" I said.

"No, not GIVE. Say it like this, GI-*VE*!" he said, creating a second syllable.

It didn't matter if I said, give or GIVE! or GI-IVVVE, it was not happening. Seamus shook his head from side to side, clenching the white plastic thing in his jaws before he dropped it on the muddy bank.

"Maybe he'll do better—I'll do better—this next time," I said.

"Give me that dog!"

He led Seamus to the edge of the water, made him sit and wait, and then threw the dummy. Seamus waited.

"Okay!" my father said, then stepped back a few feet from shore.

Seamus launched. Swam. Picked up the dummy, swam back, and as soon as his paws hit the muddy grass, my father pulled him in close.

"*Give!*" he shouted.

On a short tether, Seamus did the same old dodge and weave. *See? It's not me!* Good thing my father had worn his knee-high rubber boots because, at one point, both he and the dog were in the water.

"*No!*" my father growled. Seamus spat the dummy out. Progress?

He repeated the drill. Threw the thing, sent the dog, dog retrieved thing, swam back, came up on shore, my father gave the *give* command, and once again, Seamus performed the evasive hard-mouth tango, but this time, my father was quick. He grabbed the dog by his scruff with one hand and shouted "*No!*" accompanied with a quick jerk. For an eighty-three-year-old man, my father was remarkably coordinated.

The next toss and reel was performed not to perfection but something close enough. Less of a hard mouth. When my father said give, Seamus gave.

"See? You're not so dumb!" He gave Seamus a scratch behind his ears, then turned to me. "Don't be afraid to show the dog affection!"

He should talk, Mr. Not-A-Hugger.

"All right, you can put him away. We'll end on a high note."

I put Seamus in his kennel feeling a little bit like I had prepared for the test but had found out I had taken poor notes or read the wrong chapters. Dad took a seat on his mud-covered, bloodstained, upturned five-gallon bucket.

"I don't get it, Dad. I worked with him. Just like you said!"

He had trained all his past champions since they were pups. Sit.

Stay. Heel. Repeat. Repeat. Repeat. Bad behavior was nipped in the bud with a firm, loud, as-close-to-primal-as-a-human-could-get growl.

"Dad? You don't think Seamus is like your old dog Duke, do you?"

Poor Duke. He was supposed to pick up where my father's first dog and first champion, Belle, left off, but you know that adage: you never want to be the person who replaces a legend; you want to be the person after the replacement. So maybe Duke was doomed from the get-go.

Duke had a huge head and a small brain. He used his hard head to crash his way through field fencing, into boulders and tree stumps, in order to get to a dead pheasant. He retrieved decoys instead of ducks. He never won any trophies. His preference for faux ducks got him and my father disqualified from many a field trial. Any other handler would have given him away or, worse, had him put down, but to my father's credit, he did neither. There was something endearing about Duke. If a dog were graded for effort, he would get a solid A+ every time.

My mother and father had gone out of town and left the dog duties—feeding, watering, kennel flushing—to Linda. She went to feed Duke and noticed blood all over the floor of the kennel. Duke was hemorrhaging...from what? The dog was only five! He was still alive, but just barely. Linda wrapped him in a blanket, put him in her car, and sped to her vet, a guy who used to be the veterinarian at the zoo, instead of the one my father had been using.

Duke could be saved...but it was going to be expensive. "Listen," she told the ex–zoo vet, "my father always said if he were in a boat with my mother and the dog, and one of them had to go overboard...it wouldn't be the dog."

Duke had contracted parvovirus, even though my father had had him vaccinated for it. Apparently, the dose his vet had administered wasn't a good batch or the booster was given too late, whatever. Duke was saved. My father switched vets. And my mother was still in the boat.

"Yeah, poor Duke," he said, shaking his head. "He tried."

"Seamus is trying—" I said.

"To kill me," my father finished for me.

Dad made a joke! And I laughed! There was something in his voice...a lightness? Was he glad that Seamus was such a handful? Maybe he liked the challenge of turning my dog into...a real dog?

"That dog," he said, taking off his boots, "he ain't no Duke, that's for sure!"

CHAPTER TEN

GUN-SHY

M$_Y$ SISTER AND I were latchkey kids. We didn't see a lot of our father because he worked from 4:00 p.m. to midnight. If he arrested someone, then he had to go to court and sometimes he didn't get home until 3:00 a.m. He'd be sleeping when we left for school and gone by the time we got back. My father usually had precooked a wonderful dinner that just needed reheating on our heavy, white, boxy, Odin-brand stove. We were home alone for an hour and a half, with specific instruction to do our schoolwork and then our chores. Linda was supposed to make coffee, and my job was to peel the potatoes, so when my mother walked through the back door from her office job at 4:45 (5:00 if her bus was late), she had a nice, hot meal waiting for her.

When we were in grade school, on the third Thursday of each month, we had permission from Sister Augusta to leave the school grounds during lunch. My father picked us up in the blue Chevy Impala station wagon and took us to McDonald's. We'd eat our burgers and fries while he'd make jokes about this and that. We'd talk about school and stuff. Quality Dad time.

●　●　●

I hadn't eaten fast food in years, but after we were done training, Dad asked me if I was hungry (sort of) and would I like to grab a burger, his treat. He took me to the same fast-food restaurant he used to take my mother to when she would go and watch him train dogs.

"Mom always ordered a cheeseburger and fries."

"Oh. Uh-huh."

"And she got a coffee."

"Um…I'm more of a tea person."

"Oh." He sounded disappointed. Should I have ordered what she had?

We sat at the same table they had sat at, which was kind of sweet but kind of sad. I waited while he ordered, and my mind went into movie-montage mode, scenes of them in their early retirement years, eating and chatting, laughing. Cut to a few years later: nothing changed except they had more gray in their hair, then my mother becoming slower, eating less, talking less, laughing less. Then Dad, sitting alone. Fade to black.

I had to stop torturing myself with these dismal mental images of my father living in a depressing documentary, hopeless, alone, and brokenhearted. It wasn't helping me move forward. What stage of grief was I in, anyway? I wasn't in denial. I wasn't angry. Bargaining? Weren't things beyond the point of bargaining?

I still had to force myself to do things, like eat, do laundry, stand in a field while my father yelled at me because I wasn't paying attention to what the dog was or was not doing. So…depressed? Yeah, that sounded about right.

I had suffered from chronic depression with general anxiety disorder for years and was on medication. I had thought that Mr. Wellbutrin would wash away the top layer of grief that had been added to my gloomy layer cake. *You call yourself an antidepressant? You should be ashamed.*

My dad unwrapped his chicken tenders and ate his fries. I ate my not-what-Mom-ordered fish sandwich. Neither of us said anything. Was he thinking about her? Was this even a good idea, coming here? I should have suggested a different fast-food place. Wait. He was the one who had suggested it.

"Hey, Dad..."

"Yeah?"

"Father's Day is next week." The only reason I knew that was because I'd had a text from my daughter asking if I had any ideas as to what she and her brother should get their father for it.

"It is?"

"Yep."

Last year, before Mom went downhill, he'd sent out an email, "What You Can Get Me For Father's Day" in the subject line. He had a short list that year: Nikon Buckmaster 9 x 40 rifle scope, a St. Croix fishing rod, or a sweatshirt—"no ridiculous sayings on the front."

I usually made him a card with a vintage family photo, and I'd write something witty to go inside. This year? Maybe a picture of him with a dog? Something about a retrieving fail? Would funny be appreciated? Should the card I make for him say how much I loved him? Or would that be too...not us? Would too serious be...too serious?

"So...is there anything special you want?"

"Um, not really." He balled up the paper napkin and put it in the middle of the table.

"Come on, Dad. Nothing?"

He took another bite of his crispy chicken tender, finished chewing, and said, "Other than having your mother back? No. I can't think of a thing."

I had nothing. No comeback. His words hung there, above our

table, like circling turkey vultures near a landfill. If I could have had her back, I would have the seventy-year-old version of her back. She was still in the game. Fun. Funny. Self-deprecating. Still driving herself from point A to B. Volunteering. Sewing. Knitting.

There was a story on the TVs hung in the corner of the restaurant about a spaniel that had adopted a baby raccoon, and they were together, on a sofa, curled up to each other.

"Hey, Dad," I said.

"Yeah?"

"Why did you get a springer spaniel? Why not a Lab?"

"I was going to get a Lab. Remember Shadow?"

Shadow was our longest tenured family pet. I was five when she came into our world. She was a mutt of spaniel and Labrador lineage, conceived during a whirlwind courtship out on the mucky marsh. Hunter A sent his in-heat female Lab out of the duck blind to retrieve at the same time Hunter B sent his spaniel from his duck blind, and the two of them met in the middle, on a muddy bank, for a little bit of retriever romance.

She arrived on the heels of our previous family-pet fails—a parakeet that my mother couldn't stand for all the squawking and seed spillage. One day, as she was cleaning the cage outside, she just *happened* to leave the wire door open and…problem solved. Then there was a guinea pig that my sister claims was killed by two-year-old me. I have no recollection of this. But she does, after several gin and diet tonics.

There were dime-store turtles and goldfish that had been purchased with good intentions of recreating their environments in a deep, square plastic bin that was kept under the kitchen sink and used for my mother's hand washables. Swimming around, looking at a kitschy mermaid or spending the rest of my days staring at four red, plastic walls probably would have killed me too.

Shadow lived in the garage, in a doghouse with burlap bags for bedding. The only times she was off the property were when my father took her hunting and when she went missing for three days and got herself in trouble. She gave birth to four puppies on the weekend my father was fishing in Canada, forcing my mother into doggy midwifery.

Shadow was the constant in our silent 8 mm home movies, sauntering through graduations, lounging under a picnic table as we mouthed "Happy Birthday to You," languishing next to a lawn chair on Father's Days. I was the one who found the egg-sized lump under her leg pit. A few days later, I came home from high school to a limp chain, an empty doghouse, and a to-the-point note on the kitchen table: *Shadow had cancer. Dad.*

"So…anyway, why did you get a spaniel?"

Pure happenstance. He wanted a purebred Lab. All his cop and hunting buddies were Lab men. But it just so happened that somebody knew somebody who had a litter of springer puppies.

"I went to look, and you know how it is—you can't just go and look at a litter of pups and *not* buy one."

In fact, I did. I had gone to look at someone's aboveground swimming pool for ideas, because my husband and I were entertaining getting one for our yard, and the pool people just happened to have a litter of golden retriever puppies, and I thought, *Well, I'm here. I'll just take a look at them.* After we paid $350, we had ourselves a dog named Harvey and forgot about the pool.

"You know," he said, taking a long draw of Pepsi from his straw, "we had a dog before Shadow."

"We did?" News to me.

"Maybe you were too little to remember. I bought it for Mom. Oh, it was a cute dog. We called it Cinnamon."

"How long did we have this Cinnamon?"

"Well, this is hard—" He broke off. Took a sip of his Pepsi. He had wanted a dog to hunt with, and he thought a cocker spaniel would fit the bill. "But, you know, back then…and I hate to admit this, now, but…I thought that you just bought the dog and it already knew how to hunt and retrieve."

"No!" I said as if he had just told me he was going vegan or wanted to date a younger woman. This was shocking for two reasons—one, that my always-knowledgeable father had thought this, and two, that he would admit to his mistake.

"Yeah. I thought somehow it was all instinct. And it is, but you still have to train the dog."

I didn't know what to say. I just sat there and let him get on with the saga of Cinnamon.

"So I took it hunting, and I shot my gun, and…" He shook his head, then got up from the table and disposed of his trash. Were we done here? Should I follow him? I still had fries. He still had fries. And his Pepsi.

He came back and wiped the crumbs off the tabletop, before he put his elbows on it, like he had done so many times at our kitchen table—bad news normally followed this gesture. I braced myself for whatever revelation he was about to make.

"Did you…shoot…the dog?"

He took in a deep breath. Exhaled. "No—well, at least I don't think so. I mean, it took off. Boom! Gun-shy."

"And you never found it?"

"No. Never. I looked until it got dark. And then I had to come home and tell your sister and your mother that I lost the dog," he said.

There were tears in his eyes. I sat back in my chair, relieved. Not for me but for him. How could he have forgiven himself had he shot the dog? He had never opened up to me like this. It was a little hard for me to wrap my brain around it...but I felt like he and I were bonding in bigger ways. Better ways. And the bond was lifting me slowly up and out of my depression. We both sat there, eating our cold french fries. Too bad we're not a hugging family.

CHAPTER ELEVEN

SIGNS

I KNOW I SHOULDN'T have lied to my father about why I couldn't attend the next dad-daughter-dog training session. I told him I had to see a doctor, and that was *kind of* true. I knew if I said *doctor*, then he wouldn't ask for specifics about the whys or the what-fors, because anything medical could possibly be related to my lady parts and those were outside his jurisdiction. Tangled web averted.

I needed to talk with someone. A professional. It was for the best if he didn't know that I was going to see a psychic.

After Mom died, I waited for her to send me a sign. Why didn't I have any dreams that she sat on the edge of my bed and told me she was okay, like her mother had done to her back in 1957? When my mom's oldest sister—and my favorite aunt, Ellen—died, a Baltimore oriole landed in my birdbath. Up until then, the birdbath had been visited only by the drab and average. When my fun-loving, should-have-been-in-showbiz Aunt Jane passed, a cedar waxwing showed up. The only cedar waxwings I had seen up until then were in books. Mom had passed in April, and so far? Nothing. What was the holdup? Was she stuck in orientation? Why wasn't she coming around?

I needed something to convince me she was okay, because in the last-time-I-saw-her-alive scene that kept playing over and over and over in my head, she was at the rehab place, and she kept telling me she was cold, and I told her that I would bring her a down-filled comforter when I saw her again the next day.

"Am I dying?" she asked.

"Not today!" I said, accompanied by a pooh-pooh wave of my hand, a gesture I meant to come off as assuring.

"Are you sure?" she said.

"Positive!"

I said good-bye, gave her a smooch on the top her head, and walked out of her room, down the hall, passed the dining area. Her roommate, Helen, was in a wheelchair near the elevators. She wanted to tell me something, but I had to bend over to hear her.

"Don't give her false hope," she whispered in my ear.

What did she mean by "false hope"? Perhaps Helen knew more about my mother's situation than anyone else did or wanted to admit. I got into the elevator and pushed the *L* for the lobby. Four hours later, after watching Fred and Ginger spinning across a dance floor, with the taste of frozen custard lolling on her tongue, Mom was gone.

I knew the veil separating the world of the living from that of the dead was a permeable membrane. I knew this from my past guilty pleasure—being a regular watcher of psychic Sylvia Browne on the *Montel Williams Show*. I could not get enough of what some would call her "shtick." People from the audience would come to the mic and ask questions regarding their loved ones' deaths, and Sylvia would respond in her smokes-six-packs-a-day-with-a-shot-of-Jack voice, "Oh, he/she is standing in back of you right now," or, "No, honey, the car crash didn't kill him. He had a heart attack; then he hit the tree."

She knew exactly how the deceased contacted the survivor: "Every time you smell a cigar, it's him," or, "She'll move things around, like your car keys," or simply, "Feathers." The audience member looked so relieved. I didn't think she was causing any harm. I mean, she gave people peace of mind and closure. What's wrong with that? I needed closure. I needed peace of mind. I needed feathers.

How does one choose a psychic? The Internet! I did a Google search and clicked on "The Best Psychic Directory," because, well... Best. Psychic. Directory. What I was looking for? Someone who was definitely local, not expensive, and didn't look like Morticia Addams. I did not care about Tarot cards, and I didn't want any career or relationship advice. I was not impressed by résumés that listed an ability to channel the Archangel Metatron who walked the earth as Enoch, or the person who claimed to have a Native American spirit guide or the woman with a degree in spirit medium–ship.

The more I read about spirit realms and metaphysical soul retrievers from the various websites, the more I worried about my immortal soul because of my fourth-grade nun, Sister Mary Marcelline. She had found out that Gail and LuAnn and I had played with a Ouija board during a sleepover at LuAnn's house (how she knew, I never found out) and we were summoned to her desk during recess. "Sure, you think it's just a game... Tell that to Satan!" But I wasn't in fourth grade. I was fifty-eight and needed answers. To hell with Sister Marcelline. To hell with Satan. I went back to the Google search page. I scrolled, scrolled, scrolled. The listing *beneath* the Best Psychic Directory made me go, *Whoa*. First of all, the psychic had the same name as my mother—Marian—and second of all, her suite number was 817, and when is my birthday? August 17! I called and left a message. I was careful not to supply any information other than my name, my cell number, and that I was requesting an appointment for Wednesday. She sent me a confirmation text for 9:30.

I got there a tad early and had to wait in the hallway. She arrived scant moments after me, looking just as I had hoped—Judi Dench-ish with a heaping helping of Helena Bonham Carter, exactly what I wanted in a person who would be giving me the skinny on the goings-on in the spirit realm.

"You'll have to give me a minute," she said.

I heard her checking her voice mail through the office door.

>beep< Hi, it's Sharon! I just wanted to call about my soul contracts. Call me. Bye!

>beep< Hi, it's Anthony, and I forgot what you said about my star chart, so pleasepleaseplease call me!

>beep< Hi, it's Sharon again. The dog's not eating. Is it because she's mirroring my issue with food?

Her door opened. "You can come in now."

The office was *Mad Men* meets the great and powerful Oz. The patchouli smell took me back to...college? 1974? Astrological gewgaws—crescent moons, stars, Ouija board planchettes—were arranged across the top of a sleek postmodern credenza. The potted fern near the window needed repotting.

She motioned for me to have a seat at the round, cloth-covered table, while she corralled a few gray strands of hair that had escaped from the higgledy-piggledy mess of her updo. I pushed my fifty-dollar bill across the pentagram-patterned tablecloth and felt a rush of heat up my pant leg. A hot flash? Or hellfire? She lit the regulation psychic-medium candle.

"How can I help you?"

"Well, see, um, my mom...died, and I'm—I need to know if she's okay."

"How long ago has it been since she crossed over?"

"April."

"Ooh, that's recent!" She got her laptop from her cluttered desk.

Laptop?

"What time did she die?"

"Like nine in the evening. I think. Or maybe before that, like around eight?"

She typed.

"And when was she born?"

"May. 1929," I said. She continued typing.

"Hmm. So, she was eighty-three, almost eighty-four? That's a long life."

True. But not long enough for my liking.

"Did you bring anything of hers? Like a ring?"

Shit! Was I supposed to come prepared? I had my mother's engagement ring. My father had handed it to me at the funeral in a small, velvet bag. I didn't bring it with me because it was still at the jewelers, getting the shank replaced, worn thin by seventy years of cleaning up after other people.

I told Marian the Psychic about the last time I saw my mom, my thoughts during that day, the "false hope" thing, and how I had maybe, kind of contributed to her death. "I was in my car, and I said something out loud about how I wished that she *would* go home for supper or shopping for shoes with her sister Ellen."

"I don't understand."

"She told me she heard her mother calling her home for supper."

"Oh…I see."

"And that her sister Ellen had come to visit, but Ellen died a year ago."

"Well…yes. Uh-huh."

She didn't say anything. She didn't type anything. She just looked. At me? The wall? Mom?

"Your mother…was…confused."

"Yeah, toward the end there, she'd call me up in the middle of the night and ask me where my dad was because she was at the airport and she was waiting for him to pick her up."

"No, I mean, she thought she was dreaming."

"Oh, you mean—"

"When she crossed."

"Was she alone?"

"No, there were two women."

Aunt Jane? Aunt Ellen?

"They came to get her. One of them—oh, how can I say this? Was rather…plain looking—"

My mother's old maid aunt Anastasia? From Philly?

"—and the other…was quite pretty…with a big hat that was a deep red-wine color."

Ho. Ly. Shit.

My mom had a black-and-white picture of her parents taken on their wedding day in 1922. It hung in her kitchen in the alcove above her sewing machine, and in it, my grandmother wore a dark suit topped off with a big-brimmed hat that my mother always told me was "a deep red-wine color."

Maybe the hat was a good guess, but the color? "What about a sign? How come I don't feel her around me?"

"You've got to give her time," she said.

"It's been four months…"

"Sometimes they need time to figure things out. Time for them is not what it is for us. There's no clock. No calendar. Certainly no deadlines."

"So she's still getting used to, you know, being dead?"

"Well, I wouldn't say 'dead' because her energy is still around."

"It is?"

"Of course! Don't be so impatient. She'll get in touch. When you need it most."

I could have used a sign in those early weeks trying to find my new north. I could have used her hand on my cheek, giving me a "there, there" from the beyond when I was sleep-howling.

"And you have to be receptive. Maybe she's contacted you in a way you haven't been expecting."

"Such as?"

She gave me no answer, just a shrug. "Well, I'm afraid our time is up." She thanked me for making the appointment, and if I had any other concerns, I could always contact her for another session.

I felt a little bit duped. I had expected pseudo-Sylvia to say something like, "Oh, she says you shouldn't worry, that she's with her sisters," or "Your mother thanks you for that hot fudge sundae you brought her in the hospital," or "Having your father work with your dog was all her idea."

Had she said any of those things, I would have had closure, big-time, instead of feeling big-time stupid. But…there was that hat thing. And the part about the two women. Okay, I'd give her that.

When I got back home, I called my father to reschedule.

"I tried to call you," he said, "but I kept getting this message, something about your inbox being full. Are we on for next Wednesday?"

We were.

It had been a while—months—since I had purged my machine. I started to listen—robocalls, hang-ups, dial tones, relatives asking how my mother was doing, my father sounding stressed about hospital stuff—delete, delete, delete. And then I got to the end. Saturday. April. 14. 9:33 a.m.

> "Hi, it's your mom. I'm doing much better today. Uh, I got up, and I ate my breakfast, and I just… I'm doing better, so you don't have to worry about me… If you were going to worry…don't worry. Bye."

Was this it? My sign? The psychic had said Mom would be in touch, and what better way for her to do it than on my answering machine?

CHAPTER TWELVE

I HOPE YOU'RE HAPPY

The day was lining up to be a scorcher. All the TV weatherpeople were using their best Armageddon voices, dire with ozone warnings, heat indexes, and the importance of keeping hydrated. I hated the heat, the humidity. I merely tolerated summer. Give me cold and dreary. Rain, sleet, or snow. I live for sweater weather. Nothing like a bulky fisherman's knit to conceal one's figure flaws.

The sky had that hazy glow of heat. There was no wind. Dad had pushed our training time two hours earlier: 8:30 a.m.

The kennel club's vegetation had a tropical feel. The dew was still on the tall grasses and dripped off the leaves. The cicadas sounded like a band of bagpipers droning one long, sustaining note. My father rolled down the window of his dusty truck, which meant I had to roll down mine in order to hear him.

"Let's do water work today. It'll keep him cool! We'll go to the big pond. He's getting too used to that puppy pond. He needs a challenge. Follow me!"

The sun wasn't yet above the tree line and already my shorts were sticking to my legs. Dad was in his Notre Dame T-shirt and had his baggy jeans held up by red suspenders. He looked to me like he was beginning to gain some of the weight he had lost. His jeans were a bit on the saggy side, but physically, he looked less wilted. Maybe my plan of all this standing and sweating and swearing at a dog was starting to pay off, make him feel better. And as for me?

My husband had noticed a difference. "I can tell when you've been out with your dad and the dog," he said.

"Because I smell?"

"No, you seem, less—you know… More like your old self—not that you're *old…*"

The big pond was at the bottom of a long, gradual hill. It was more out in the open than the puppy pond was.

"So, what's the plan?" I asked.

"Oh…you'll see," he said and gave me a wink. A wink? Well now.

He went around to the back of his truck and got a bucket full of dummies—one orange with nubs, a familiar white one with hexagonal ridges, one half-black, half-white with hexagonal ridges, and an articulated one that looked like a dead mallard.

"Why is that one black and white?" I said.

"Easier for the dog to see on water or land. They don't see color; they see the contrast."

"What's with the orange one?"

"Easier for the handler to see."

The faux dead duck was self-explanatory.

"Before you open the kennel door, tell him to wait." Hadn't I been doing that for—what? The past four months? Why was he giving me instructions for something that he'd seen me do over and over? I blamed my crankiness on my sweating. "Make sure he's sitting."

I checked to see if Seamus's back end made contact with the plastic floor inside his kennel. Usually he did a half-assed sit, more like a very low crouch, his muscles at the ready for immediate launching. "Sit!" I said. And he did.

"Now, as you open the door, tell him to wait."

"Why?"

"Just do as I say!"

I hadn't heard him use that command in quite a while. Years. Decades. I remembered, one time, when I was nine and Linda was thirteen, we had just sat down to dinner. Dad was home because he was off duty—technically he was never *off duty* because crime fighting is a 24/7 job. He told Linda to get up and get him a glass of milk and she said, "Why?" and he said, "Just do as I say!" and Linda pointed to my mother and said, "Why can't *she* get it?" Dad hit the table with his fist, got up, pushed his chair back so hard it hit the window and broke it, then he stormed out of the house, got into the Chevy, and burned rubber out of the driveway. I, who had not caused the glass-shattering, skid-marked chain of events, sat there and bawled. Linda sat there with her arms folded across her chest, defiant. My mother simply sat down and said, "I hope you're happy!"

I took a deep breath and opened the kennel door. "Wait!" I said, and winced because I knew Seamus would be flying past me at any second. Any second.

"Now, just leave the door open."

"Won't he jump out?"

"If he does, make him go back in."

"And why are we doing this?"

"Because we're waiting for him to get a little steady. He's got to know that he can't just explode. And you've got to remember that you are in control."

"Yeah, right. Me. In control."

"Well, aren't you?"

"Not all the time."

"You should be."

I have to say, I was surprised that when I opened the door, Seamus just sat there, panting, his nose taking in all the kennel club smells, his eyes looking at me, then back at my father, then back at me.

My father spoke slowly, with a measured calmness in his voice. Like he was instructing me how to dismantle a bomb. "Now, take the lead and clip it to his collar, keeping him at a sit. And then, once you've got him and yourself ready, tell him to heel."

I clipped the lead to his collar. He stayed sitting.

"Whenever you're ready, tell him…"

"Heel!" I said. Seamus walked himself out of the kennel and sat down at my side. No pulling. No yelling. No false starts. "Who is this dog, and where is Seamus?" I said.

Why hadn't I been doing that earlier? Why hadn't Dad figured this out weeks, months ago? I could have saved my shoulder socket some wear and tear. Perhaps he hadn't because he hadn't been fully engaged in this dog-daughter training? Maybe he had been a little pre-occupied? Maybe, now, the Mourning Marian room in his brain was becoming a teeny bit smaller? Or at least less messy?

Dad took the bucket o' dummies with him on the long walk to the other side of the bigger and more challenging pond. Seamus sat at my side. He seemed calmer. I felt calmer. Or was it the heat? Seamus didn't take his eyes off my father as he walked through the tall, damp grass, then down the road, then over the footbridge, around the bend, and directly across from us.

"Well, aren't you a good dog! Sitting here. All attentive." I said to Seamus. He held his gaze toward my father, even when he took a moment to scratch.

"Ready?!" my father yelled from a little high spot rife with cattails and probably mosquitoes that could be carrying West Nile virus. My father doesn't apply insect repellent. He doesn't have to. Mosquitoes don't bite him. I think they're too intimidated. And as for sunblock? *That's for women.* I held up my hand—our "ready" signal.

Dad threw one of the white dummies, and it landed flat on the surface of the water. Then he threw the other farther and to the left. Splat! And then he threw the orange one, backward, into the tall reeds. He cupped his hands to his mouth and called, "Send your dog to the first one!"

I pushed Seamus's face in the direction where the first dummy had fallen. "Okay!" I said. He bounded into the water and went right for it—good dog!—but on the way back, he spotted dummy number two, spit out dummy number one, and swam over to his preferred choice, so when he brought me number two, I didn't know what I was supposed to do. Correct him? Show him affection? What?

"Take it," my father said, a little winded from the long walk back.

"Yeah, but, it's not the one—"

"Send him back in to get the other one."

"How will he know which one?"

"Just do as I say."

Seamus swam out and got the dummy he should have retrieved, swam back, brought it up on shore, sat, and gave it up. He shook off before I could give him his allotted affection. I didn't mind getting wet.

"Send him back. He's got one more to find."

Seamus was panting. Too tired to go back in? "The one in the reeds? How's he going to—"

"He'll find it."

My father seemed so sure of Seamus. I was not in that camp. He'd have to swim across the entire length of the pond, which was more like a small lake, complete with a dock, boat, and a sign about catching and releasing fish. Then he'd have to go over a rise and through a small channel, then find the hidden treasure and make the return trip.

"Okay!" I said, and he ran into the pond like Frankie Avalon after Annette Funicello.

He swam across and trotted out, then scurried up the distant shoreline. He ran to the left, his nose to ground.

"He can't find it," I said.

"He'll find it."

"Well, what if he can't?"

"He *will*." My father seemed so certain.

Seamus ran back to where he had exited the pond and turned to cover the ground on our right. Then he doubled back and went to the left again.

"He looks confused. Should I blow—?"

"Sometimes…you have to *trust* your dog."

We lost sight of him. I assumed he had made it to the reeds—they were moving wildly, flapping like one of those wacky, inflatable, waving tube men in front of car dealership grand openings.

"Dad?"

"What?"

"Has your dog ever lost a dummy in here?"

"Never."

"Never?"

"Never."

Seamus appeared, then disappeared back into the reeds.

"As a matter of fact, I've had to send him to find the ones that somebody else's dog didn't."

Seamus was the only game in town. If he couldn't find it, somebody else's dog might have to. The reeds parted. Seamus appeared with an orange thing in his mouth.

"Ha! He's got it! Call him in."

I blew the whistle. I watched the dog swimming for a couple of seconds, then shifted my focus to my father's face.

He was beaming. "I told you he'd find it."

Seamus walked up onto the grass, ran behind me before I coaxed him to my side, and coughed up the dummy along with half the lake before he shook off all over us.

"Let's give him a rest. Put him back in his kennel," Dad said.

"Should I give him a drink?"

"Nah. He gets enough water swimming."

I put Seamus back into his kennel after he took a long pee. Dad and I sat down on the empty five-gallon buckets that once held the dummies. Like father, like daughter. It didn't feel uncomfortable as we sat in silence. For the first time in what seemed like forever, my mind wasn't filled with maudlin thoughts but with doggy-related questions.

"Hey, Dad?"

"What?"

"What do you think of dog parks?"

He scoffed. "Dumbest things ever!"

"Would you ever consider taking a dog to a doggy day care?"

"Hell no!"

"Why does the dog do three or four okay retrieves, then falls back into his old bad habits?"

"Either he gets complacent, or you give up and then he gives up."

"I give up? What do you mean?"

"Oh, I don't know, maybe you're bored or don't want to be here, and the dog…he picks up on that and he figures, 'If she don't give a shit, why should I?'"

"No! That's not true." Well, okay. Sort of true. I didn't want to be there that day. Sweating, sticking to a plastic bucket at 9:30 in the morning.

"Or you let him get away with stuff and he gets sloppy."

He was right. I had lapsed back into my old la-di-da approach to dog training because I hated the reprimanding. Funny, I didn't have any trouble yelling at my children when they did something stupid.

"Don't forget, he's got to relearn stuff; you've got to relearn stuff. Sometimes, training the dog is secondary. It's all about training the trainer."

"My psychiatrist kind of told me the same thing," I said.

"Your what now?"

"Psychiatrist."

I waited for Dad to say something about me going to see a psychiatrist, something like, "A shrink? What the hell?!" but he didn't. He took a long swig of water from his kennel club water bottle. "Want some?"

I wiped off the top of the bottle with my shirt and took a drink. The water had a stale plastic taste.

I had gone to see the psychiatrist on Monday because…getting out of bed was still hard, and I needed to get some pointers in grief management. The psychiatrist's office was surprisingly similar to the psychic's, except without the occult accents. She even started the session with the same question: "How can I help you?"

I told her about my mother's death and how if I didn't have to do this dog thing with my father, I probably would be under the covers or catatonic.

"And, speaking of my father," I had said to her, grabbing a tissue, "he's so...sad...and...it's killing me!" I blew my nose. Hard. Loud.

"Of course he's sad!" she had said, not in a "well, duh" way, but as more of a clarification.

"But I hate to see him that way!" I needed more tissues.

"Look at it this way—his sadness is a testament to his love for your mother."

I stopped midblow. *His sadness is a testament to his love for your mother.*

"How would you feel if he wasn't affected at all?" she had said, crossing her legs and leaning a little bit forward in her chair.

"Yeah, that would be weird..."

I thought of a friend of mine, whose father had started dating two months after her mother had died. My friend wanted to see her father happy again but not quite *that* happy.

"You can't deny him his sadness."

"So I shouldn't feel bad that he feels bad?"

"I think you should see his sadness in a different light."

A different light.

I had told her about the dog and the training and my manufactured scenarios of my father in a bleak, black-and-white documentary.

"And stop manufacturing scenarios."

"Yeah, I tend to do that."

"The time you and he and the dog are spending is what you should be focusing on. He's out there with you and the dog, and that's great!"

She was right. It *was* great. I may not have had my druthers when Dad and I were drenched in sweat, waiting for the dog to come back, but...I felt good afterward, usually on the drive home. I attributed the warm fuzziness to my socks drying out.

"So are you ready to get back to work?" my dad said, shaking me out of my reverie.

Ugh. Not really. The rise in humidity correlated with my drop in enthusiasm.

"I've got an idea," he said. "Let's see if we can get him to come back to you in more of a straight line. Bring your dog to heel and follow me."

I asked Seamus to wait while I opened his kennel door. He did. I attached my thick lead to his pinch collar. We followed my father down an overgrown, rutted road. "What I want you to do is stand here, while I go down there. I'm thinking that because this is narrow, he might not run wide."

Seamus sat, panting, drooling down my leg. My father walked on, stopped, and turned toward us. He threw the dummy high, not far. It landed in a poof of dust, with a dull thud.

I slowly unclipped the lead while I told Seamus, "Wait!" Then, after a few seconds, I gave him the "Okay!" He ran toward the target like an arrow, but on the return, he repeated his bad habit and ran wide of me. Without having him attached to a long rope, I was clueless. He wasn't listening to my whistle. Or my growling.

My father had enough time to walk back to us and grabbed the scruff on either side of Seamus's neck. He lifted the dog off the ground and shook him, punctuated by "NO! NO! NO!"—a kind of dog Heimlich maneuver. Seamus dropped the dummy and sat there looking at me.

"I hope you're happy!" I said to him.

My father picked up the dummy and threw it a couple feet. Dad gave Seamus the okay, and instead of his usual blur, he approached the dummy with measured steps, picked it up, returned in the same path, sat, and dropped it at my father's lugged soles.

"Okay. That's it. We're done for the day."

"We are?"

"Yep! Always end the session on a high note."

"Don't you think Seamus has improved?"

"Yeah, he's getting there. Still runs wide of the mark, but yeah. He's better than he was."

He *was* getting there. I felt like I was getting there, and by "there," I meant back to some new kind of normal.

"You know," he said wiping the sweat from his face with a paper towel, "I was looking at some pictures of your mother, and…there were some of her taken a couple years after our fiftieth, and…her smile wasn't her smile, you know? Like it was more of a reflex, I guess is the word? If only I would have been able to see…"

"Oh, Dad…how could you have known something was going on with her? You saw her every day, and it's hard to recognize…"

"Yeah, yeah. You're right. No sense in beating myself up."

I had noticed something different about her back when my sister, my niece, and I took Mom on the trip of her lifetime to the old sod, Ireland. My mother had dreamed of going to the peat-infused land of her foremothers ever since my father had taken her to see the movie *The Quiet Man* in the 1950s. She wanted to go back to the tiny town that her grandfather had left back in 1880-something and get in touch with her inner Maureen O'Hara. Too bad for her that my father was a see-the-USA-in-your-Chevrolet kind of guy. He wasn't going to take her anywhere unless he could drive there. His only international experience was his yearly border crossing into Canada for the fishing and the cheap over-the-counter codeine.

I had attributed to jetlag her inability to figure out how to flush Irish toilets, open Irish doorknobs, her relentless anxiety about being left alone or behind, or whether we were taking her to the poorhouse. But on a tour of Trinity College to see the Book of Kells, when I asked her what she thought of seeing the illuminated pages in person, she turned to me and said, "I miss my oven."

I had noticed it, but I hadn't wanted to notice it.

"Oh…by the way…I need you to come over and go through Mom's, uh…stuff." Dad had arrived at that place—ready to part with her things, only not willing to do it himself. Of course I would come over and help, and not because I wanted something. I had her engagement ring, which I wore every day. The only other thing that I would have treasured would have been this very Jackie O clutch—sleek, black leather with a square chrome clasp. It had been my mother's wardrobe staple for weddings, brunches, rare evenings out with my father. The last time anyone had seen it was the night it went to prom with my niece, Amanda, probably left behind in some backseat, along with her virginity.

"Your sister's coming over tomorrow around two—"

I see. He wanted me to come over and balance out her crazy.

I told him I'd be there.

CHAPTER THIRTEEN
CLUTCH PLAY

Iᴛ ᴡᴀs ɢᴏɪɴɢ ᴛᴏ be another sticky, icky day. Seamus seemed quite content to stay home in the air-conditioning, and lie on the cool tile floor in the back hallway, his back up against the door—a Labrador version of a draft stopper.

"I'm going over to Grandpa's. To go through Grandma's stuff. Auntie Linda will be there. Wish me luck," I said.

He lifted his head and puffed air out of his flap of lip.

I arrived precisely at two. Plastic bins blocked the kitchen cabinets. Several boxes of large-capacity garbage bags were on the floor, pairs of Mom's shoes on the table. I noticed a half-empty bottle of gin and diet tonic water in the tangle of hangers.

"Your sister's here!" my father said. He seemed buoyant. Perhaps seeing my mother's things in closets, in cabinets, in her crafting corner of the basement had kept him from moving forward.

Linda came into the kitchen, her recently re-hennaed hair in a messy bun that would have looked good on a twenty-year-old, but on a sixty-something-year-old woman, it came off more cat-lady crazy than sexy casual. She wore a too-large-for-her Hawaiian shirt over black capri leggings and black wedge sandals. She added more gin to her tankard and used her middle finger as swizzle stick because she didn't have an index finger. It had been bitten off by a bonobo twenty or so years ago, and please, do not make the mistake of saying *monkey*, because you will be admonished: "A bonobo is a chimpanzee, not a monkey!" It's a long story that involves a cup of juice and a primate with issues against a specific zookeeper—her. She keeps the finger in a plastic bag inside her freezer because, as she told us last Christmas, "I'm thinking of making it into a pin."

Our plan was to have three piles: hers, mine, and Goodwill. She slid open the closet doors and revealed a plaid jacket that Mom had worn at her and Dad's fiftieth wedding anniversary party, a photo from which we used for her obituary; her collection of elastic-waisted pants; turtlenecks that my father had zippers put in to make getting her dressed easier; the robe she wore the night the paramedics came to take her to the hospital; her sleepwear, all lifeless and droopy. I'd expected to become emotional, but I didn't. They were just clothes now. Just shoes.

Dad walked into Linda's and my former-bedroom-turned-TV-room and offered to broker any deals if my sister and I came to a stalemate or blows. Us? Blows? We preferred the passive-aggressive approach. It left no visible marks. We used the rapid-fire yes-no method gleaned from watching cable shows about hoarders.

We moved onto the other bedroom closet and discovered several wrinkle-free shirts, a bin full of Mary Tyler Moore scarves circa 1974 that Mom had worn when she worked in a big office building in downtown Milwaukee. She got the job because my father had been risking his job by moonlighting as a housepainter, a flower deliveryman, and loading crates of produce onto trucks, all police department no-nos. Mom was going to work just long enough for us to get over the hump. She ended up working for forty years. Some hump.

My sister's collection grew into a clothing Everest—socks, leather gloves made from deer killed by Dad, boots, shoes, a London Fog trench coat, loungewear, pajama pants, wallets, not one but two double-breasted peacoats, a velvet blazer, and a wool dress coat with strands of silver Mom hair on the collar that prompted a collective "awwww." Linda was small in stature and would fit in most of Mom's clothes.

I hated to admit it, but we were having fun, and, shock of shocks, we were of one mind. We agreed to donate Mom's winter outerwear and old-lady boots to a homeless shelter, and not to separate the intimate apparel from the other items going to Goodwill. "Let it be their problem," we said. And then we flew too close to the sun.

Our talk turned to how things would go down AD. After Dad.

"I want the tool chest," she said. My dad had a wooden box in the basement that my grandfather had made. All his tools were inside. It had history. Patina. I had often thought about giving it a second life as a cool coffee table.

"Then I get all his police stuff," I said. I knew he still had some uniform coats in the attic with brass button that depicted the City of Milwaukee seal.

"Fine. Then I get the duck decoys," she said.

Damn! "What are you going to do with them? Sell them? I'm the one with the dog!"

"How are things going in there?" my father yelled from the kitchen.

"Fine!" we both said, singsongy without a tinge of venom.

"I want the old camping gear," I said. I wanted it only because she'd told me last Thanksgiving she wanted it.

"The cuckoo clock…mine," she said. It came from Germany and had caused quite the family schism. My uncle brought it back from World War II and gave it to my grandmother, but when she died, my aunt thought since *her husband* had brought it back, she should get it, but instead, it had gone to my mother, and my aunt gave our family the cold shoulder for forty years. She showed up at Mom's funeral, though, so either fences had been mended, or she was sniffing around, laying the groundwork, cuckoo-clock-wise.

"I'll give you the cowboy coffee cup for the cuckoo clock," I said. The cowboy cup and matching saucer had been purchased at a gift shop when we went to Mount Rushmore in 1963. It was the family vacation that ended up being biblical: we were hit with a plague of locusts; we got stuck in the middle of the open prairie in a hailstorm that smashed out our car windows; and my sister got lost in the desert. She didn't wander for forty days, just forty minutes—and for forty minutes, I entertained blissful thoughts of having my own room.

"Fine," she said. "Then I get Dad's hunting stuff."

"You're not getting his rifles!" I said, throwing pairs of white socks into the Goodwill pile.

"*You're* not getting his rifles!" she said, threatening me with one of Mom's slippers.

"What are *you* going to do with them?" I said.

"I'm—" She had been pulling items out of Mom's dresser— hankies, gloves, long underwear—when she stopped midpull. In her clawlike, four-fingered hand, she clutched...the Clutch!

I'm generally not one for gasping, but at the sight of the thing that I thought had been left at a heavily body-cologned formal event by an irresponsible teenager, I gasped.

"I think we have a problem," she said, her eyes narrowed. "Or maybe we don't. I mean, *you* got the ring."

"Like it was going to fit on your fat finger that even a monkey didn't want!"

"Chimp-*pan-ZEE*!"

My father's dealings with domestic disputes as a police officer made him a skilled negotiator and good assessor of situations. He had been busy in the kitchen, then doing stuff in the garage, then going into the basement, doing what I don't know, and we must have been loud enough for him to hear us sans hearing aids. He seemed delighted to be called to duty, acting as mediator, entertained by our who-gets-what debate.

"The question is," he said, his arms folded across his chest, cop-like, "what is the clutch worth? There has to be something…"

There was something clutch-worthy, but unfortunately it too was MIA. It was a Lionel O-gauge train that my father had bought in 1955. It had a big, black, heavy, metal engine that blew smoke, a coal tender, a couple of boxcars, a grain car, a flatcar, and a caboose. It ran on an oval track my father had bolted to a piece of half-inch plywood that he dragged underneath our Christmas tree every year up until our teen years, when none of us gave a shit about it and didn't care if we ever saw it again. And then, in the early 1980s, as my sister's marriage was on the rocks (unlike her gin and tonic), she became obsessed with it. Every Christmas, she'd bring it up: Where was it? Who had it? Was it sold? Had Dad thrown it out, like her Beatles card collection she claimed could have put her kids through college?

"Too bad we don't have the train," I said.

"Admit it! You"—she pointed her remaining index finger at Dad—"threw it out!"

"Threw what out?" he said, playing devil's advocate. Pusher of my sister's buttons.

"The train. *And* my bubble-cut Barbie! *And* my Spiro T. Agnew T-shirt! I saw one on eBay for sixty-five dollars! All *my* stuff. All *my* memories. Thrown out. Cast aside! Without any consid—"

"I know where it is," Dad said. It was as if he had thrown a bucket of ice-cold water on her. "It's in the attic." My father's comedic timing has always been impeccable. This? The way he said it, as if everyone knew it had always been in the attic except Linda? Genius.

I expected a why-didn't-you-tell-me-this-sooner tirade, but I got something much, much better.

You know the Tasmanian Devil? The cartoon? When he spins like a tornado? Out of control? Yeah. Like that. She ran out to the garage, got the green ladder, ran back inside, dragged the ladder into the narrow hallway, climbed up, balanced on that thing that isn't a step, pushed up the secret panel in the ceiling, and gathered enough upper-body strength to hoist herself into the attic crawl space, just like women who lift cars off their children.

I let her go. There was no stopping her, and I didn't care about the train. I cared about the clutch. She could have the train. I didn't know what she was going to do with it. Her house was already full of stuff she had to have but didn't know what to do with.

We stood by and listened to her crawl around. "Stay on the plywood! I don't want your foot coming through the ceiling!" Dad yelled.

And then we heard a muffled "*Aha!*" followed by some scraping, dragging, and an "*Oh, shit!*" before an orange box, with *LIONEL* written in blue lettering on the side stuck out of the ceiling. She handed each box to my father. I took possession of the clutch.

Dad and I pushed everything into her Mini Cooper until it looked like all the air bags had deployed. There was just enough room for her to squeeze behind the wheel.

"I bet she sells half of that stuff on eBay," I said to my father as we watched her back out of his driveway.

"I don't care what she does with it. Oh, by the way," he said, "you're a half second too slow with some of your commands."

We're talking dogs now? "Oh. Okay."

"You have to remember, don't go *to* the dog; he has to come to you."

"Right. Don't go to the dog. Got it."

"More than two steps is too many."

"I'll make a mental note... Why didn't you say anything about the train being in the attic all these years? All those Christmases. Her rants. We could have all been spared."

He looked down at the cracks in the driveway. Then squinted up to the sky.

"For the entertainment value!"

I got into my car with my meager acquisitions—a purse, some sweaters. I waved to him. He looked relieved. I think we all were. My sister had her train. I had the clutch. And Dad had...closet space.

CHAPTER FOURTEEN

THE SEED, PLANTED

Sᴏᴍᴇᴛɪᴍᴇꜱ I ᴍɪꜱꜱᴇᴅ ᴛʜᴇ kennel club's driveway and had to turn around a half mile down the two-lane highway, in the K-9 Kampus Kennel's establishment. I threatened to leave Seamus in one of its rows of empty, rusty-wire barracks if he didn't change his hardheaded and hard-mouthed ways. This time, the kennel club driveway was clearly marked with bunting and flags and a big, hand-painted sign:

Annual Hunt Test! Open to All Dogs!

There was a routine to our arrivals. I'd pull into the parking lot, Dad would wave his hand, put his truck in gear and he'd take off. Sometimes, he'd go down the better-graded road; other times, he'd turn and drive down the bumpier, potholey-er road. I never knew what he had in store for us on any particular day. Maybe he didn't know either. Maybe he didn't think about it until he was on the two-lane highway, heading west out of Milwaukee. Training with him was like having a pop quiz every class on things I didn't think were germane and thus hadn't prepared for. And what were Seamus and I preparing for, anyway? I'm a person who needs a goal, a carrot, something to shoot for, which is why I'm really good at losing weight but can't keep it off because once I reach that number... Cake!

Fall was coming. Dad seemed to have more vigor. He made more jokes. He was quicker with a quip, a rib, a tease. He kids because he loves. He had more stories. We'd be standing next to each other, waiting for Seamus to find the planted dummy, and Dad would say, "Did I ever tell you about the time your mother…" and he'd launch into a story that I might have heard before, but I let him tell it to me anyway. Our Wednesdays at the kennel club had become a new regular routine—and I found that comforting.

When Dad and I weren't at the kennel club, we were *talking* about the kennel club—the state of the algae growing in the ponds, the members who had been complaining that the grass was cut too high in the far field, or who I should be talking to when the time came for me to get another Lab puppy. *Wait. What?* And I used phrases like "hard mouth," "deliver to hand" and "blind retrieves" as punchlines in jokes only Dad and I understood.

We changed into our boots, put on our vests, and stuffed dummies into the pockets of our vests. "Annual hunt test?" I asked.

"Yeah, it's in three weeks," he said. "There're demonstrations— blind retrieves, quartering, shooting, food, a raffle, that kind of thing." Sounded interesting, but not interesting enough for me to suspend my usual Saturday morning of staying in my pajamas until the afternoon, reading between the lines on my friends' Facebook pages.

"Did you scent the dummies?" he asked.

Of course I had.

"Oh, and uh…" He paused, then he said, "There's a fastestretrievercontest."

"A what?" I said.

He coughed out, "Fastest retriever contest."

"Really? Fastest retriever? Hmmm."

My father knew me. He could hear the gear mechanism in my head turning, clicking, spinning. Was he afraid to tell me because he knew I'd get all hell-bent on entering Seamus before he was ready and then suffer through his inevitable crash and burn? *FAIL* stamped in big red letters across our permanent records? Or maybe I interpreted his tone all wrong. Maybe he really wanted me to enter, and his gruff nonchalance was all an act? Think of how impressed my father's kennel club friends would be—my dog, an untrained mess until Dad stepped in and worked his magic! My ears perked up. I cocked my head to the side. "Dad! We could totally do it!"

"No, no, no. I'm telling you...I don't think he's—he won't deliver to hand...he's got a hard mouth. They might be using real birds, and we haven't been using real birds. What's he going to do with those—"

"But, Dad, think of it. I'd get that bad sports-show juju off my back!"

He winced. Rolled his eyes. It was his I-don't-want-to-burst-your-bubble look, the one he gave me when I was seven and wanted tap dance lessons. I borrowed my second-grade friend Rhonda's patent-leather tap shoes and clickity-clacked on the basement linoleum, choreographing a routine that I was sure would impress him so much, he'd beat a path to Miss Trixie's School of Tap and enroll me immediately. His instincts of passively not encouraging, not discouraging proved correct later, when I auditioned for high school musicals and didn't even get called back for the role of townsperson number five.

"Let's just see how things go," he said. "Let's just see."

I couldn't stop thinking about this. It was the perfect setup. No pressure. No audience in bleachers, possibly a few people here and there on picnic tables or in folding camp chairs. The event would be in the same field that we'd been practicing in for months. *And if Seamus didn't do well? If he bolted and ran around like an idiot? So what? It will be just for fun!* This is what I told myself as I tried to push thoughts of sports-show vindication and payback from my mind. *Fun? Like hell it's fun.*

For the next few weeks, no longer was our one hour in the field a game. I became a taskmaster. A drill sergeant. Things that I had let the dog get away with—scooting on his butt when I told him to wait, a sloppy, sideways, not-at-my-heel heel, excitable jumping—I didn't put up with. I yanked. He yelped. I growled. He cowered. He pinned his ears flat back against his head and had a different look in his brown eyes. *What happened to my regular woman?* We worked for fifteen minutes in the yard every day, twice a day.

Heel.

Wait.

Okay!

Give. Repeat. Repeat. Repeat.

At the next training session with Dad, Seamus showed marked improvement. He didn't run around *as much*. He didn't chomp on the dummy *as much*, and, ta-da, he gave when I said "give," and yet… something wasn't right.

I noticed he had stopped coming into the living room. He stayed inside his crate under the kitchen table. "Seamus, come on! I'm watching *Pit Bulls and Parolees*!" I moved the pile of dog-centric magazines to make a space for him next to me on the sofa. Maybe he was just tired.

"Where's my TV buddy!?" I yelled. I heard him get up and pad from the back of the house and into the front room. Usually he wouldn't have broken his stride and gone up onto the sofa to sprawl, but that was before I had turned into Vince Lombardi with my relentless two-a-days.

"Come on. You can come up!" I patted the vacant spot next to me. He didn't budge. He just sat there. His facial expression was the dog equivalent of *What am I to you? A work dog? A pal? You can't have it both ways.* He turned his head away, then got up and left. I heard him crawl into his kennel and plop onto the floor with a heavy sigh.

Dear God, what have I turned into?

Two weeks before the allegedly fun trial, we were at the kennel club. "Dad, I'm having second thoughts about this whole fastest-retriever thing," I said as we unloaded our gear near the pond.

"Why?"

"Wouldn't competitiveness ruin everything by taking the fun out of it? I mean…it's not like I want to win or anything"—*lie!*—"it's just that—"

"I know…you want your dog to do well," he said. "I know how that is. Did I ever tell you about the time I got kicked out of a field trial?"

My father? Admonished? No. He was the one who doled out the right and just punishments to us civilians.

"What do you mean, you got kicked out?" I said. Seamus demonstrated his opinion by peeing on the kennel club's signpost.

"Well, my dog was in the finals, and he flushed up a bird, and when I sent him, he hesitated, just a bit, I mean a second, two at the most. I thought it was no big deal, but apparently"—insert classic Dad eye roll here—"one of the judges, some dippy broad—"

"Dippy broad" is his term for a woman who he believes is out of her league, whose sole purpose in life is to muck up his men-only world. My sister and I have tried to wean him from his sexist terminology, but either he doesn't hear us because he's not wearing his hearing aids, or he does and doesn't care.

"—she tells me to get my dog, that he's disqualified, and that's when I kind of said some words…uh…something to the effect of…she's full of you-know-what, and…uh…I may have called her the B word, dropped a few F bombs."

My father never used bad language when we were little. Never. I heard him say, "God damn it" once, and that was when he couldn't get the strings of Christmas tree lights to light up.

"Geez, Dad. Was Mom there?"

"Oh yeah, she was there. Saw and heard the whole shebang—"

Knowing my mother, she probably stiffened herself to stand by her man, come what may.

"—and then I was put on probation. I couldn't come out to the kennel club for six months. I couldn't enter any trials. Nothing. And…I had to go before a tribunal."

Who did these people think they were? He's the law. He's got the badge.

"I had to get an attorney…pay a fine…three hundred dollars."

"Jesus!" I said. So that's why, that one year, when I asked about the dog and the kennel club, my mother gave me the zip-the-lip signal behind Dad's back.

"I wasn't going to pay it. Screw it!"

"But…you did, obviously. What made you change your mind?"

"Your mother. She said to me, 'Do you enjoy working with the dogs? Do you like doing this kind of thing? Well then, pay the damn fine and shut up!'"

Mind. Blown. A, that my mother told him to shut up, and B, that he listened to her. I could see something like that happening to me, with

Seamus. At this trial, maybe I'd lose my cool and pick the dog up by the scruff and do the doggy Heimlich or grab a bucket and wallop him upside his head.

"No. I'm not doing it. Not entering the dog. No. You're right. He's not ready. I'm not ready." I decided I'd show up sans dog. That way, I could scope out the competition, play armchair quarterback.

●　●　●

The grounds of the kennel club were full of manly pickups and macho SUVs with vanity plates like: LABMAN, SPRNGR, FETCH, and the baffling STSTAHL (sit, stay, heel—it took me a while). Hatchbacks, tailgates, and truck caps were up or opened to reveal built-in custom dog kennels made from ergonomic molded poly-whatever, with heating, air-conditioning, cushy liners, and stainless steel screens. Some were duplexes, others single family.

No expense was spared on dog transportation or outfitting, and not the froufrou kind. No Swarovski crystal–encrusted collars, no little plaid-jacket ensembles—well, I take that back. Yes, there were ensembles in the form of chest protectors, vests, and matching boots that were designed to keep the dog from harm as it ran through thick brush, burrs, and thorns. Totally serviceable and practical, not like dressing a dog in a tutu.

I had a hard time finding my father among all the similarly clad, graying gentlemen in their blaze-orange game vests and Wellingtons, with their double-barrel shotguns casually slung over one shoulder. He was near a display of all things retriever, being chatted up by some of the "young" guys who had just retired and were now finally able to devote all their days to their dogs. Forty years ago, he had been the young guy and was taken under the wing of a club elder named Wally who taught him everything he knew about dogs and training, and now he was the club elder passing on all he knew to…me?

He seemed happy. He was in his element. He introduced me to his springer spaniel posse as his "daughter who went over to the dark side and got herself a Labrador." He regaled them with stories of Seamus's antics and my unskillfulness, and while I could have taken umbrage with his interpretation of how I blew my whistle, I didn't. I was fulfilling my role as comic relief.

"Retrieving will be done at the pond. Not the one we use, but the other pond, the big pond," he said. "Follow the signs."

We hadn't been using the big pond for a couple of weeks because it had been thick with weeds. The last time Seamus swam it with the long rope attached to his collar, it had trailed behind him, collecting aquatic debris that almost dragged him under—but it had rained a lot, and the water was high. The organizers had deemed it good enough for the noncompetitive fun-ness.

The other Labs (mostly black, though there was one chocolate with nuts) were leggy, their faces not so boxy, their heads a bit longer than Seamus's. The field was being marked off for the fastest retrieve when my father finally caught up with me. He had been busy directing participatory traffic. He came up and stood next to me. Close. "See that dog? Over there?" he said without moving his lips, so that no one would see him.

I looked over there, but in a way that made it look like I wasn't looking "over there," or if I was, I wasn't at all interested in whatever was going on over there. And what was going on? Two men who looked as confused as the dog were trying to get it to pick up a dead pheasant, but it would have none of it.

"Geez," my dad said, "that dog is dumber than yours!"

"Um…thanks?"

The course was finally ready. Forty yards. Each way. All the dog had to do was run, get the retrieving dummy, run back, cross the finish line. Simple. No live bird. No dead bird. No delivery to hand. Was it too late to drive home and get the dog? *Damn!*

First up was a seven-year-old black Lab who preferred a measured trot to a bolt. Next up was another black Lab, whose owner told me he was six years old, but he looked more like sixteen, was overweight, and might have had hip issues. His muzzle was more white than black. He made contestant number one look like a blur. Then a vizsla that had impressive speed but overshot the target, then a Boykin spaniel that picked up the dummy, dropped it halfway, and had to go back to get it. Twice.

The chocolate Lab and its owner/handler took their places at the start. My father leaned in closer. "Who the hell wears a white dress shirt and Crocs?" he said. If it hadn't been for Brett Favre and his sexting, my father would not have known what Crocs were.

"That guy," I said.

His crisp white shirtsleeves rolled up just enough to expose the TAG Heuer on his evenly tanned wrist, Mr. Crocs steadied his dog, then sent him. It was like a jet-fueled dragster on too short of a track.

"That's one hell of a fast dog!" my father said.

Just as I was feeling all jealous, it ran past the dummy and kept going. Mr. Crocs jumped, yelled, and attempted to run in Crocs over the field, past the first parking lot, until we lost sight of his bright-white shirttail. "That dog is probably in another county," my father said.

"Dad, maybe you should offer him your services? To that guy, to help him train his dog."

"Nah. I've got enough work with your dog."

"Come on! You have to admit, Seamus is getting better!"

"Uh…if you say so."

"What are you saying? There's no hope?"

"No, no. There's hope. There's always hope. He's not stupid, remember?"

Seamus and I were getting better. According to me, anyway. Even my husband noticed how much better behaved he was. How he came when called. How he sat and waited by his bowl of food, a long string of drool dangling from his lips, until we gave him the okay to gobble.

Why hadn't I entered Seamus in this fun Fastest Retriever Contest? Why? Because I had taken my cue from my father. He was the one who'd said the dog wasn't ready, but that was before we had found out there weren't real birds. Was I mad at him? A little bit. A teensy bit. Those dogs were so inept, and at this stage of our training, Seamus was so…ept.

• • •

When Dad and I were back at it the next Wednesday, Seamus did everything I asked him to do. No hard mouth. No goofing around. We ended like we always did—on a high note.

"Boy!" my father said. "I don't know what you did, but…he is like a different dog!"

"I think he's turned a corner, Dad."

Was Seamus the Labrador equivalent to Eliza Doolittle? If he was, then was I Henry Higgins…or was my father Professor Higgins and I was that other guy?

"Maybe you're the one who turned a corner. Train the trainer, remember?"

I *had* turned a corner. Ever since the psychiatrist had given me "permission" to let my father experience his sadness and me, mine, I had felt lighter. I had been able to actually think of things, like getting new window treatments or having our kitchen cabinets resurfaced. I started to talk with my mother, like it was a one-way phone conversation. I'd tell her about the dog, what Dad and I were up to, Seamus's shenanigans.

My father sat down and pulled off his boots, then his socks. He put on a fresh white pair, then his clean shoes without pond scum, mud, and dog poo embedded in the lugged soles. A few fun trial stragglers came up and asked him how he was doing. "Oh, pretty good. Pretty good."

They were sorry to hear about Mom. He thanked them. He was gracious. Didn't make a joke. Didn't tell anyone not to make a fuss.

"That guy?" he said to me, putting his wet shoes in the ammo box. "Just lost his wife, to cancer."

I used to not know what to say, but that was before my mother had died. "That's gotta be rough," I said.

"And that other guy? The one over there getting into the big red pickup?"

I looked at the field-turned-parking-lot-turned-field; it was almost empty, except for the one red truck, idling with a large, white-bearded man in the driver's seat, checking his phone. "He just had to put his wife into a nursing home." My father shook his head and gave a what-can-you-do shrug.

"At least...Mom, didn't...you know. She—we didn't have to go through *that*." I said it not knowing how he would respond, but I felt like I had to say it, because she hadn't lingered; she hadn't been in a hospice situation; she had spared us that.

"You know," he said, "I kind of hate to say this..."

Oh no. Had I said something about Mom that I shouldn't have said? Did I cross a line? Ruin his upbeat mood?

"What is it, Dad? Go ahead. Say it." I held my breath, waited for him to say whatever he had to say. Hopefully it wouldn't be something that would cause me to descend into a shame spiral. He climbed into his truck, collected his keys, put them into the ignition, and started the motor.

"Um…yeah, you know, I think your dog could have won that contest."

CHAPTER FIFTEEN

SAINT ROCCO

DAD SAW ME PULL into the kennel club's gates and, without so much as a hi, how are you, he took off, either eager to get the session started or miffed that I was late, because Seamus had gotten stair stuck. Every once in a while, he would forget how to go up the steps. He would freeze. On the landing. Unable to go up or down. Eventually I'd have to put a leash on him and pull him until he got some momentum going.

My father pulled his truck over to the side of the gravelly road made narrow from a prolific growing season, got out, and walked over to my rolled-down window.

"I want you to see something," he said.

We walked to a clearing of sumac that had just begun to flame out. The air had that dry, leafy smell that I loved. The grass was a bit crispy. It was that season in between summer and fall, when it's sweater weather one day and short sleeves the next. That day? Sweater.

A dog and its handler were in the big field next to the marshy pond. They were performing an exercise in precision—dog and man in sync, like a pair of Olympic ice dancers. A hand went up, the dog stopped; a hand waved left, the dog ran left; a hand waved right, the dog went right. "That's called quartering," my dad said. On the next pass, the dog abruptly stopped. Its tail shot up like a flag. I knew what that was called, or at least what it meant in Seamus-speak. *Skunk!*

He had been sprayed not once, not twice, but three times. The first encounter was a direct hit to his face, and he went mental, running and rubbing himself on the patio bricks. I would have thought he would have figured out that black and white with a bushy tail meant, *Run away!* But that's me.

The second time he met Mr. Skunk, he ran into the house before we had figured out what had happened. Big mistake. The sulfuric/burned-coffee/rubber/rotten-egg smell permeated the walls, the wood floors, the pots and pans. I thought we'd have to call one of those services that cleans up after murders. On humid days, I can still smell it.

The third time he got hit was a month later, around ten thirty at night, on his final pee before bed. Luckily it was warm outside, and I could apply the Dawn dish soap, baking soda, and hydrogen peroxide concoction to him on the patio, but I might have left it on too long, because in the light of the next day, Seamus had gone from a black Lab to a Labrador with cheap highlights.

Back in the field, the dog's tail-as-flag meant *Pheasant!* And the pheasant took off, flapping. A second man, called a gunner, stood a few feet from the handler. The gunner took aim, then *Bang! Bang!* The bird did a midair cartwheel before it fell. The dog sat and waited for the signal to retrieve. The handler pointed toward the dog—like a football ref signaling a first down—and in a few seconds, with bird in mouth, it came trotting back, sat at the handler's heel, and released the bird. No farting around. No running amok.

"See how the dog is steady from wing to shot?"

"Wing to what now?" I said.

"Wing to shot. That means when the bird is flushed, the dog has to stop and sit and wait for the handler to tell it to go."

Did my father expect Seamus and me to perform at this high of a level?

"See? That's how you do it! Come on. We've got work to do!"

Inadequate is too inadequate a word for what I felt. Clearly that dog had been in training from day one. Its brain was programmed: *I get signal, gun go bang, I sit.* In Seamus's brain: *Woman make sound, now what?* We were trying to get the dog to unlearn things, then relearn new things and make different associations—sort of what my dad and I had to do in this post-Mother landscape.

There was a plastic grocery bag on my father's front seat. "What's in the bag?" I said.

"A frozen, dead duck."

Who drives around with a fully feathered, frozen, dead mallard in the front seat of their truck? The same person who drives around with a shotgun behind the backseat, ropes, a bottle of bleach, gloves, plastic dropcloths, rubber boots, duct tape, and ammo. Not a serial killer. My dad.

We did a couple of warm-up retrieves with the familiar dummy. Seamus waited at my heel. I sent him. He swam, got the thing; I blew the whistle; he came back and zagged, but not too badly—if the highly trained pair had scored perfect tens, I felt that Seamus and I would have gotten solid fives.

"Let's change things up a bit and see what happens." Dad tucked the frozen fowl inside his game vest and walked to the other side of the pond.

"Keep your dog at heel, then give me a sign when you're ready!" he shouted.

A sign? Was there a standard? A thumbs-up? A wave? Dad interpreted my hailing-a-cab-in-Manhattan signal as my "ready" and threw
the duck, using its head as a handle. Seamus and I watched as it arced
skyward, then fell into the pond with a hefty splash. I counted to twenty
and sent him. He swam in a straight line toward the duck-berg, but
when he made contact, he spit the thing out. He tried again. Got a taste
of a webbed foot in his mouth before he went *blah!*

Unbelievable! He'd brought me rotting fish carcasses and feasted
on feral cat poop, but this was beyond his palate?

"Call him back!" my father yelled.

I whistled the "come back" whistle command, but the thing-that-
wasn't-a-dummy vexed him, and he kept circling and circling and circling it.

"Call him!"

I called him. He kept circling.

"Call him again!"

I called him. Harder. He kept circling. Harder. My father stood
on the opposite shore with his arms folded across his chest, shaking his
head in disgust, and started the walk back to my side of the pond. I was
this close to putting on a pair of waders and dragging the dog out by the
scruff of his neck, but I gave one last blow of the whistle, and he turned
and came back to shore, leaving the duck behind. My father put his
hands on his hips and looked down at the dripping Seamus.

"One thing I have to say, dog, you are persistent!"

"Yeah, and that persistence almost killed him," I said.

Seamus had been about two when I decided to take him for a walk
along the same stretch of beach that was across the street from my old
all-girl Catholic high school, verboten to me when I'd attended school
there. At fifty-something years old, with my high school no longer in

existence but the buildings still there, I'd felt like I should have been looking over my shoulder for Sister Lucretia, with her clipboard and wad of detention slips.

Seamus and I had been there a couple of times, and it had been a joy to watch him romp in the waves. On that day, I decided to bring a bright red, doggy-friendly Frisbee along for him to run after and catch. I had thrown it maybe three times, and he had bounded into the lake after it, timing his leap like a wide receiver, catching it midair, always bringing it back for me to throw over and over, which I did.

Until I threw it too hard, and it caught too much air. Before he could get it, it had sunk. Game over. I called him to come back with a cheerful clap, but he would not retreat. He kept swimming around and around and around looking for it. I'd called him, "Seamus! Come on! Let's go!" But he wouldn't. Didn't. Couldn't. And then he broke his pattern, and I thought he was going to head back to me, but no. He had spotted...ducks? Near the breakwater.

I continued to call his name, and he continued to swim out, out, out. I switched over to "Suppertime!" which always got him running to the back door no matter what, but not this time. I tried another reliable—"Car ride!"—accompanied by me jumping and waving my jacket. A runner stopped to see why the crazy woman was screaming, jumping, and waving her jacket.

"What is it?" he said, squinting.

"My dog!" I said.

"Way out there?"

"Yes!"

"Uh-oh."

He resumed his run.

If I stretched my arm straight out from my shoulder and held up my thumb, like I had done in Drawing 101 for perspective, Seamus's head was no bigger than the tippy tip. How far out was the breakwater? A hundred yards? A mile? How could I, a lifelong Milwaukeean, not know this?

I stood on the shore, alone and out of ideas, telling myself, *Don't panic. He's a Labrador. They're bred for swimming in the cold Canadian water, retrieving fishing nets and, if necessary, fishermen.* It was mid-March, and while that means the end of winter for some places on the map, Wisconsin doesn't pay much attention to those kinds of things. The day had started out partly cloudy and warmish, but had turned into something resembling a scene from a Brontë novel.

At what point did I call it? When I couldn't see his tiny Labrador head anymore? Maybe he'd be one of those dogs that appeared in the newspaper that would be found miles from where he started?

I had a phone, but who would I call? 911? The Coast Guard? The fire department? I did the only thing a person in my situation could do—I prayed.

Growing up, prayer, like our telephone, was only to be used in case of an emergency. I was brought up during the Cuban Missile Crisis 1960s. I was also brought up Catholic and the daughter of a police officer, and we had what was called a "limited line," meaning we were only allowed one outgoing call per day. Calls to friends were out of the question. Incoming calls from people other than my father were to be kept short and to the point, because how did my mother put it? "If your father is trying to call and gets a busy signal, then gets shot, it will be on your heads!"

I figured if I prayed to A-listers—God, Jesus, Mary, John Paul II—they had a lot on their prayer plates, so why waste their time?

I stood on the sand and opened my arms out wide, tilted my head back, and let a prayer rip to Saint Rocco, patron saint of dogs. "Rocco! Come on! Do me a solid!" And that was the moment that the ducks flew toward the shore, and I saw what I hoped was still my dog turn and head west.

Seamus trotted out of the lake. He was a little winded but none the worse for wear. He had been in the cold water for almost thirty minutes, and once he shook off, he barked at me.

"Are you kidding?"

He barked again.

"No, no, no. I think we've had enough fun for one day."

I clipped the lead to his collar. I wiped him off with my jacket and sat inside the car, breathed in the wonderful aroma of Lake Michigan Labrador while I made a check out to the Humane Society at the behest of Saint Rocco.

CHAPTER SIXTEEN

FOURTH AND TWELVE

It was September and that meant field trials. My father is an expert marksman, and his services as one of two people needed to shoot down flying pheasants during field trials were in demand. The kennel club was also busy, and our favorite fields were often in use by other Labs or spaniels. According to protocol, if there was someone training in a field, you had to wait until they were finished before you released your dog.

Dad and I had come upon another Lab man working his Lab, kind of a wide receiver to Seamus's running back. I sat there on my bucket and watched as the guy gave whistle commands. At one point, the dog ran from the top of the hill, down and into the pond to retrieve a dead duck. When it was halfway back to the shore, the man blew one blast of his whistle and the dog stopped swimming, midswim, duck in mouth. Who knew Labradors could tread water?

"I hope you don't expect me to—Seamus to—"

My father laughed. Hard.

Fall also meant football. This would be the first football season my mother would not be watching and giving her special brand of color commentary on. I don't know when, why, or how my mother became a football fan. She grew up in a big baseball household. When her father died at the age of ninety, he was buried in his faded Milwaukee Braves baseball hat and jacket, holding a Warren Spahn–signed baseball instead of the typical rosary.

Mom's fourth-down conversion must have happened after she and my father were married. That's when they began their yearly pilgrimage, via train or family station wagon, from Milwaukee to South Bend, Indiana, for Notre Dame football. Why Notre Dame? They weren't alumni—hell, they hadn't even gone to college. I think it was the Catholic thing. The win-one-for-the-Gipper thing. In 1972, when I was in high school and thinking about going to college, I asked my dad why he wasn't a fan of the Wisconsin Badgers. I mean, hello, home team? "Too many Communists," he said.

I attended Notre Dame games via 8 mm home movies. Silent scenes of my mom as she walked across the parking lot toward the stadium in a tweed suit pinched at the waist, a yellow chrysanthemum the size of small planet pinned to her lapel, then a cut to the stadium interior and a long shot of the marching band, with a high-stepping drum major, and a slow pan of a pass play made me think, *If only I had been a boy, then I could have been the one who would have attended Notre Dame, played football, been drafted by the Packers, securing not only my father's season tickets, but my status of favorite child forever.*

Besides my dual loyalties between Notre Dame and the Badgers (both my children were raised communist socialist liberals), I am—*we are*—Green Bay Packer fans. We've stuck with the green and gold through the thick—Bart Starr glory years—and the thin—the 1970s and '80s when Titletown didn't see a title. But still, every season, my mother held out hope that the Vince Lombardi trophy would return to where it belonged, instead of being ensconced in other places, by other teams, like the dreaded Dallas Cowboys from the city that, according to her, "murdered our Catholic president."

In the 1990s, the sinking Packer ship made a course correction—new coach (Mike Holmgren), new general manager (Ron Wolf). Enter Mr. Brett Lorenzo Favre. Mom never liked Brett Favre. She *loved* Brett Favre. Like my daughter did when she was a teenager and smitten with a boy du jour, my mother worked his name into any conversation, be it about cooking—"I hear Brett likes a good casserole!"—gossip about the choir at church—"Did I mention that Brett is Catholic?"—or politics—"Don't you think Brett would make a good president?"

She wasn't gaga over movie stars. Oh, she had her faves—John Wayne, Tom Hanks—but they remained in their proper places, on the shelf with all the other VHS tapes. She had never been like this for Bart or Lynn Dickey or Don "Magic Man" Majkowski. There was something about Brett. What? His aw-shucks-ness? His Opie Taylor-ness? "I just think he's…I don't know…cool!" She even bought a Favre jersey for Seamus—and we're not a doggy-dress-up kind of family.

After each Packer game, my phone would ring. It would be my mother, giving me her in-depth post-game analysis: "I just love it when he takes off his helmet!" and "Did you see it when he completed that pass as he was falling down backward?"

In her eyes, he could do no wrong. Even when he threw stupid interceptions that cost us the game or the championship or a chance, she came to his defense: "Oh…that's because he tries too hard!" For sixteen years, she never missed her weekly trysts with Brett.

But nothing lasts forever.

On March 4, 2008, Oprah was sidelined for breaking news. After 250-something consecutive games of getting run over and into by men the size of locomotives, Brett said he was done. My phone rang. It was Mom.

"Are you watching this? Oh…I…just… Oh, Brett!"

I really hoped she was fake crying.

143

During his whole I'm-retired, I'm-not-retired post-breakup mess, our family unit was divided: eight in the he-made-his-bed, it's-time-to-move-on camp; one in the why-don't-they-want-Brett-back, he-won-a Super-Bowl-for-Heaven's-sake camp.

Then there were the dark days when Brett was jettisoned to New York. She went through the five stages of grief.

Anger: "If I ever run into that general manager Ted Thompson, I'll slap him one. I mean it!"

Bargaining: "Maybe if I write a letter and tell them they should make Brett a backup quarterback, that would work. Wouldn't it?"

Depression: "I don't think I can watch another game unless I see him on the sidelines… What channel is the Jets game on?"

Disbelief: "I just—oh. I think someone put him up to all this."

Finally, acceptance: "I guess we're stuck with that Aaron what's-his-name."

When Brett got into trouble sexting—I wasn't going to be the one to explain to her what sexting was, but kudos to whoever did—she had a simple solution: "I know what he needs. I think he needs to talk to his priest." God love her.

Brett was gone.

Mom was gone.

She would not be seated next to her Favre-palooza tabletop shrine—a framed, autographed eight-by-ten photo, a glossy book (*Favre*), a copy of a *Sports Illustrated* with a smiling Brett on the cover, a Brett bobblehead, and a piece of the True Cross, a.k.a. a box of "Frozen Tundra" sod. Every bubble screen, every post-pattern completion, every home game, I would be missing her. If only she could have changed her mind and decided not to be dead, I'd have given her her old locker back, her starting position, even a contract extension. But a person can't play football forever.

CHAPTER SEVENTEEN

DOGGY IN A CAN

THE LANDSCAPE AT THE kennel club was quieting down from the loud greens of summer to the softer, muted palette of autumn. Seamus was working hard trying to locate the dummy my father had hidden in a little rise of tall grass the color of the raw-sienna crayon in the Crayola box. We were doing a blind retrieve. The dog had to use its nose to find the dummy. Expert handlers can get their dogs to turn their backs on the action, then turn back around and go on command. I was not an expert, and Seamus craned his head to follow my father's movements, which defeated the purpose. "Cheater!" I said when Seamus came back with a mouth full of dummy.

Even though it was early October, it had snowed. Not much. Just a dusting. Still, I wasn't prepared. My warm clothes were in the attic in their plastic vacuum-sealed bag. Winter clothes, like the furnace, weren't supposed to be put on until later, as in Halloween later. My father stood next to me and cleared his throat. I hoped he wasn't getting sick. But would it surprise me? Not after the year he'd had.

We were walking back to the truck, letting Seamus run around and sniff things, when my father said, "I had to take Aunt Florence for her, uh, final arrangements."

When Dad wasn't giving me helpful tips regarding my

retriever-in-progress, he was busy taking care of the elderly—Mugsy, his fourteen-year-old field-trial champion, who couldn't hear and didn't know what his back legs were up to, and my great-aunt Florence, who also couldn't hear, was partially blind, and, like the dog, could no longer jump up into my father's truck. Between the three of them, at eighty-four, he was the spring chicken. If my dog-year math is correct, Mugsy came in around ninety-one and Florence…714.

She lived around the block from my parents, in her own home, widowed since the 1980s. She and her husband had had no children, and because my mother and father had this 1940s Greatest Generation sense of duty, they saw to her needs: dinner, groceries, and home maintenance—jobs made increasingly more difficult as she (and they) aged.

Aunt Florence was born in 1911. She never went to high school, was the youngest of twelve. She had worked for years in the hosiery department at Gimbels—before employees were "associates" and customers were "guests," when salesladies wore black with a simple strand of pearls and got the box of stockings for you from behind the counter. She still scrubbed her kitchen floors (on hands and her original knees), kept all of her tchotchkes dust free, and somehow managed to go down the steep and narrow basement stairs to do her laundry with an old wringer-type washing machine: "It still works. Why should I get rid of it?" She didn't cook anymore; she just reheated.

My father was her meals on wheels, her groundskeeper, accountant, and snow-removal man. Not only was he responsible for her driveway (even though she didn't drive) and sidewalk, but he also cleared the drive and sidewalk for her neighbor, a ninety-six-year-old widow, whom I only knew as Jitters. He did it because her late husband had survived the Bataan Death March. "It's the least I can do," he said.

For some reason, my mother did not like Aunt Florence. I recall a series of voice messages left on my machine from Mom: "Florence is driving me nuts! I swear I'm going to kill her!" Immediately followed by another message, "Hi, it's Mom. Disregard that last message. I didn't mean *kill* her. That would be bad. Wouldn't it?"

Florence was the reason for many of Mom's phone calls.

"She's sooo needy!"

"Mom! Cut her some slack… She's over a hundred!"

"She called last night at nine and said she heard something in the yard, so your father had to drop everything and go over there—"

"Wait a sec… Mom? Are you…*jealous*?"

"Wha-what? What do you mean, jealous?"

"Of Florence. When she calls, Dad jumps. Think of it…his attention…on her…away from you?"

"Oh…Well? No! Well…I don't think so. Maybe?" She paused. "I'll tell you one thing…she'll outlive me! Just watch!" I would not have taken that bet. I would have been dead wrong.

Linda and I used to speculate as to why Mom harbored this bilious vitriol toward Florence. Perhaps there had been a secret family rift over an undetermined amount of money or a stolen heirloom or perhaps a festering insult? But my mother wasn't the type to hold a grudge.

She lived and let live. She was the one who made the first move to accept her father's second wife, Rose, a woman he met in line at the butcher shop only three months after my grandmother had passed from cervical cancer that, maybe, possibly could have stemmed from his World War I randiness—he confessed to my father on his deathbed that he had fathered a French love child.

In the days after my mother died, I took Florence her small meals and sat with her while she ate because my father wasn't up to it. My sister had the I-have-to-work excuse, so…me.

147

I knocked on her back door once, then twice, rang the bell several times, and eventually she opened it. "You shouldn't have gone through all this trouble!" Should I have told her the truth? That all the "trouble" I went through was cruising the ready-to-go buffet at the grocery store, plopping whatever into a container, then repackaging the food onto one of my dinner plates and wrapping it with foil to make it look like I had gone through all this trouble?

She had on a leopard-print beret, with a matching leopard-print cardigan over a red crewneck sweater. Gray pants. Earrings. A bracelet. I hated her for looking better at 101 than my mother had at eighty-three. And when she complained about her intricate system of supplements and medications—"I have to take sixteen pills a day!"—how she couldn't do the things she used to do, like garden and change her window treatments per the seasons—"Oh, I wish I were ninety-eight again!"—I wanted to scream at her, "You're here! Living! In your own house! You're over one hundred years old!"

"Oh, how I wish the Lord would take me! Why am I still here?" she asked, scraping the remnants of a piece of pineapple upside-down cake that I'd let her believe I'd baked. Why *was* she still here? I would have sold my soul for a Florence and Marian switcheroo.

I sighed and shrugged. "It's a mystery to me," I said.

Seamus trotted at our heels. He looked good. His fur glistened in the sun. I gave him a good-dog scratch behind his ears.

"What do you mean, Florence's final arrangements?"

"You know...*final* arrangements. She doesn't want a religious service, no coffin, and she wants to be cremated." He wrinkled up his nose.

"What's with the face?"

"I don't go for that cremation stuff."

Wait, wasn't he the guy who said something about his ashes put into shotgun shells?

"Yeah, but Dad, it's what *she* wants."

I sat down on my bucket, and Seamus plopped down in the grass next to my father. I settled in for a session of Dad-Florence venting.

"Florence has been bugging the you-know-what out of me. She keeps complaining, 'I can't see. I can't hear. I'm so weak. Why won't the Lord take me?'"

"Seriously, Dad, why won't He?"

My father shook his head and let out a sigh. "She called me yesterday and told me she was going to kill herself."

"How? Pills?" It wouldn't surprise me. She took so many—for her heart, her blood pressure, when she retained water, vitamins, supplements, sleeping pills…

"No, she's got this gun, so…I tell her not to do anything stupid and stop talking crazy, and I go over there, and first of all, the gun is so old and rusty—"

"Where did she get it?"

"She claimed she's had it since the war."

"Which one? Spanish-American?" I said.

"She could hardly lift the thing, let alone shoot herself, so I took it. But when she gets that way, wondering why she isn't dead, I don't know what the hell I'm supposed to say." He reached down and gave Seamus a pat on his big, blocky head.

"I've tried to talk her into moving to assisted living, but she won't go."

I could see her point. What am I going to do when (if) that day comes with Dad? And we have to have the talk? Or will he be more pro-active and pragmatic and sit Linda and me down to say he's selling the house, moving into a senior facility? I shivered a little bit. Not because I was cold, but because I wanted to shake that thought out of my brain.

"She could fall down those steps," I said.

"Well… If she falls down and dies at this point…" He shrugged.

"Dad…did you ever think that maybe the reason why she's still alive is that…maybe she's a vampire!?"

It felt good to see him laugh. I gave my dad's back a rub, his shoulder a squeeze.

"Um, so…Dad? How've you been?"

"What do you mean?"

"You know…like, how have *you* been?"

"Oh. Well…uh…during the day I'm busy, but at night, I've got no one sitting next to me on the sofa to watch TV with, no one to talk to, no eyeballs looking back at me."

I didn't understand how my father could come home to a house made emptier by my mother's physical absence and not have a dog in the house. Sure, Mugsy was there, but he lived outside. Mark and I had made a pact that we would never be without a dog; that's why we had the backup, so when the old dog had to go on the last car ride to the vet, there was a wagging tail waiting for you at home.

"Sounds to me like somebody needs a puppy!"

"No. When Mugsy goes, that's it. No more dogs."

He couldn't mean it. No more dogs? Maybe he felt like that now, but next year? My father *always* had a dog. Ever since I could remember. For him not to have another dog would be harder than it was getting used to seeing him without my mother.

"How are you going to know… I mean, when it's time for Mugsy to…you know… Don't you want him in a box? On the bookcase? Next to the ribbons and trophies he won?"

"No."

"Why?"

"Why should I?"

I liked my collection of dead dog receptacles. There was a can with our first dog, Bob. I'd had the final arrangements handled by the vet, and I was never sure that what I got back was just Bob, so I swore that when it came time for our second dog, Harvey, to go, I would take matters into my own hands.

He was the golden retriever that I'd bought when I went to look at my nephew's friend's aboveground pool. He had epilepsy that was managed with drugs and had been seizure free for years, and then, I think he was around eight when I found him in the kitchen, standing with the top of his head pressed up against the wall, and I thought, *Well, that's a strange way to have a seizure.* Not a seizure. Liver cancer.

A lobe was removed, and he was cancer free without any additional issues until he turned eleven. That's when his house of cards started to fall. Cataracts, a scratched cornea, congestive heart failure, and then his larynx collapsed. He couldn't walk up any stairs. I had to get a sling-type thing with a handle that made him into a golden retriever carry-on. I entertained the thought of maybe…maybe it was, you know…time? We had our backup pup (Seamus) in place, so… I admit there was a degree of selfishness to my maybes—only one dog…less poop…fewer vet bills. But every time I hinted around and asked our vet, Dr. Bob, "Do you think… I mean… Wouldn't it be better if—how will I, you know…know?"

"Oh, these old guys, they have a way of letting you know."

Wasn't he letting me know?

One day, as puppy Seamus romped around the yard, I spotted this congeal-y blob that Harvey had left under the maple tree. I'm no vet, but it didn't look good. I dropped him off at the clinic and ran errands, expecting to pick him up in an hour with another prescription, but when the assistant called and asked me if I minded being put on hold because the vet wanted to talk to me, I kind of knew… Dr. Bob said that ol' Harv was bleeding internally, he suspected from tumors in his liver, the spleen, stomach. "I mean, you could take him home, and let him bleed out, but if he were my dog…"

I told the vet to wait until I got there, that I wanted to be with my big old galoot of a golden one last time. Harvey wobbled over to me, then to the door. He wanted to go home, but I had to tell him he wasn't going home—well, not to our home. He was going Home home. I stayed with him, said my good-byes through my tears, until his big head fell, lifeless into my lap.

"I'm going to put him in my car and take him to get cremated," I said. Harvey's body was placed in the back of my car on a waterproof blanket that was part of a picnic-themed raffle prize that will now never be used for a picnic. Would you drink wine, nibble on cheese and a fresh baguette, on something we now called the "dead-dog blanket"?

The pet crematorium place was appropriately hidden at the end of a dead end. The road was unpaved, unmarked, overgrown. I passed two sets of rusted, forgotten kennels that would have been depressing to me that day had they been new before I came to a rustic pair of buildings—I use the term "rustic" as in real-estate speak, like "handyman's dream" or "needs a little TLC." Nothing was plumb or level. A hand-painted sign that looked like it came from Jed Clampett's cabin hung outside the door and read "Office."

A woman—a generic, high-school-office-lady type—was on the phone. A man sat on a chair, his stained work shirt unbuttoned, exposing a bony set of clavicles, blurry tattoos, and several scars. He made the Tilt-A-Whirl guy at the state fair look like an Armani model.

"Excuse me," I said. "But, um, I have my dog in the car."

"Dead?" he said.

"Yes, dead."

The woman hung up the phone and offered me her sympathies, got out her pad of paper, and took down my information. "For a single, we charge by the pound. Weight?"

Harvey had lost ten pounds in the past week. "Sixty pounds," I said.

"*Finally!* A good-sized golden!" said the man I'll call Igor. "Some a them run a hunnerd pound!" Which, he went on to tell me in graphic detail, made his job just that much more of a challenge.

You're welcome?

He pulled on his greasy work gloves and made a beeline for the door. I followed.

"Look," I said, "I don't want to see you take him out of my car. It's unlocked. Just go and get him and I'll wait here until you tell me that you've taken him wherever it is that you take him." I couldn't bear seeing what was still, in my mind, Harvey plopped into a wheelbarrow like compost.

I was back in the office completing the transaction when Igor poked his head in. "Um, you want that blanket back? 'Cause…some a them got a flame retardant on 'em and I can't get the ovens up to white-hot—"

Could he not have been so specific? I was in mourning, for Chrissake!

"Yes, I want the blanket back."

The lady said she'd call when my cremains were ready. *Cremains?* She directed me to a showroom filled with samples of memorial plaques, headstones, urns, and mini-coffins and wondered if I'd be interested. No. I knew I wanted to put Harvey in something fitting, but I wouldn't

153

know what it was until I saw it, and whatever it was, it wasn't there. Igor came back and told me the coast was clear. I got into my car with the empty blanket in the back and sobbed. When I walked into my Harvey-less kitchen, puppy Seamus was waiting to be fed.

I wanted my father to get another dog, because…I needed him to get another dog. That would mean life would continue as it had always, minus my mother. For him not to get another dog? No. I would have to face facts. He was getting old. I was getting older. And nothing stays the same.

CHAPTER EIGHTEEN

OLD WHAT'S-HER-NAME

OCTOBER 28 WAS MY parents' wedding anniversary. When I got up, fed the dog, then had to follow him outside on his route around the perimeter of the yard to make sure I got to the pile of feral cat poop before he did, I knew that a few miles down the road, my father was waking up alone on his anniversary for the first time in sixty-two years. He had to face the day without his lovely wife, Old What's-Her-Name—that was his pet name for her, which made my sister get riled up when she was in her women's-studies phase.

"It's like she's a nameless nothing!"

I wanted to call him, but I didn't want to call. What would I say? I couldn't wish him a happy anniversary. Problem solved—he called me.

"Today would have been sixty-three years." He sighed.

"Oh, Dad! I know. I know," I said, followed by a pause. Then I asked, "Dad? Why did you call Mom Old What's-Her-Name?"

I heard him chuckle. "Oh, yeah. Um, well, there was this guy on the radio, kind of a comedian, and he used to talk about his wife, and he called her Old What's-Her-Name, and I just thought it was funny."

"Didn't Mom object? I mean…what's-her-name?"

"Nah. If she did, she never said anything."

I thought maybe he needed to reminisce. That it would help him get through the first anniversary minus Mother. Even though I knew how they met, I asked him, "How did you and Mom meet?"

"Uh…we met at the park…ice skating," he said. "Yeah, I was around twelve, and me and my cousins Richie and Lefty were playing a game of girl tag, and I skated up to your mother because she was short and I stole her mitten."

"So, you've known—*knew* Mom since you were twelve?"

Their romance began like all good romances, with disdain and annoyance. My mother told me Dad was a pain. He pestered her. Followed her. Always knew where she'd be, so he could just happen to ride his bike and bump into her, literally.

Life was scripted: meet a girl in high school, date, graduate, get a factory job, get engaged, get married, buy a house, have kids. They went to the same high school and sat next to each other in band—she played the clarinet; he played the trumpet. She was taller than he was until he was a junior and grew a foot over the summer. They started dating when they were sixteen, and back then, in 1944, no one went to college. They were engaged at eighteen and married at twenty-one. I wondered if he regretted throwing out all the old anniversary cards she'd given him because they had impinged on the opening and closing of the drawer in the hutch they were shoved into. She personalized them with "You've still got what it takes!" and "To my knight in shining armor!"

"Yeah. That's what…seventy years?"

He went on, talking about how he saved up his earnings from digging graves to buy her an engagement ring and how he used to bring her flowers.

"Please, Dad, tell me you didn't give her dead people's flowers?"

"Why let them go to waste?"

"So you and Mom…did you ever break up?" I don't know why

I'd never asked my mother this, not even when I would call her in tears because the man I thought was the One wasn't.

"Well…there was one time I left my wallet at her house, and Mom found it and thought she'd bring it to me, and then…uh…she kind of saw me with this other girl, Dodie—"

"Jesus, Dad. Dodie?"

"Hey, she was a cute little blond! Anyways, your mother sees us, and she threw the wallet at me, and for two weeks she gave me the cold shoulder."

"As well she should have!"

"Yeah, well, then I find out she was stepping out with a kid from across the street…oh, what the heck was his name…Dick? Don? Leo!"

"Who?" This was shocking because my mother always told me she never dated anyone else, that she knew he was *it*. And now? Well, this was like finding out she had dentures all over again.

"He lived across the street from her. I always told her, if she had married him instead of me, she'd have been a rich woman, because his family owned a door business."

Had my mother married this Leo person, where would I be? Still lurking in the cosmos somewhere? Or would I be here, only a different version of myself, perhaps a cat person, more of a girlie girl? A man? A Labrador?

"I always wondered why you got married right in the middle of hunting season."

"Yeah, well…that was kind of an interesting story…"

He hadn't planned on getting married in October, but Mom kept bugging him to set the date and he remembered a trick his Uncle Hienie had pulled. Hienie was one of nine brothers—a confirmed bachelor, but not for the reasons one might think. I think he was a lifelong bachelor because of his propensity to eat cigars. Eat. Not smoke. He had a Cro-Magnon unibrow and a Wolfman hairline, and whenever someone wanted him to fix the whatever or install the something, he'd say, "I'll be over on the twenty-eighth!" not specifying the twenty-eighth of what month, so the next time my mother whined about setting the date, my dad said, "Okay. We'll get married on the twenty-eighth!" And she ran home all excited, got out the calendar, and the only date that fit the Saturday wedding requirements fell on October 28.

"Did you go on a honeymoon?"

"Mom insisted on Chicago."

"How romantic! You and Mom, twenty-one years old…two young kids…alone…in love…in the big city…" I pictured a George Cukor–esque romantic comedy, Jean Arthur as my mother and a rugged Joel McCrea as Dad. I had obviously just seen the 1943 movie *The More the Merrier* on TCM.

I heard him clearing his throat. "So…are we on for Wednesday?"

I got it. He wanted to change the subject. I felt bad for bringing it up. Wait, *he* brought it up. He called *me*. This dad-daughter dance of grieving was tricky. Who leads? Me? Him? Oh, that's right—he doesn't dance.

"I'm not sure if the weather will cooperate." There was a threat of severe weather. Possible snow. Sleet.

"Let's make it a game-day decision," he said.

"Dad?"

"What?"

"Well, think of it…if you hadn't gone skating on that day…"

"Yeah, and I usually didn't go to that park, but Richie insisted."

"…and if Mom hadn't been there…"

"Did I mention it was at night? And she almost didn't make it because it was her turn to do the supper dishes."

"...I would not be sitting here talking to you. I might be talking to someone named Leo or Dodie."

"Yeah, it is funny how stuff works," he said. "All because of a mitten."

CHAPTER NINETEEN

THE EPIPHANY

I<small>T WAS</small> N<small>OVEMBER</small>. D<small>EER</small> hunting season was a few weeks away. Dad decided that, yes, he would be spending five days, from sunup to sundown, in the north woods with his retired cop buddies and their friends. A good thing? Did I want him to go? He was eighty-three, and if he shot a deer, then he'd have to track it, find it, gut it, and drag it out of the woods to the road three—four?—miles. Was I worried he would stumble, fall, shoot himself, and bleed to death? Or have a heart attack as he was dragging the carcass and lie there until the guys came to look for him or my mother came to take him? Um, I think you already know the answer. On the other hand, if he hadn't accepted his deer hunting pals' overtures, I would have worried that he was wallowing, maybe getting depressed. And dealing with a parent who's depressed and who doesn't believe in psychiatry…the universe wouldn't do that to me, would it? Going deer hunting meant he was in a good place, even if that place was in a tree stand waiting to kill something majestic.

● ● ●

He started our next training session with a question. "What do you want your dog to do?"

"In general or today in particular?"

What exactly did I want the dog to do? I had thought retrieving would have been enough, but…then I'd seen the need for him to deliver to hand. I no longer had to chase him whenever he stole my very expensive bra out of the laundry. Whistle commands also came in handy in the yard. I kept my whistle at the ready, hanging from a pushpin on the bulletin board that was cluttered with expired coupons. I can't tell you how many opossums I'd saved from a real death, not a pretend opossum death, by calling the dog off with my firm *toot, toot*. All this training…to what end? Hunting? Field trials? No. I would have to learn to shoot a shotgun. I wasn't about to go all in.

I enjoyed our Wednesdays out in the open air, learning about dogs and other stuff, like why Dad can't watch *Lady and the Tramp*: "When that dog gets hit by the dog catcher truck? Oh. Boy. I get choked up."

I was going to say something about wanting Seamus to get back to his Labrador roots, blah, blah, blah, when the area of my brain designated for wacky ideas and schemes lit up. It had been dark after Mom died, then dimly lit by a twenty-watt bulb, and now it was like Lambeau Field for Monday Night Football.

"Dad?" I said. "I know what I want Seamus to do!"

"O-kaay."

"I want to enter him in the Fastest Retriever Contest! The big one. Not the kennel club one. The. Big. One."

"The one where he wouldn't go up the stairs?"

"Yes!"

"The one you got kicked out of at the sports show?"

"Yes!"

"The one that brought shame upon our family?"

"Dad, I—I just want to be able to do it! I need to be vindicated! What do you think?"

He turned over his empty five-gallon bucket, the one that housed all his training materials we were using, and sat down. He pursed his lips. Rubbed his chin. Put his hands on his knees. Squinted off into the distance, like John Wayne when he scanned the horizon for Apaches.

"Hmm. Let's do a little test," he said. He went to the back of his truck and pulled out some thin white dowels.

"How far do you think the run is?" he said.

"Uh...forty yards?"

"Stand with your dog here." He dropped a white dowel at my feet. "That's going to be the starting line." He marched forward, counting as he went until, he said, "This is forty yards!"

Looked very doable. I got Seamus at my heel, made sure he was steady. Dad, forty yards downwind, tossed a dummy a few feet to his side. I sent the dog. Seamus broke the sound barrier on the way there, but on his return, he ran wide of the mark (me) and did his little dance of avoidance.

"Okay, that's enough. I can see that's not going to work," my father said, collecting his dowels. The contest was in March. That meant we had four months to figure out how to get the dog to pick up a training dummy and come back to me in as straight a line as possible.

"I want you to practice in the yard, while I'm deer hunting."

"Speaking of deer hunting, Dad, do you go out in the woods in a group?"

"Not all the time. Why?" He crawled up and into his truck cab to stash the sticks in one of the compartments. He had the truck insert put in, with benches and cushions that folded out into a bed, so he could sleep inside instead of in the deer camp cabin.

"What if, say, there's an emergency? How would anyone know?"

"We have a couple walkie-talkies—hand me that bucket." My father had designated spots for everything.

"One walkie-talkie for each guy?" I said.

"A couple. That's two!"

"Two? For how many guys? Six? Who gets to have one? You?"

"Nah. What do I need a walkie-talkie for?"

"Dad! What if you fall or get shot or have a heart attack!"

"Well, then you and your sister can fight over who gets what."

In the throes of my future grief, when my sister and I are in a dispute over Great-Grandpa's World War I sharpshooter medal, the wicker game baskets, the old Flexible Flyer sled that's in the garage rafters, will I be able to laugh and say, "Dad would have loved to have seen this"? No. Maybe. I don't know.

He barked last-minute orders. "Take in my mail. It usually comes in the morning,"

"Okay."

"Push the garbage cart to the curb on Tuesday."

"Okay."

"And put some lights on, so it looks like someone's home. I don't want to come back and find the house ransacked." I don't know why he was so concerned about a break-in. He lived in a neighborhood populated with police officers (active and retired) and deputy sheriffs who were heavily armed and could sense criminal intent days ahead, miles away.

"Oh, and one more thing—while I'm hunting, I want you to read a book called *Training Your Retriever* by James Lamb Free."

CHAPTER TWENTY

THE TAO OF DAD

I PICKED UP A COPY of *Training Your Retriever* from the library. It should have come with a surgeon general's warning. Whoever had it last must have chain-smoked their way through the three-hundred-plus pages of practical advice on training a retriever for, as Mr. Lamb Free put it, the lazy man. Anyone who writes a book about how to do something for someone who has accepted their laziness and who says, "There's nothing to it that a fairly bright moron couldn't figure out for himself," well, that's my kind of book. It was full of practical advice, like:

> Never give a command you can't enforce.
> Give short, frequent lessons.
> Don't give him a chance to be bored.
> A retriever's work should be his fun.

> Give your dog a cookie every time he does what he's supposed to do, if you like. But it's a useless precedent you're starting and will become a nuisance. If he learns to expect these tips, there will come a time, out in the field, when you run out of tidbits. If you never start this practice, he'll be just as happy without it.

So that's where my father had picked up the tidbit on treats. I was a little insulted when I read that house dogs are sloppy and confused. My dog? Sloppy? Confused? Mr. Lamb Free addressed Seamus's issue with a hard mouth. "It is the blackest of all the retriever crimes." Ouch. I was sharing my living space with a fur-bearing felon.

The more I read, the more I discovered that the book wasn't just a how-to guide; it was my father's Tao.

> A woman is at a disadvantage in dog training. Her voice is simply weaker, and higher pitched, than a man's. She can't bellow like a top sergeant. But, even so, if she really tries, she can get that ring of authority into her commands. And when necessary, she can get fine results by throwing away her inhibitions and yelling like a fishwife.

I was starting to understand dogs. And Dad's "dippy broad"-isms. There was a chapter called "Spare the Rod," dedicated to the use of walloping as a disciplinary measure, but it was too *Nicholas Nickleby* for me. Mr. Lamb Free stated that a dog, unlike a child, never reaches the age of reason, and, therefore, he gave the green light to a smack, which didn't make sense to me. Although, I did understand the part about the dog not being a child—probably why I wasn't a good fit for doggy day care.

I remembered back when our daughter went off to college and my son was in high school, so his mothering needs had diminished to nil—my role had been reduced to shuttle driver, maid, and short-order cook. Writing hadn't proven to be as lucrative as I had envisioned, and I needed a little extra income, so I had applied for a job at the doggy day care. It was in a repurposed warehouse not too far from where I lived, and if I got the job as playground supervisor, my plan was to ride my bike to and from work—get a paycheck and lose weight!

The only indication that this was a place for dogs and not human children was the lack of carpeting—oh, and maybe the collars and leashes. There were standard day care–issue cubbies; coats and boots neatly arranged; doggy artwork hung on the primary colored walls— not *of dogs*, but *by dogs*—bins of balls, stuffed animals, springy jiggly toys, squeakies; and treats that looked quite tasty. I picked up on a strange vibe. Nothing bad. Or evil. Just…off.

I met with the director, a girl in her twenties. Her office, littered with dog toys, bones, throws, and blankets, was more dog bed than office. She shared it with a Great Dane–Irish wolfhound–horse mix. "This is Daphne," she said. Daphne raised a mud-flap-sized ear. "She wants to know why you think you'd be perfect for this job."

"Well, I get dogs. I'm not exactly a dog whisperer," I said, unsure where to direct my answer. "I'm more like a dog *shouter*."

"Hmm. I see," Ms. Director said, looking down at her desk covered in half-eaten dog toys and photos of her dog family.

"Any experience?"

"I've had other playground experience—my son's middle school. Talk about your wild pack of animals!"

"With animals?"

"I worked at the zoo."

"The zoo?" Her ears perked up. "How long were you there?"

"Oh…a summer."

Thank God she didn't ask me to go into more detail. I only lasted two weeks due to an, uh, unfortunate incident in the petting ring. FYI: never put a python in the compartment next to the teddy bear gerbils. Sunnydale Elementary learned all about the circle of life that day!

"Have you ever worked at a doggy day care before?"

"No, but I have dogs," I said.

"How many?" she asked, while Daphne chased rabbits in her sleep.

I told her that I currently had two dogs, a Golden that was circling the drain, so to speak, and the other a Lab puppy that was the backup dog.

"Backup?"

"Right, see, when it's time for…you know…I don't want to come home to that empty-house feeling."

"How can you be so cavalier about end-of-life issues?" she said. Cavalier? I thought I was being emotionally preemptive. I saw Daphne's sphincter pucker. In dog body language, I knew what that meant—prepare for a room-clearing fart.

"Would you like to see the area you'd be working in?"

"Yes, please!"

We left Daphne to lie in her fetid cloud.

Ms. Director took me to an outdoor area covered in pea gravel. Several dogs nipped at each other and romped with a large playground ball, the same kind I remembered having in grade school. Others gathered under a spindly tree, and a few more napped in the sun. A brown dog with a curled-up tail and a border-collie type looked like they were about to have a go at each other over a chew toy, a good time for me to impress with my skills. "*Hey!*" I yelled, clapping my hands.

"Oh, no. No, no. That's not how we like to do things." She tsk-tsked me. "We use what's called positive reinforcement." She said it slowly, emphasized each syllable, as if I had never heard of it. Like it was a brand-new concept. *I raised two children. I took psych 101!*

"First, we redirect." She grabbed a different chew toy and offered it to the brown dog, who couldn't have cared less. "Sometimes Sasha can get possessive over chew toys. She may have to go into a time-out." The director grabbed Sasha by the collar and ushered her out and into a different fenced-in area, while praising another dog that had just made a nice pile of poop. "Way to go, Judy! Nice work!" And that's when I knew what the vibe was that I had picked up on in the beginning. I'm not one of these people. I don't understand doggy time-outs, play dates, and sleepovers. I couldn't see myself filling out the detailed intake and outtake forms:

> *Jeremy had a couple of loose stools this a.m. We worked with him on his issues with leaves.*
> *Betty had a dominance issue with Troy over the Kong ball.*
> *Please bring fresh socks for Chester. He started a new lick sore on his hind leg.*

She offered me the job, but I declined.

Was it the money?

No.

Was it the three hours of standing?

No.

I admitted that I had a bias against dogs like Sasha. "I don't know what it is, but dogs with tails that curl up onto their backs seem kind of douchey." I continued. "I feel that this prejudice will prevent me from giving any positive reinforcement; therefore, I'd be creating an unhealthy and unbalanced state that the dogs would pick up on, and they would probably end up devouring each other." It was either that or tell her I thought she was nuts.

My father called me to tell me he was safely home from the deer hunt.

"I only almost shot myself once, when I tripped and fell into a small hole."

"Oh, well. No worries, then!"

He wanted to discuss our next scheduled round of training; with the weather being so nasty, we'd play it by frostbitten ears. He asked if I enjoyed the book. I told him I had, that I found the tone to be amusing, and I told him how I could see why he had recommended it, but I felt it was my duty to complain about the sexism.

"Dad, he's got a whole chapter called 'Even the Ladies Can Do It'!"

"Well, they can, can't they?"

"Well, yeah, but...never mind. How's the plan for fastest retriever coming along?"

"I've got an idea. You might not like it," he said.

"Why?"

"Well, I think it's time we use the shock collar."

Dear God. What would Daphne think?

CHAPTER TWENTY-ONE

SABOTAGED

So far, the first year without my mother had been full of hurdles, but the upcoming holiday season was going to be a triathlon. First up? The long, emotional swim through the lumpy gravy of Thanksgiving, then the uphill ride of Christmas and the shin splints of the New Year. It was my sister's turn to cook the turkey and be the hostess for Thanksgiving, but she couldn't find her dining room, so it was all up to me to plan the first Big Holiday with a Giant Hole in Our Hearts. I turned to Seamus for advice. He was curled up in a dog ball on the chair next to my computer.

"How am I going to handle this? Do everything the same as last year? As if nothing happened?" He opened one eye.

Last Thanksgiving, we had been worried Mom wouldn't make it. She'd had trouble with three steps. How was she going to go up my thirteen front steps? "Don't worry," my son had said. "If I have to, I'll just strap Grandma to the front of me in a giant BabyBjörn." To her credit, she made it, Björnless albeit with a lot of help.

"Seamus, what about the table? It has to be set just right for maximum mood uplift. Should I go with something formal and fancy? Wash the family heirloom stemware?"

He exhaled and yawned.

"No, you're right. Formal might be too fussy, and fussiness would make people uncomfortable…but…if I go casual, it might look like I didn't care."

He got up and found a better spot on the rug.

"I could use my transferware dishes that I've been collecting, with scenes of idyllic English countrysides in greens and browns? Do a mixy-matchy kind of thing."

The rug muffled the thumping tail of approval.

"What about Mom's apple pie? Should I attempt to make one this year or just let it become the stuff of family legend?" He repositioned himself to scratch an itch.

My mother's apple pie is—was—the star of any dessert table. Other desserts were merely extras—pie #2, dessert #4. She mailed, UPSed, and FedExed her pie to comfort the grown-up grandkids' homesickness and soothe their bouts with mono, strep throat, the flu. An apple pie from her helped to mend hearts after breakups and divorces. I'm not saying it had healing powers—I'm just saying.

I worried that this year's dinner would be a lot of heavy sighs, no sassy banter, no loud pontificating, just the soft clinking of forks on plates—that is, if anyone even felt like eating. What then? All that food gone to the dog…except for my sister's green bean casserole. I don't know how it came to be a Thanksgiving staple. No one requested it, and yet, she insisted on bringing it along, like a bad boyfriend whom everyone merely tolerated. There have been dinners when it needed a last-minute warm-up to crunchify the onions, and, oops, it was forgotten, left in the oven, remembered after everyone was well into pie mode. One year, she held up dinner for over an hour because she had left it on her kitchen counter, and despite our niceties about how we'd just have to soldier on without it, she had to drive home to get it.

Was I overthinking? My responsibility would be for dinner and the pies. Pumpkin. Pecan. Apple?

Last Thanksgiving, with my mother's arm strength not what it used to be, she'd decided to relinquish her rolling pin. To me. My apple pies? The crust tended to be gummy, the apples dry. I've followed her handwritten, stained, and blurry recipe to the letter: 2/3 cup of shortening, 2 cups sifted flour, 5–6 tablespoons cold water, 1 tsp. salt. Four ingredients mixed together in one bowl. So simple yet so hard. "Come over, and I will show you," she'd said. I would be her understudy.

I loved baking with my mother. Elementary-school me would sit there while she rolled and cut her dough for butterhorns, apple tarts, and pies, and ask her questions.

"Mom? What did you want to be when you grew up?"

"Oh…I always wanted to be a teacher."

"Really?"

"Uh-huh. Put a spoonful of the apples in the center of the square."

"Why didn't you?"

"I'd have had to go to college, and we didn't have the money. Wet your finger and pinch the ends of the dough together."

"You're kinda like a teacher. You teach *me* stuff."

"That's true! Put the pinched ones on the cookie sheet. Those are ready for the oven. What do *you* want to be when *you* grow up?"

"Oh…I don't know. What do you think?"

"Hmm. Well…I think…you should be…whatever you want to be."

Last year, I had packed up my just-like-hers rolling pin, my canister of flour, a peck of MacIntosh apples, and sticks of shortening. It wasn't that I thought her ingredients or tools to be inferior; I just needed to make sure that my stuff wasn't the reason for my crust fail.

"Is today the day we were baking pie?" she'd said, sitting on the padded seat of her walker. Hadn't I reminded her of our plan two hours ago? I'd expected to come into the kitchen and see the big yellow mixing bowl and the measuring spoons waiting on the table, not still in the cabinets, the drawers.

My father was dressed in his kennel club clothes. "I want to talk to you," he said, and motioned for me to follow him into the garage. "Mom is... She's, uh...getting forgetful," he said.

Why was this such a concern? She had been getting forgetful for a while. "I went to the store and came home, unpacked all the groceries, and she sat there, watching me, and when I got done, she asked if I was going to the grocery store."

I didn't know what I was supposed to tell him. That it would be okay? Not to worry?

How much was he doing for her? I only saw the two of them whenever they came over or I went there to knit, and Mom was up and dressed, her coffee cup half-full next to her on the doily. Did he have to... There was a skyscraper of Depends in the linen closet...

"Dad? Is it getting to be too much for you? I mean...when will you know if you need to..." I was going to say something about assisted living, in-home care, but I couldn't get the words out. I was too afraid of what the answer might be. He had turned his head away from me.

"I'm going to the kennel club. I'll be back in a couple hours."

When I walked back into the kitchen, my mother had been coming out of the bathroom, and she said, "Oh! When did you get here? Is today the day we're baking pie?"

I cored and peeled, while she talked about her prescriptions, what she suspected the neighbors were up to (I didn't bother to correct her regarding the Nelsons, who hadn't lived down the block for forty years), and the birds that came to her bird feeder.

"Don't put the sugar and cinnamon on the apples now. Wait until they're in the crust; then do it." Really? My MO was to mix the sugar and cinnamon and apples together in a bowl, then dump everything into the bottom piecrust before I baked. I measured the flour and sprinkled the salt.

"Now I have to sift, right?" I said.

"No. I never sift."

"Then why does the recipe say 'sift' if you never sift?" She shrugged her bony shoulders. Up next? The critical cutting in of shortening. I went to the silverware drawer and pulled out two forks.

"Not those." She scooted over and pulled out two different forks from a previous lifetime.

So…it's the forks!

"You have to lift and cross. Fluff!"

I asked her if she was a natural. Did crusts come easy for her?

"Oh, no. As a matter of fact, the first pie I made almost killed my brother."

She had bought a box mix for the crust, somewhat of a novelty in the early 1940s. The pie turned out beautifully, and as it cooled, the smell wafted out the kitchen window, just like in one of those cartoons where the tentacle of steam wraps itself around the unsuspecting victim and carries him back to the source.

"My brother was six or seven at the time and couldn't resist it."

It only took a few minutes for him to plow his way through half of it before his digestive tract rebelled. She blamed the box mix. "That was before there were any of those dates stamped on things, and who knew how long it had been sitting on the shelf? He thought I was trying to get back at him for stabbing me in the hand with a pair of scissors."

I didn't know what my father had been so worried about. She remembered that. And how to make pie.

"Now, I add the water?" I said.

"Cold. It has to be cold."

"Why cold water?"

"I don't know. It just does. And don't just dump it all in. You've got to put it in one tablespoon at a time."

"What difference does it make if it all gets mixed in, anyway?"

She shrugged. I sprinkled and resumed fluffing until the dough looked like crumbs.

"And now, you make a ball and split it in half and roll it out."

This was it. The big moment. I was unsure of myself and my technique. Would the dough stick to the table no matter how much flour I put on it? Or it would fall apart like a piece of old newspaper? I took a deep breath, gathered it up, split it in half, and sprinkled a bit of flour on the table.

"What are you doing? Don't you have a sackcloth?"

"Sackcloth? Like the kind worn by martyrs?"

She wheeled her walker over to the sink, opened a drawer, and pulled out a flimsy white rectangle. "You roll the dough out on this, but first put a little flour on it and only add more flour onto the rolling pin, not the dough."

I didn't comprehend how her method would work. Any other dough I had rolled—pizza, bread—I always put flour on the table and the top of the dough to keep it from sticking, but I did as she said, and guess what? It never stuck to the rolling pin. It rolled out evenly. It wasn't a perfect circle—it looked a little bit like France—but it was big enough to fit into one of her pie dishes. Hers were not like the one I had purchased at an upscale cooking store. She used the inexpensive glass types sold at hardware stores, usually next to the canning supplies.

"I use these because they let you see how the bottom crust is baking. The one you have, that stoneware one? I could never figure out how you could check the bottom crust. No offense, dear, but it was always a tad on the soggy side."

I gently lifted the crust into the scratched and battle-worn dish. The apples were next. The sugar, the cinnamon.

"I add a little bit of butter to the apples, tucked in, here and there."

"Butter?"

"It adds a little extra flavor."

So it's the butter!

I rolled the top crust with a lot more confidence and placed it over the buttered, sugared, and cinnamoned apples.

"Wet your finger with the water, and go around the bottom edge before you press it with the fork tines. That way, you'll make sure you've made a good seal."

The top crust required a bit more patching.

"I've never rolled a top crust that didn't need patching."

So her crusts weren't exactly perfect. She had to work at them.

"Now, you take an egg white and mix it up with a little bit of water and then you brush the top crust with it. Make sure you poke a few holes here and there for the steam, and then sprinkle cinnamon on the top. We like a lot of cinnamon."

We do? Since when?

The pie had been cover-of-a-magazine perfect. It was the closing act to last year's Thanksgiving dinner—*her* last Thanksgiving dinner. The pumpkin pie went unnoticed; the cheesecake was an afterthought. It was the apple pie that everyone wanted. I was nervous to make that first cut, because the first cut is always the one that makes or breaks it, but the first slice came out intact. The filling held together; there was just enough juice, the bottom crust firm, the top crust golden and covered with cinnamon.

I remembered how I'd waited in the kitchen for the reviews, too nervous to face my audience. The around-the-table silence didn't help. Were they struck speechless by heaven on a plate? Or had the crust stuck in their throats, making swallowing and talking impossible? After a long five minutes, the critiques came in:

"A valiant effort!" from Adam, my New York City nephew.

"Serviceable!" from Caitlin.

"Too much cinnamon!" from my father.

Wait. What?!

Everyone agreed that the cinnamon made the piecrust a little too...cinnamon-y.

"We don't like a lot of cinnamon," my father said, scraping the last crumbs onto his fork.

"But, I—Mom said..."

I looked over at her, sitting there, looking innocent, avoiding my eyes, petting Seamus's head.

"Oh, you're such a good boy, aren't you?" she cooed.

Had she sabotaged me? With cinnamon?

As I thought about last year's pie, Seamus got up from the rug. He stretched, then gave me a look.

"What about the obvious empty chair? The one less place setting? Do I ignore the fact that Mom won't be sitting in her favorite spot closest to the radiator?" He shook his head and used his back left leg to scratch his left ear.

How did other people in my same situation handle a first holiday sans relative? How did they make it through? I went online and searched:

- Handling the holidays when mother is dead
- How to deal with grief during Thanksgiving

178

- First holiday after death of parent

I scrolled. I skimmed. Pretty much all I got was, "It will be diffi-cult," or "It will be different."

No shit.

My strategy was to do as much of the prep as I could before the big day; then all I'd have to worry about would be the turkey (which I always remind myself is nothing but a big chicken), the gravy, and my guests' emotional health. Seamus hadn't been out to the kennel club in weeks. I did what I could in the yard, tossing the training dummy between our two large maple trees, but he'd get up a head of steam and almost slam into the trunk, and I wasn't as creative as my father was, making up little training exercises, challenges. My yard wasn't big enough for any blind retrieves. And then it iced over, and I didn't want to risk having Seamus pull a muscle or tear a tendon.

On Monday, I counted the forks, ironed the napkins, and did a tablescaping dress rehearsal, foregoing the maudlin empty-chair-as-memorial. Tuesday, I mashed the potatoes, concocted the stuffing, and made a pumpkin cheesecake (from my pureed Halloween jack-o'-lantern—how very Martha Stewart of me!). Wednesday was dedicated to brining the big chicken and baking Apple Pie 2.0.

I wore one of my mother's stained, ripped aprons for the juju. I prayed to the pie goddess, a.k.a. Mom, that my forks would be adequate enough for the lifting, the crossing, the fluffing. The dough was mixed, gathered, and shaped into two balls. I spread the Mother-sanctioned sackcloth on the table and wondered if she was nearby, on the celestial sidelines. "You can do this," she'd have said.

I rolled out a pretty decent—no, make that one helluva—piecrust. Patching? Um, what patching? I gently lifted it off the cloth and laid it into the approved dish before the quarter moons of apples tumbled in, then the sugar, the pieces of butter here and there, topped off with a sprinkle of cinnamon. "Not too much. We *don't* like a lot of cinnamon," I said to Seamus, his nose covered with a dusting of flour from investigating the edge of the counter. He wouldn't risk full-blown counter surfing with me standing there, would he? No. He'd wait until I left the room and then he'd balance himself on his hind legs and quietly, stealthily pull his target off the counter.

We could never catch him in the act, and in the beginning, we were in denial and blamed others for the bags of hot dog buns, potato chips, and artisanal loaves of bread that we could have sworn we just bought at the grocery store. I'd find suspicious-looking plastic pieces from bread bags or twist ties embedded in fecal matter in the yard, but by that time, it was too late for me to discipline him. I would have to set up a sting operation.

I tied one end of a string around a bagged baguette once, and the other end to one of my stainless steel KitchenAid mixing bowls that I filled with screws, forks, spoons, and a beer can with a few pennies inside. I left it a few inches from the edge of the counter, irresistible to a certain Labrador retriever. "Seamus!" I said. "I have to leave. I'll be back." I put on my coat. My shoes. Got my keys. My purse. And went out the back door.

I sat on the back steps and waited for the crash. It didn't take a minute. I returned to find the contents of the mixing bowl scattered all over the kitchen as planned. Seamus had scuttled underneath the table, and my baguette? Still in its sheath. It had worked! Briefly. He's regressed and pilfered pizza, garlic bread, and bruschetta. I should have set up the trap again, but that would take effort. I took the easy way out and never left anything on the counter unless it was behind a fort made out of small appliances, canisters, and cutlery.

I made sure the apples were all snug and tucked in before I painted the top crust with egg white, then sugared the hell out of it and added a whisper of cinnamon. "So, Mom," I said in case she was somewhere in the vicinity, "what was the deal with the mass quantity of cinnamon? I distinctly remember you telling me to sprinkle a lot on the pie. It's not like I'm mad or anything. I'm just curious." And with that, I slid the bequeathed glass pie dish into the preheated 350-degree oven.

Emotionally ready or not, Thanksgiving and my family arrived. My children had bused in from Madison the night before and had spent all morning in their pajamas, watching the Macy's Thanksgiving Day Parade, just like they had done when they were little. I found it comforting that, even though they were closing in on thirty, they still needed to see the big Snoopy balloon, the Rockettes, and bad lip-synching.

Dad came bearing bags of buns that I hadn't requested and bottles of Lambrusco (Mom's favorite) that no one would drink. He looked a little drawn, as white as boiled turkey breast meat. He didn't greet me with his usual gusto—he didn't greet me at all, just moved quickly past me. My sister was right behind him; Amanda and Adam behind her. Seamus was never good at handling an influx of entering guests and ran back and forth, back and forth, bunching up the area rugs as he ricocheted around the room. My father gave him a swat with the buns. Better those than the Lambrusco.

I went in for a hug. "What?" he said, pulling back just a little.

"I don't know…just…thought you needed a hug, that's all—this being the first, you know…without Mom," I said.

"The game on?"

My sister clenched my forearm. "You just had to go and say something!"

Well, yeah, I had to. There. Done. Mom's not being here had

been addressed. Not formally. Not with a ceremonial something. But addressed. I felt a little bit of pressure had been released, and it felt good.

Everyone ended up in the kitchen, trying to "help," and got in my way. Seamus took up his usual spot right in the middle of the high-traffic lane until his tail was stepped on; then he retreated to the safety of his kennel.

I had prepared for this contingency, unlike years past, when they'd disrupted my choreographed serving assignments. I put Post-it notes on the serving dishes so my "helpers" wouldn't screw up my plan:

The flat rectangle—canned cranberry with ridges, the only kind my father would eat.

The Waterford bowl was for the made-with-actual-cranberries-as-God-intended relish.

The big green bowl—mashed potatoes.

Great-Grandma's platter—dark meat.

The heavy stoneware one I carried on the plane back from Ireland—white meat.

My sister posted a picture of my system on Facebook, and within seconds, it got twenty-five likes. *Were those I-love-this-idea likes or this-person-is-nuts likes?*

After everything was in the proper dishes (bean dish in the house!) in the proper places, and Seamus was under the table at the ready—we didn't need a ten-second rule in our house because he never let anything touch the floor—I called everyone to the table.

This would have been the time for saying grace, but we're not a big grace-saying family. I don't know why. I think it has something to do with stating the obvious. Well, yeah, we're grateful for the food, etc., and since God is supposed to know everything, why risk insulting Him/Her?

That might be the reason we're not a big "I love you" family. Of course we love each other. Would we put up with each other if we didn't?

If not grace, then a toast? Last year, my dad had stood, hoisted his glass, and said, "To my family!" But this year, he made no move. He made no eye contact.

Please, someone say something.

My daughter looked at me.

My husband's eyes met mine. They said, *Make a toast before your sister says something totally inappropriate.*

I stood, cleared my throat, and then raised my glass of much-needed wine toward my favorite black-and-white photo of Mom. It was circa 1950s, and she was looking very Rita Hayworth in a hammock, wearing Ray-Bans and a sassy little sundress. "To Marian!" I said.

"To Marian!" We clinked our glasses. That was it. That was all. That was enough.

We plowed through the plates of food, stopping to pass stuffing and stories. "I, for one, cannot wait for the Winter Olympics," Caitlin said. I gave her a thank-you-for-starting-the-conversational-ball-rolling pat on her shoulder.

"Grandma fell off a chairlift once," my father chimed in. "Hey, no sweet potatoes?"

"I forgot them. They're in the oven!" I said. I got up and put on my Ove' Glove to remove the dish from the oven. From that point on, I would only be sitting in short bursts. My sister needed more ice. My father needed more butter. Wineglasses emptied quickly. Bottles needed opening, platters more turkey.

"She did what?" asked Adam as he made a depression in his mashed potatoes with a spoon for his gravy lake.

"Maybe 'fell' isn't the right word, because she never really got on," Dad said. "Who wants cranberries?"

"I do," Linda said, "but seriously...Dad, you are aware that *real* cranberries don't have ridges on them from a can?"

"Yeah, I know!" he said.

"You went skiing?" my son asked him in that way children do when they realize that their parents, or in this case, grandparents, had one time, long, long ago, had a life.

"So...she fell off a chairlift how?" Caitlin, always the journalist, needed facts.

"She was half-on and half-off, and I had to hang on to her by the collar of her parka—pass the stuffing—but it started to choke her, and—"

"Was the lift moving?" asked my sister with a mouthful of food.

"They stopped it—you got any pepper?—anyway, a ski patrol guy skis underneath, and he yells at me to let her go."

"So...you *dropped* her?" Caitlin said.

My husband said nothing. He was busy eating. Over the course of our thirty-year marriage, he has learned that at times like this, when everyone is talking at once, he is better off keeping silent.

"Well, she didn't fall far, and besides, she fell on top of the ski patrol guy!"

Laughter felt good. We were used to getting together most Sundays for dinner, but since Mom died, regular dinners had fallen off the calendar, and it had been a while since we had told stories with mother as the punch line. She would have approved.

The topic shifted faster than the plate of congealed cranberry.

"I have a funny Mom story," I said. "When Linda and I would argue—"

"You two? Argue?" Dad said.

"Yeah, believe it or not! Anyway, to get us to stop, Mom would say, 'I'm going to call your father!' and she'd walk over to the phone we had on the wall in the kitchen and dial, and we got all scared 'cause we thought she was calling Dad at the police station, but she really called the weather."

My son was confused. "What do you mean, she called the weather?"

I had to explain about life before the Internet and unlimited calling and texting—when we dialed a number for the forecast or for the correct time, and the fact that we were allowed to make only one outgoing call per day.

Amanda put down her forkful of mashed potatoes. "You could only make *one* call *per day?*"

"That was back when our phone number had the Lincoln exchange," Dad said. He still had the same phone number that I'd had to memorize when I went to kindergarten. *What's going to happen to that number when he dies? Will it go into the phone number hopper? Get reassigned to a stranger? No. I can't allow that to happen. It's our number.*

Linda interrupted my thoughts. "How come no one is eating my bean dish?"

"Why do you even bring it? You're the only one who eats it!" Amanda pushed the Pyrex dish rimmed with crusted and burned beans out of her sector of the table.

"I thought you liked it!" Linda already had several stains and smudges on her Thanksgiving-themed sweater, complete with a smiling pair of pilgrims.

"No, Mom. Never."

"Yeah. I have a rule," Adam said. "I never eat anything that color."

"It's green!"

"No, it's taupe."

My father took some on his finger and offered it to Seamus. He sniffed at it and turned away. Then sneezed.

"Even the dog won't eat it."

I sensed tension building over in the southeast corner of the table, between my sister and her daughter and son, so I changed the subject.

"Uh, Dad, when did you get your first dog?" I asked.

"My first dog? Oh, geez... I had a Sealyham terrier when I was in grade school—pass me the biscuits. My pa got it from some guy he worked with at the foundry, but I didn't have it long. It got distemper. Then, when I was around fourteen, I worked in a garage, and one day, in walks this dog, and when it was time to go home, the dog was still there, and I said, 'What about the dog?' and my uncle says, 'You take him.' So I did—gravy? Who's got the gravy?"

I commandeered the gravy boat from my son and passed it to my father.

Dad continued. "I called him Major. He was some kind of spaniel, which explained why he liked to chase ducks, and one day, see, we lived right across the street from a park, and he...uh...ran...into the road, and..." He couldn't finish.

My sister leaned over to me. "Nice work, bringing up dead dogs," she said.

Caitlin switched the topic. "Grandpa, how was deer hunting?"

"Lousy! Didn't even *see* a deer."

"Did you go with the same guys you always go with?" asked Caitlin, pouring herself another glass of Pinot Grigio.

"Um, yeah, pretty much."

He regaled us with tales from Deer Camp 2013. "Those guys get a snoot full and like to howl, which is why I sleep in the truck."

Howl? What exactly did that mean? I pictured old, white, wrinkly men running naked in the woods, getting in touch with whatever was left of their primal selves, which put me off the white meat.

"The guys had the TV inside the cabin turned up so loud, I could hear it a mile down the road, and I can't hear for shit!" Dad may not have killed a deer, but he was killing the room! With each spit take, the dark clouds of grieving lifted.

"Were there any young guys? You know, the next generation of hunters?" I asked. Not because I was concerned that the hunt was dying out, but because I wondered if there was someone with the upper-body strength and a healthy heart who could have helped a certain old man drag a dead deer out of the woods or call for help in case…well, in case.

"Oh, yeah," he said.

"Oh, like who?"

"The Johnson boys."

"How old are they? Like twenty? Thirty?"

"No, more like seventy-nine-*ish*."

The banter had returned. The loud pontificating that had to be held in check whenever someone brought a prospective suitor to the table—so as to not scare them away, but they were scared away anyway—ran wild and free. Seconds were served, then thirds before the leave-room-for-dessert call was made. Dishes were cleared. Wineglasses topped off. I came across a jar of freeze-dried Maxwell House Coffee (Mom's preferred brand) in my kitchen pantry. I had doled out a small teaspoon into a coffee cup and filled it with hot water, leaving room for Mom to pour in the Coffee-mate. It was ten years old and still had a lot of teaspoons left. I felt it was only fitting that I put it out on the table. "Awwww! Grandma!" was the collective reaction.

Real coffee was ground and brewed. It was time for pie, but not just any pie.

Before I made the initial cut, I looked up and said, "Mom, you owe me a solid."

Solemnly, reverently, I presented the first piece to my father. He turned the plate around to get a closer look at the filling before he did a few exploratory pokes with his fork. "It *looks* pretty good," he said.

A *pretty good* from my father was pretty *damn* good.

"The true test...according to your mother...was"—he put down his fork and grabbed the piece of pie with his bare hand as if it were a slice of pizza—"if you could hold it in your hand. If it stayed intact, then it was..." It stayed intact, and I'm not just saying that. I have witnesses, one hostile. He took a bite and chewed it slowly, with his eyes closed.

"Dad?" I said.

He continued chewing.

"Well?" I said.

He took a sip of water. Dabbed the corners of his mouth with his napkin. "I would have to say"—he took another sip of water, put his hands on the table—"could use a bit more cinnamon."

CHAPTER TWENTY-TWO

STUFFED

Getting out of bed on Black Sunday (or whatever the Sunday after Black Friday is called) was difficult. I still felt like a python that had ingested an antelope. The Christmas season was officially official. I didn't want to think about it, but how could I not? My favorite satellite radio stations had all gone Holiday weeks ago. I drove through tears during the many versions of "Silent Night" and had to pull the car over whenever Judy Garland wanted me to have myself a merry little Christmas.

Even Seamus seemed logy. He had to be coaxed to get the paper. Maybe he had reached that point in the Labrador timeline where puppyhood ends and old age begins? He gobbled his morning food as per usual, then turned to me and hacked it up, intact, in a neat pile on the kitchen floor.

The puking part by itself wasn't a cause for concern—with a Lab, it was pretty much standard operating procedure—but when he seemed like he couldn't poop or lie down, that's when my worrying became acute. According to my best-guess degree in veterinary medicine, I diagnosed some sort of obstruction. What could he have eaten? All earrings, cords from phone chargers, and socks had been accounted for. So what now? A turkey bone shard? A stick? Because these things always seem to happen on weekends, all signs pointed to a visit to the emergency vet.

Cha-ching!

Trips to our regular vet's office made him über anxious. It usually took two assistants to hold him still—if they had experience corralling pigs; three if they didn't. Since I had taken my rightful place as alpha owner, maybe this time Seamus wouldn't be so…Seamus-y.

The emergency vet car ride didn't start out promising; he was not keen on jumping into the kennel in the back of the car. I had to lift him, just like I'd had to lift Harvey for the last ride to the vet.

Dear God, no!

Upon our arrival, I opened the kennel, and instead of his usual snake-in-a-can exit, he oozed out in slo-mo.

Nothing about this place screamed "easily hosed off." It looked more like a luxury hotel than a vet's office. An effervescent girl in purple scrubs with "Kayla" stitched above the pocket greeted us in the lobby/ Zen garden and excitedly typed in our symptoms—lethargy, vomiting. She had a considerable drop in enthusiasm when I answered no to her bloody-stool question. We took a seat in the crowded, woodland-themed waiting area.

There weren't any people with birds. No cats. No guinea pigs. Just dogs—a chocolate Lab, a yellow Lab, and two black Labs. Did I say Labs? I meant cash cows.

"So what brings you here?" asked Mr. Yellow Lab.

"I think he ate something," I said.

They all nodded in been-there-done-that agreement.

"This is our second visit in three weeks," Ms. Black Lab #1 said. "The first time? A pen." She produced it from her purse. "Look. It still works!"

"I'm missing a pair of Spanx, and I think I know where they are," said Ms. Chocolate Lab.

Black Lab #2 had an appetite for asphalt.

Kayla came in and led Seamus and me to a small examining room. It was tricked out with all the latest in diagnostic equipment—the same machines that I could have sworn I'd had seen in my mother's hospital room. I let Seamus off the lead. He took a short lap around the perimeter, then he came back and put his big head on my lap. For a black Lab, he looked pale. His usually low-maintenance high-luster fur was dull. "Don't worry, buddy. We'll figure it out," I said as he hacked up bile onto my jeans.

The vet looked like a young Burt Lancaster. I'd have said something about this to him but doubted he knew who Burt Lancaster was.

"What's up?" he said.

"Well, he seems to be trying to poop but can't, and as you can see"—I pointed to the fresh, pea-soup color stain on my pants—"he puked, and he keeps lifting his hind leg, like he can't put it down."

"Hmmm," he said.

He palpitated. He squeezed. He listened to lungs, chest, and stomach via stethoscope. I noticed he wasn't wearing a wedding ring. Had I been more on my game, I would have figured out a way to work my single, naturally blond, leggy PhD-candidate daughter into the conversation. We could certainly use a vet in the family, but *some other time.*

"Well, I have to say, I do feel *some*thing, but…I can't tell what it is for sure unless we get an X-ray."

"Uh…how much is that going to run?"

He looked at me like I had just told him to put the dog down.

"Uh…about five, seven—"

Thousand?

"—hundred. You can wait. It won't take long."

The waiting room had emptied of other Labradors. I took a seat next to the contemplation waterfall and contemplated. *What if he ate a twist tie, and it went rogue? Dear God, has anyone heard of poisoning by bean dish? Wait. Why am I always the one who takes the dogs to the vet? I don't think my husband even knows who our vet is!* And then I thought of...the last time I was in an emergency-type area. It was with my mother when she had become severely dehydrated and slid off her lift chair, and this time—unlike the chairlift episode—my father hadn't been able to save her, and she'd ended up slipping further and further away.

I felt a little sick to my stomach. I wanted those feelings of sadness to please go away. What if Seamus had to be put down? My mother always said, "Death comes in threes." I thought we already had that covered with the two aunts, then her. What if this was a death leap year and it came in fours? That might be the thing that pushed me over the edge of the contemplation waterfall.

One by one, the other Labs came out of their private examining rooms, looking eager to get back into digestive trouble. How long had I been sitting there? An hour? Two? I checked the clock. Two and a half hours! I spotted Kayla with a tablet as she crossed the indirectly lit lobby and into the Garden of Eden–ish waiting room. "Seamus's mother?" she called. When did I become my dog's mother? I did not give birth to him, and if I had, I would have alerted the *Weekly World Examiner.*

She directed me to another, more private waiting room that took tranquil to a whole new level. *A koi pond? For real?* I should have removed my salt-encrusted boots, worn my better, a.k.a. cleaner jeans and a free-trade organic-cotton T-shirt. Dr. Lancaster returned. Seamus was not with him.

"Hello again!" He opened his laptop and turned it so I could see the image on the screen.

"See this big area here?" He pointed to a milky blob near what looked like ribs. I was never good at discerning things on X-rays or ultrasounds—when the technician told me I was having a boy, I couldn't even tell if the blurry image on the black-and-white screen was a baby.

"This looks very suspicious," he said, circling the area with his indigestible pen. "It could be gas. It could be an object... I think we should do further tests."

"Like, what do you mean, 'further tests'?"

"Well, I would suggest an ultrasound—"

"Uh-huh."

"Then if that isn't conclusive, we'll do a barium X-ray—"

"Uh-huh."

"And then possibly surgery."

"Surgery!? How much?"

"Well, anywhere from two up to maybe five thousand."

"I have to talk to my husband."

"Sure, sure. Take all the time you need."

I called home and told Mark all I knew. We decided to go as far as an ultrasound and hoped barium and surgery weren't in the cards. I gave Burt Lancaster the okay to proceed up to our financial threshold.

This was not how I wanted to spend a Sunday. I would have liked to be on the sofa, watching football in my elastic-waist pants. I should have gone outside with him, instead of just opening the back door and releasing him on his own recognizance—maybe I could have prevented him from eating whatever it was that was causing the backup in his intestinal interstate. Stupid me!

Kayla summoned me back into the serenity suite and Dr. Lancaster showed me the latest image on his laptop. "I'm afraid that a barium X-ray and surgery is back on the table."

Shit.

"Can I ask you a question?" I said.

"Certainly."

"Um…is this…life threatening?"

"Uh…well—"

"Let's say this was your dog. What would you do?"

"Me? Well, I'd do the surgery—"

"Of course you would. Dumb question."

In comparison to the to-shunt-or-not-to-shunt decision we made regarding my mother, this was nothing. Gut-wrenching? Not really. Seamus's guts were the ones being wrenched, not mine.

"Give me the dog," I said. "I'm taking him home."

Dr. Burt shrugged and gave me an I-hope-you-know-what-you're-doing look.

I did.

Did I?

Kayla retrieved Seamus from the bowels of the building, but not before I signed the credit card bill that canceled any hope of us having a top-notch Christmas. I put him back in the car and said a prayer to Rocco, my go-to saint in these types of situations, and to my not-officially-sainted mother.

"Please. Mom. Rocco. All I ask is for the dog to take a good, old-fashioned crap. Too much?"

When we got home, Seamus scooted past me and went to his favorite pooping spot under the maple tree. He spun around a few times before he assumed the comma position. As he strained, he looked back at me, as if to say, "I could use some help here!" I moved in and lifted his tail with authority just as Dr. Burt Lancaster had done.

There was something.

"Hold that thought," I said to him. "I need to get gloves."

With my Playtexed hand, I grabbed what I could and gently guided it out—a little bit, a little bit more, like a magician pulling multicolored scarves from a brown, puckered sleeve.

Pieces of a woven...finger-shaped something emerged. Then shreds of the same with...speckles of blue rubber?

Uh-oh.

Two days ago, after the last of five loads of dirty Thanksgiving dishes were cleaned and put away, I had texted my sister: My Ove' Glove. I want it. Back.

Ove' Glove? she texted.

My oven mitt? Looks like a glove.
Made out of Kevlar. Got it at the state fair. As seen on TV.
You used it to remove your damn bean dish from oven.

No. Used a towel.

Where is it, then?

How the f**k should I know?

I knew.

It was on a pile of snow in my yard, in shreds.

For the next few days, it found its way out of the catacombs of Seamus's large intestine. A finger here. A finger there. I washed the biggest intact portion—partial palm and remains of a cuff—and hung it on the refrigerator, as a warning of what happens when a certain dog decides to ingest something that clearly is not part of any food pyramid.

I thanked my one-miracle-under-her-belt mother and Saint Rocco, and seriously considered making a call to my sister to apologize.

Nah.

CHAPTER TWENTY-THREE

GROUND RULES

W̶HEN SEAMUS AND I had entered the fastest retriever contest five years earlier, my mother was still able to climb steps, was still going to choir practice, and hadn't been pulled over for speeding on a return trip from the bakery. When the "nice policeman" asked for her license, she had offered him a cheese Danish.

And five years ago, there wasn't a Facebook page full of pictures of previous contestants and stats. The time to beat from last year's field was 10.4 seconds, but, remember, I didn't want to win; I just didn't want to get disqualified. That meant I had to avoid signs of aggression to another dog or person and leaving the stage area, entering the water/pool located on stage, or not returning the retrieving dummy to the handler.

The official rules read:

> Each contestant will have two timed runs; official time will be the better of the two runs.
>
> This is a land retrieve—going after a retrieving dummy. The retrieve is thirty-five to forty yards each way. Owners may bring their own retrieving dummy or use one provided.

Dog and handler will stand at starting line on one end of the main stage. The retrieving dummy must be dropped within the designated area at a distance point on the other end of the stage.

Contestants may bring someone with them to drop (toss) the retrieve to the designated spot, or the show will provide someone.

Handler will release their dog. The dog will be timed from the moment they cross the start line to when they cross the line back to the handler with the dummy. The dog will be disqualified for leaving the stage area, entering the water/pool located on stage, or not returning the retrieving dummy to the handler.

And did "not returning the retrieving dummy to the handler" mean he had to deliver to hand? Oh, and excuse me, but I didn't see anything about a pinchy collar.

I told my father that I had done some research and found the "official rules"—albeit from 2010—online. I read the description verbatim.

"Read that part to me about the finish line again."

I complied.

"I don't get it, Dad. Does that mean he has to give me the dummy? Or can he just cross the finish line with it in his mouth?"

"Tell you what, let's keep working on him...get him to deliver to hand, because if he does, great, even if he doesn't have to."

The kennel club had a light dusting of dry snow, the kind that only required sweeping from my front sidewalk. The ponds were still open water for the most part. It was cold but not uncomfortable.

We set up a forty-yard course, using the same white dowel and bucket system as we had before, only this time we were next to the big pond, a.k.a. "water distraction." My father went to the other end of the course, while Seamus and I waited at the start/finish line.

"After you send him, take a few steps backward."

"Why?"

"Well…that way he'll keep running full tilt while he crosses the line. If you stand right on it, he might pull up short."

We decided to use the dummy that Seamus didn't get that mouthy with, heavily scented. My father tossed it a few feet to his side, while I coordinated my whistle, the dog, and the stick and bucket (just in case). I made sure I turned on my stopwatch phone app.

"Okay!" I said to Seamus, and he took off. Straight line. A heat-seeking missile. He got the dummy, I blew my whistle, and Seamus turned. He was looking good when two-thirds of the way back, he started farting around, going off course, shaking the dummy.

"Use the stick!" my father yelled.

I had been using my phone to time him and had let the stick drop somewhere. By the time I found it and put my phone in my pocket, he had already crossed our makeshift finish line and the window of correction had shut.

"Here. You go down there. I'll stand here. Leave the stick."

We swapped positions. I tossed. My father sent Seamus. He bolted there, got the dummy, started back, and did his stuttered stop, shake, farting around. My father let the bucket have it. Bam! "No!" he said. Seamus went flat, tucked in his tail.

We resumed our regular positions. "Now, if he screws around, I want you to bring the stick out and don't do anything with it."

"I don't hit the bucket?"

"No. Trust me."

We tried again. This time, no screwing around. No drum solo necessary. He crossed the finish line at 10.65 seconds.

"Whoo! Good dog!" I said.

We did it again. He flubbed the pickup, so his time was a tad slower: 11.10 seconds. The last one for the day was the best: 9.75 seconds. And the best part? No stick.

"When you practice in the yard, have the stick and the bucket sitting there."

"Like, just on the patio table?"

"Yeah. Make sure he sees it."

"What about the bucket?"

"You wont need it."

I was confused. I had just gotten the hang of the bang. "Why?"

"Because...trust me."

CHAPTER TWENTY-FOUR

POLAR VORTEX

THE FASTEST RETRIEVER REDUX seemed less and less of a good idea with each drop in windchill. Standing in a frozen field, facing the bluster of wind, and Dad was getting (c)old. Having our backs to the wind, while a lot more comfortable to us humans, wasn't optimal for Seamus's olfactory mechanics. He didn't mind. Cold. Wind. Sleet. Snow. Nothing seemed to penetrate his thick coat or his thicker head. For him, a day in a bleak, Siberian landscape was a day at the spa. For me? Well, let's just say…not.

We were paying a price for the last couple of mild and relatively snowless winters. Hello, my name is Polar Vortex. The relentless snow, the negative ten degrees, negative fifteen degrees punch-in-the-face (after a point, what difference does five degrees make?) was, in a strange way, comforting. It pushed global warming farther down on my worry-o-meter—Dad took the top spot, then my kids, husband, the political landscape, the future, lack of money, whether I was doing right by the dog, and whether or not I should grow out my bangs.

The regular snowfalls and corresponding shoveling reminded me of winters past, when Mom and I would go out after supper to clear the front sidewalk. What is it about shoveling at night? The snow looked fake—too fluffy, too sparkly. We'd be out before the plows came through. The snow covered any demarcations of curbs, driveways, and front steps, making our little lot expand so that our yard looked like it ended across the street at the neighbors' front door. After we'd finished, and Mom had deemed the job Dad approved by proxy, we would hang our shovels on the designated nails on the garage wall studs. My glasses fogged up as soon as the back door opened. I flew blind for a few seconds, going by feel down the basement steps before I found the rag rug, a.k.a. boot parking lot, with my foot. I took off my parka and hung it on the nail next to Dad's deer hunting jacket.

I knew there'd be a cup of marshmallow-less Swiss Miss in the heavy mug with the cowboy on the bucking bronco waiting for me on the kitchen table. Mom would cup my cheeks in her hands to warm them, and I'd feel the delightful pinging sensation of skin being thawed, just like my top lip after a dental procedure.

Because the past several winters had felt more like Southern France than Southeastern Wisconsin, I had become lax in my cold weather wardrobe maintenance. I hadn't kept up with glove repair, long underwear renewal, or wool sock replacement. I had to piece together something I hoped would be warm enough for field conditions by layering:

Saggy long underwear bottoms that had lost the ability to snap back to firmness after a washing, much like my collagen-challenged face.

Jeans.

A mismatched pair of wool socks.

A mock turtle with a stretched-out neck.

A jacket that I pulled from the pile destined for Goodwill.

A not-quite-a-pair of insulated, nylon gloves with several burn holes in the fingers from handling hot logs in the fire pit. (I had given my only pair of mittens to my mittenless daughter because that's what mothers do.)

I topped off the outfit with a slouchy, multicolored hat that I'd knit for my hipster son for his last birthday, but when he'd opened the box, he'd looked more pained than appreciative. I could have guilted him into wearing it, told him how I had labored for hours, days, just like I had when I gave birth to the nine-pound, eight-ounce him twenty-five years earlier, and he would have taken it. But I had a feeling he would regift it to some undeserving girl who would then break his heart. I took it back and saved future me from going all Jerry Springer on future her.

There was a sheet of ice on the big kennel club pond. The only open water was near the shoreline and way out in the far corner, where the spring came burbling up. My father was out of his truck and raring to go. He was bundled in his poufy, down-filled deer hunting getup, a blaze-orange hat with ear flaps that can be tied up or down (today was a flaps-down kind of day), his Sorel boots, and mittens with a flap for his trigger finger. The only skin exposed was his face. He looked like an eighty-four-year-old toddler, grossly overdressed for a day of sledding in the backyard.

"We're not doing water retrieves, are we?" I said, reluctantly leaving my heated car seat.

"No. The ice is too thick. I've sent my dog into water with thin ice, and when he hit it, he broke it."

"Like a crème brûlée?" I said.

"Cream of what?"

I opened the back hatch. Seamus's whiskers quickly frosted over. He bounded out of the kennel, unfazed by the stinging cold. He failed the first few long retrieves due to operator error—I couldn't locate my whistle from underneath my many layers in time to call him back and he didn't deliver to glove.

Seamus had made peace with the bucket and stick method. At one point during my yard work, he grabbed the stick from the patio table and ran around with it. What was it going to take to get him to come back to me? I was afraid of the answer.

"Did…you bring…the shock collar?"

My father had given it to me years ago. I was supposed to use it on Seamus to get him to stop jumping up on people. But I couldn't bring myself to use it. And it wasn't just a collar. There was a remote control, a charger and batteries, an additional collar without a shock box, and a Betamax videotape from 1982 that—surprise!—I could play because we were probably one of five households who still had a working Betamax machine.

The nic button on the controlling mechanism was the trigger that provided a brief jolt, "like a static electricity shock," according to the instructor on the video. Had he ever lived in Wisconsin during January? Our static electricity could reanimate the dead. There was another setting, "Constant," but it wasn't like the dog was getting a constant shock; it would only give eight seconds' worth of "stimulation" to get the dog's attention. But in dog years, that's like, what? Two months?

I kept the shock collar and its accessories in the bucket in the garage, hopefully never to be called into duty.

"So? Did you bring it?"

"Yeah, I got it."

"Well…put it on him!"

I tried to avoid Seamus's eyes, which shone with unconditional love while I strapped the conductive gizmo to his throat. I'm sure that to Seamus the collar was just another collar. All he cared about was flying down the hills, locating something that smelled bird-y, and bringing it back (more or less) to me.

"You gotta make sure it's tight and that these prongs are pointing into his neck."

Prongs? Into his neck? Maybe I should get some thigh-high boots and a black rubber suit?

"It gets results. I bet you'll only have to zap him once. He's pretty smart. And the other advantage to the collar is it's flat, kind of like his around-the-house collar, so maybe you won't have to use the pinchy collar on him for the fastest-retriever thing and risk getting kicked out."

Hmm. He had a point.

"Let him run around first," my dad said. "Then we'll get down to business."

Seamus left his steamy mark on a rock, a stump, on the truck's back tire while we set up our reasonable facsimile of the fastest-retriever run.

"Okay, go ahead. Get your dog."

I grabbed Seamus by the evil collar in order to get him to a heel.

"What the hell are you doing?"

"Um—I'm—we're heeling?"

"Use the collar!"

"I am!"

"Not as a handle! Tell him to heel, and if he doesn't, give him a jolt!"

"Can't I give him the benefit of the doubt?"

My father shook his head no and put his mittened hands on his down-filled hips.

I walked away. Seamus followed, saving me from pressing the button. Good boy!

"Now turn," my father said.

I turned. Seamus didn't follow.

"Tell him to heel!" my father yelled.

"Heel!" I said to Seamus, but he didn't.

"Nic him!"

I winced and pressed the nic button. Seamus wasn't fazed. My father yelled at me to repeat the procedure.

"But…if I say it again and give him a nic, doesn't he associate the nic with the command in a bad way?"

"No. You say 'heel,' he doesn't heel, and then he gets the jolt because he didn't."

"Isn't that what I said?"

My father took the remote on a rope from around my neck because I wasn't doing it right. "Tell him to heel."

"Heel!" I said. Seamus didn't follow. I saw my father's trigger finger come out from its hiding place and press the nic button. Seamus was too busy deciphering a scent.

"Is this on?" he said.

He turned the top dial up from ten to twenty. "He should feel it now!"

Seamus didn't. Feel it. Or he acted like he didn't. He wandered around, found another thing pee worthy. "Okay, let's go with thirty."

"Heel!" I said. Again, the dog meandered.

"Are you sure you've got it on right? Are those prongs in his skin?" One thing was certain, my father's exasperation was producing heat, because he opened the top snap of his poufy parka.

"I'm pretty sure they are." They probably weren't.

"Let's crank it up to forty."

"Forty?!" I said. "Won't that hurt?"

"Criminy. You sound just like your mother," he said.

I did sound like my mother. More and more. Not just in what I said, but my intonations—a certain lilt in my voice when I became frustrated, my propensity to use the idiom, "For heaven's sake!" It wasn't just *me* hearing *her*. I saw glimpses of her when my son tilted his head when he laughed, the way my daughter talked with her hands when she got excited. Was this the I-feel-her-around-me feeling I had been waiting for?

"Okay, tell him to heel."

"Seamus! Heel!" I said.

The dog ignored me. My father shook the remote, then held it up to his ear before he checked the little side switch.

"No wonder! You've got it set on 'page,' not 'shock'!"

"Page?"

"Page means he's just getting a vibration."

"Oh…I wondered what that *P* and *S* on the side meant."

He let Seamus go and sniff before he told me to give him another command, this time phasers set to stun. Seamus didn't heed the command, and Dad pressed the button with his trigger finger. Seamus turned and trotted back. He didn't wince. I did.

"That was the problem. He wasn't getting any juice!" He handed me the remote control and explained how things were going to go down. "When he comes back with the dummy, you say 'give,' and if he doesn't, you zap him once. Got it?"

"Sure?"

"We've got until when?"

"March 5."

"Christmas is coming up…and the guy doesn't always come and plow the roads and parking lot, and even with my four-wheel drive, if the snow is too deep, I can't get into the fields, so who knows when we'll be able to get back out here."

"Okay, okay."

We assumed our positions—the dog and I at the starting point while my father walked forty yards away. I worried. Had there been any studies done? Were there any lasting, long-term effects from pulsating electric shocks? Near a thyroid? I pictured myself and a much older, whiter-faced Seamus at a future vet appointment, getting bad news about some kind of strange, fatal cellular mutation running rampant in his body. "By any chance, you didn't use a shock collar on him, *did you*?!"

Dad dropped the dummy. I gave Seamus the okay. He took off. I had a few seconds to find my whistle, insert it in my mouth, and position my fat, gloved finger on the nic button before he turned and ran back. I held out my hand and said, "Give!" and when he didn't, I gave him a nic. He dropped the dummy, sat down, and gave me a what-the-hell look.

"Let's try it again, only see if you can get your hand under his mouth before he drops the dummy on the ground!" my dad yelled. He tossed. I sent the dog. Seamus picked the dummy up and came racing back to me. I held out my hand. "Give!" He placed the frosted and frozen dummy into my gloved hand. No nic! We tried another. Three. Four. Five more times. Each time he was flawless and nic-less. Maybe my father was right? About the shock collar. About Seamus being smart. It was sooo easy.

On the way back to the car, I told Seamus to heel, but he wasn't at my *exact* heel, so I gave him a nic. Then I told him to sit and wait while I opened the hatch of my car, but he jumped on the bumper, so I gave him another nic. I let him have a sniff by the trees. I waited until I couldn't see him to call him back, but he didn't come, so I gave him a nic, and when he didn't come again, another nic and another nic.

"Jesus!" my father said. "Let the guy take a dump!"

Oh. My. God. Was this the stuff of the Stanford prison experiment?

Since Seamus had responded so well to his electroshock treatment, my father decided to up the ante. "Let's see what he'll do with a dead bird." He went to the back of his truck and pulled out a dead pigeon from a different five-gallon bucket, this one labeled "crap." We already knew what the dog did with a frozen duck. Why would a dead pigeon be any different?

"He might take to this because it's smaller. We'll just try it."

My father walked with labored steps up the hill, the dead pigeon in his mittened hand. He was a bit more hunched over than he had been in July. Was his back bothering him? Or was he protecting his face from the wind? Jesus rays broke through the clouds. Dad's trudging, the sun, the snow, the wind—it all became the final scene of my old-man-walking-off-into-the-sunset kind of movie.

EXT. OPEN FIELD. DAY. WINTER.

```
The sky is heavy with clouds. There is snow on
the ground. We see an old man, dressed in hunting
gear, walking slowly up a hill. His head down.
The wind whips the snow behind him. He keeps
walking. Wearily. He is alone. There is a break
in the clouds just as he is about to reach the
crest. The snow blows. The sunlight blinds. The
old man disappears.
```

I didn't see him give me the sign to send the dog through my frozen tears.

"Pay attention!" he yelled. Grizzly old guy still had life in him.

I sent Seamus. He ran past my father. Up the hill. Down the hill. Then back up. Then over to the left. The right. Was this good? Was this what he was supposed to do? Should I nic him? Dad was a bit out of breath by the time he walked back to me. "That's good. He's using his nose."

"Yeah, but he's not finding it. Should I give him a nic?"

"No! He's doing what he's supposed to be doing. Give him a chance. He'll find it."

Back and forth. Up and down. Left. Right.

"I don't know, Dad. Maybe he won't—"

"He's got it!"

I blew my whistle. Twice. Seamus overshot us on the downhill return—not a nic-able offense considering velocity and gravity. He found me and coughed up the bird along with a few feathers.

"Praise him!"

"Good dog!"

"Okay, let's try another one, only this time, don't let him see me."

Seamus's pretty good retrieve had made the weather seem a lot warmer and seemed to have given Dad more energy for his second ascent. Turning Seamus around wasn't as hard as it had been in previous attempts at a blind retrieve. He didn't rubberneck. Perhaps he was worried I'd nic him. Truth be told? *I* was worried I'd nic him. He and I stood—well, he sat; I stood—with our backs to the wind and my father. It felt good, not having that pins-and-needles feeling on my face.

I couldn't see where my father was or what he was up to. *I probably should turn around to see that he hasn't fallen into a divot or tripped, possibly hitting his head on a rock.* He'd want to go that way. Doing something he loved. Not in a hospital bed. Or at a rehab center. I had to admit, I too would prefer it if he went that way. I wouldn't want to see him become feeble. It would be too hard. He's the rock. He's the guy who I still see as serving and protecting...me.

People don't live forever. Neither do dogs. Someday Dad won't be a phone call away. Who am I going to ask why Seamus has started to shy away from the forsythia bush? Or whether or not I should buy a ramp for him to get in the back of the car when he gets to be a senior dog citizen? Google?

My father returned from the summit. "Okay, get him turned around, and use your hand to direct him to the bird."

"What do you mean?"

"Take your hand and put it on the side of his head and get him focused."

I put my right hand up, like a blinder, and pointed Seamus in a southwesterly direction. "Okay!" I said, and he took off northwest.

"That worked."

"Well, you'll get better with practice."

I *was* getting better. Dog-wise. I *mostly* commanded. I *told* more often instead of asked. And most of the time, Seamus obliged.

Seamus ran back and forth, up and down. Left. Right.

"He ran right past it!" my father said.

"How do you know where you planted it?"

"I marked the spot with a stick."

Of course he did.

Seamus had doubled back.

"You know, he's beginning to be a real good—well, sort of a good dog."

"Yeah?"

Before all of this dad-dog stuff, I had thought of Seamus as a kind of human-dog hybrid. I let him on the furniture. We watched TV together.

I gave him kisses. I talked to him. When I wasn't with him, I missed him, sometimes more than I missed my husband. My father's admission that Seamus was a real good dog made me feel all warm inside.

"He's got it!"

I whistled him in. On the return, he didn't overshoot; he came right up to me and politely dropped the balding, de-feathered pigeon at my well-insulated feet.

"Good dog!" I said, picking a few feathers from his whiskers.

"That's enough for today. You got the bird?"

"Me? I'm supposed to carry it?"

"Well, if you had worn the game vest…"

All this up-the-hill, down-the-hill nonsense was making me sweat. Steam rose from my de-mittened hands. Seamus's retrieves had plucked the bird's neck down to the pink flesh, its wings the worse for wear. I bent down and picked it up, bare-handed.

We started the descent, Seamus happily lagging back. My father started up his truck and put the heat on full blast and waited outside for it to warm up. I opened the back hatch of my car and didn't have to tell Seamus to get in; he jumped cleanly into his kennel. I removed the shock collar.

"I cannot believe this thing!"

"It works because it's an immediate corrector. But you gotta be careful. If you use it too much…that's not good either."

I gave the plucked bird back to my father. He put it on the seat next to him, the head dangling over the edge.

"Let's play the next session by ear, okay? We're supposed to get more snow!" he yelled at me through the exhaust of his truck.

"Okay!" I yelled back to him. I hoped he heard me. He drove off and into the late-afternoon sunset.

CHAPTER TWENTY-FIVE

I NEVER WAS
A HAT PERSON

I HAD JUST DELIVERED a hot meal to Aunt Florence. My father needed a break, and my sister was on set making another obscure zombie movie and couldn't be disturbed. My eyes felt hot. Did I have a fever? Was I getting a cold? The flu? I was in the mood for a spell on the sofa, a little rom-com movie marathon along with a heart-pounding, used-for-making-meth decongestant.

When my mother was in and out of hospitals and rehab centers, getting a seasonal flu shot was not a priority. I expected to get sick but didn't, and this year, I thought, *Why bother getting a shot?* But I just happened to be at Target, and the nice ponytailed pharmacist offered, and it was free, so how could I say no? It made me feel invincible. *I don't need your Sani-Wipes for my grocery cart, thank you!*

The thermometer was in the back of our medicine-cabinet-overflow closet. It was the kind you stuck in your ear, which my mother bought because she was afraid my children would chomp down on the old, mercury-filled glass one that had been good enough for my sister and me but didn't meet her strict safety standards for all things grandchildren.

My temperature had risen to 101.4 degrees.

I couldn't remember if a temperature taken via the ear canal was off one degree up or down. That would have been the kind of thing I'd have phoned my mother about. But she wasn't there. And my father would probably say, "Beats the hell out of me!" So I took two Tylenol, staggered to bed in the room formerly known as my daughter's, now the guest room/respite from my husband's snoring. But more recently it had been used as the sick room.

At 1:23 p.m., I felt a lot hotter. No wonder. My temperature was 102.6 degrees!

I wasn't congested. Didn't have a cough. No sore throat. According to WebMD, I was either getting a cold, the flu, or was in the early stages of dengue fever. During *Andy Griffith* reruns, it was 103 degrees. I drank fluids. Took more Tylenol. In the morning I checked my fever. It was definitely going in the wrong direction. My husband kept his distance. He knows that in the early stages of sickness, I tend to growl and snap, and then I turn into something a little bit like my mother the martyr, who always yielded the last piece of food, the warmer blanket, the better seat to someone else because she suddenly was full, warm enough, or had developed a fondness for standing.

My husband checked up on me before he left for work.

"Are you sure you don't want me to bring you anything? You sure you'll be okay?"

"You go to work. I'm fine." (Subtext: I'll just lie here, waiting for the dog to bring me a cold compress or for death, whichever comes first.)

I wasn't going to call my father to tell him I was sick. I thought that it would set off some kind of PTSD, like two weeks ago, when my uncle had been admitted to the same rehab place that Mom had been in only seven months earlier—to me it seemed like it had been seven years. My father thought twice about going to visit his brother-in-law, but his Greatest Generation–duty thing kicked in, and he went.

"Thank God he wasn't in the same room; otherwise, I don't think I could have gone in."

But I had to call. How else would he know whether or not we were on for our next fastest-retriever rehearsal?

"Dad, I'm sick. I can't go training."

"Okay."

He was a little too quick with the okay. No *How come?* No *That's too bad?* No *What's the matter?* Mom would have asked. Mom would have wanted to know the symptoms. She'd have given me advice, told me the measles story about when I was three and my fever was so high, I had to sit in a dark room and couldn't look at books because "the doctor said it would affect your eyes." Mom would wax nostalgic about how our doctor made house calls. I knew he was coming when she made me put on clean pajamas, moved me onto the sofa, dusted, and vacuumed.

My father wasn't going to ask about symptoms, so I offered, "I think I've got the flu."

"Oh. Okay."

"I've got this temperature, and I feel like I'm going to barf and then—"

"Okay. Okay. Uh, well, take care and call me when you feel better."

I heard Seamus pad up the stairs, trot into the bathroom. His toe-nails clickity-clicked on the tile floor. Then silence.

"Seamus, you better not have a towel!" He liked to retrieve the nicely folded, fresh, and fluffy towels from the rim of the claw-foot bathtub; then, unsure what to do with them, he would whine until I came and got them. He proceeded up and down the hallway with urgency, like he did in the field when he couldn't find the dummy and it drove him nuts until he located it in the brush. Was he looking for me? Was I the dummy?

"Seamus?"

Whine.

"I'm in here."

Whine.

"You can come in. Come on!"

For some reason, he never crossed the threshold of this bedroom. It was the only room where socks and underwear left on the floor were safe. We used to put a piece of cheese inside the room just out of his reach, but he wouldn't come in to get it. He'd stand in the hallway and bark at it until he'd worked himself up into a lather. I'm sure that, over the house's 120 years, someone must have died inside. Maybe in this very room. Was I in bed surrounded by specters? Or…

"Please tell me you don't have to go out!"

Whine.

"Can't it wait?"

Whine.

"It's times like this I wish you were a cat!"

My blotchy, too-much-like-Mom's hands gripped the railing. I took one step. Paused. One more step. Paused. Seamus leaped three treads ahead and was already at the bottom, jumping, twisting, bolting back and forth like I had just returned home from a tour of duty.

There were advantages to the Polar Vortex: a cold blast to a fevered face felt good. And the dog did his business, bing, bang, boom. Going back up the stairs? To bed? Too much. A small taste of what my mother's last years were like? Those stairs—a mountain. And I wasn't feeling very Sherpa. I suggested to Seamus that maybe he and I could snuggle up on the sofa and watch some TV.

He ran off and returned, dragging the afghan from the drafty front room into the sunnier family room like a lion with a fresh kill, and while the accent pillow he fetched may have been a little slimy from his overexuberant mouth, I appreciated it. We settled in to catch up on the goings-on in *General Hospital*.

I could see why the ratings for daytime soaps have been declining. A viewer can't just jump in and expect to figure out what the heck is going on. Who is Lucas? What's the deal with the evil hospital administrator with the foreign accent, and where are Luke and Laura?

Brought to you by Tamiflu. According to the voice-over, I was in the Tamiflu window of effectiveness.

I drove myself to not-that-urgent care, because I didn't want to bother anyone. I waited for almost an hour in an uncomfortable waiting-room chair, trying to avoid listening to the invasive TV blaring *The Price Is Right*, before I was seen by a doctor who asked few questions and gave few answers.

It wasn't the flu.

Not a cold.

I knew it! Dengue fever!

More like a lower GI issue.

That would explain the recent wrinkle: the runs.

He prescribed antibiotics. He guaranteed I'd feel *tons* better in twenty-four hours! After three days, I still felt like I had contracted plague, so it was back to urgent-ish care and a different doctor. He looked nothing like a *General Hospital* doctor. He was short. Fat. Thinning hair. A thick accent from an undeterminable Latin American country. I told him about the fever, my prior visit, my dog's somewhat bothersome hovering, the antibiotics—

"No, no, no. Antibiotic? Is…no!"

He then digressed into a lecture about how the medical community overprescribes antibiotics, which I agreed with, but…seriously…go

217

ahead, prescribe them. If not now, when? He said I needed to let it run its course. "Running? Runs? Funny, no?"

Uh, no.

I was to follow a specific dietary regimen that he wrote on the back of an ad for Tamiflu. For the next twenty-four hours, I drank broth with a Pedialyte chaser. After three more days on the sofa with the dog and the plot twists in Port Charles becoming more interesting—two gay nurses!—the only improvement was that I had lost nine pounds. Time to get to an urgenter urgent care, see a different doctor, one with weapons-grade antibiotics. I relinquished my sackcloth and asked my husband to drive me.

If Clinton Kelly, of all things "wardrobe makeover," had seen my outfit, he'd have asked, "What do the faded flannel pajama pants, saggy sweatshirt, and those felt clogs say about you?" They said, *I really don't care if I pooped myself.*

The waiting room was empty. I was seen by a medical professional whose name I didn't catch, who if I had to ID in a lineup, I wouldn't have been able to. *The cramping! Make it stop!*

"You'll need to give us a specimen. I'll get you a hat."

A hat?

He came back with an armful of vials, plastic bags, several pairs of blue latex gloves, and what looked like a white, plastic cowboy hat. "Now, you put this in the toilet and…"

I will spare you the details.

I often complain to my husband:

"You never surprise me with flowers."

"How come you aren't like those guys in the jewelry commercials?"

"When was the last time you took an afternoon off from work and we went antiquing?"

But…driving a stool sample to the lab in his recently detailed car? I don't need diamonds and flowers; he does. Oh, and the next time he wants me to go fishing? And it's raining? I'll be in the boat, waiting.

It's not every day that I get a simultaneous phone call from the health department and an email with "TAKE IMMEDIATE ACTION!!" in the subject line. Diagnosis: campylobacteriosis, which sounded an awful lot like a plot line on *General Hospital*. But how? Where?

"Did you happen to drink any raw milk?" the health department nurse asked. She needed to find out the source, so she could enter it in the local and national database in order to pinpoint the origin.

"No."

"Have you prepared any chicken in the past two weeks?"

Oh. God. The thought of chicken… "No!"

"Have you eaten at a restaurant in the past week?"

"My husband and I are very dull people. We don't go out."

She wanted to know if I had come in contact with any fecal matter? Human or other?

"I use the bag method to pick up after my dog, and I always discover that hole in the bag when it's too late, but I wash my hands because I'm paranoid about *E. coli*."

"Have you done any baking? Do you eat the batter?"

Isn't that the reason one makes chocolate chip cookies?

"You haven't been in contact with any chickens? Say…on a farm?"

"Chickens? No. A farm? No. Uh-uh. Definitely not."

She told me to call her if I remembered anything that might shed some light on how, where, when. The only place I had been was at the kennel club…with the dog…and Dad…and…that pigeon. Pigeon?

My father called. It had been ten days since we had talked.

"How the heck are you?" He sounded concerned.

"Better."

"Good."

"I did not have the flu," I said.

"What then?" he said.

"Campylobacteriosis."

"Campa what?!"

"And I just got off the phone with the health department—"

"They *called* you?"

"I can't figure out where I could have picked it up. I mean, the only bird I've handled was that pigeon—"

"Wait a sec." I heard the gears inside his police brain going into overdrive. "You know...a couple years ago—no, maybe longer than that—there was a guy, at the kennel club, who got real sick. Uh, we called it Pigeon Fever. Hmm," he said. "Maybe, from now on, we should just stick to using dummies."

CHAPTER TWENTY-SIX

IT TAKES A VILLAGE

W E HAD A FRESH dusting of Christmas-card-perfect snow every other day. Any other year, fresh snowfalls would have put me into holiday overdrive—baking dozens of cookies while turning the house into a nostalgic winter wonderland with tasteful tableaus scattered about. But this year, I just wasn't feeling it. I wasn't up to the dragging, the hauling, the going up and down the ladder.

I decided that I would not be *celebrating* Christmas; I would be *observing* it. That was the thing I remembered from my Internet gleanings regarding Christmas and lost loved ones. Observing, not celebrating, made so much sense! That was how I would file this Christmas. I finally had a place for it, instead of that mental junk drawer where stuff I don't or can't label gets crammed. This year, that drawer overflowed and wouldn't shut no matter how hard I pushed.

Observing allowed me to not feel guilty about not feeling Christmassy. I didn't have to force it or fake it. But guess what? The freedom to *not* decorate made me want to decorate, to drag the bins labeled "Christmas Crap" out of the crawl space, and think about getting a tree.

I wasn't up to the trudging over the interstate and through the tree farm as we had done in years past. "Lots are for used cars, not a Christmas memory," I recall saying to adolescent eye rolls. Our Christmas trees have been too wide (who needs furniture?), too tall (we had to use guy-wires to hold it steady), too skinny, too prickly, too sappy—one came with a bonus rodent cornered and disposed of thanks to Seamus! None of them were forgettable. But this year, I conceded to find one that spoke to me from a lot as long as it was sincere. I judged tree-lot sincerity by the following criteria:

1. It had to be lit with strands of those big, white light bulbs.
2. Wreaths or other accessories are optional, although free boughs were a plus.
3. A fire had to be burning in a fifty-gallon drum.
4. No hot chocolate, no Santa, no music.
5. Exceptions made if there is a tree-lot retriever on-site.

We chose a tree with a crooked and twisted trunk because it had been rejected by three other couples. We are not of the perfect-cone Christmas tree camp. The more bumps, gnarls, humps, the better. Bald spots and irregular branching patterns are perfect for the display of our ornaments, especially the Borg cube, because when it comes to Christmas, resistance is futile.

After our tree with scoliosis was professionally bound and driven home, we released it from its tight fishnet stocking and put it into a sturdy stand in the front window. After two weeks, the branches relaxed and I began to transform it from an ordinary balsam into something tinseled, ornamented, and lit up—*Abies balsamea dragus queenus.*

In keeping with my plan of not celebrating but observing, decorating the tree would be my only observation. The toy tableau, the holiday-themed family photos, favorite Christmas cards from Christmases past would not see the festivities. I would limit my baking to three varieties of cookies. I wouldn't bother with cards. What about my father? Would he be decorating? Should I go over there to help, like I did for Mom?

I had volunteered to help with her Christmas decorations when her stamina for climbing ladders, stools, or kitchen chairs had deteriorated. My father wasn't going to pick up the holly-and-ivy mantle. To him it was all clutter.

"Why three Nativities?" he'd said.

"Because one is from the grandkids, and the other from the first graders I read to, and the other one with the three-legged camel and an armless wise man is the one we bought at the dime store for our first Christmas!"

Mom held nothing back. Never wanted to rotate her stock. I admit that when I volunteered to help her, I had an agenda. I thought if I took control, I could force my no-plasticky plastic rule onto her, but my mother had a way of getting her way that didn't seem at all like she was getting her way, and I found myself hanging her plasticky plastic holly garland and finding a place for her plasticky plastic poinsettias. How did she do this? Hypnosis? It's a secret she took to her grave.

I had to find places for her platoon of carolers; several Liberace-fied angels done up in gold lamé, feathers, and pearls; the horror-movie-looking elves; several Santas; and the Dickens' Village.

My mother loved her little corner of ceramic London. Her collection of all things ye olde sprang up once a year, like Brigadoon, in an area of prime real estate: the front bay window. My father made a platform for it out of three-quarter-inch plywood in his signature built-to-last (a.k.a. heavier than shit) style. Putting it into place was a two-man (make that one-man-and-one-daughter) job.

First up? Covering the plywood with a blanket of faux snow for optimum coziness that hid the necessary strands of wires, each with one lightbulb that got hot—which I remembered the hard way. Mom sat on the sofa, oohing and aahing, as if she had never seen the Counting House, the Olde Curiosity Shoppe. "Make sure you put the police station in the front!"

I'd pushed Styrofoam under the snow blanket to make hills, so that the country cottages were logically and geographically separate from the city. Wait, did I say logic? To me, the Dickens' Village meant THE DICKENS' VILLAGE, and only those pieces that came with the official label were allowed in the development. Anything else was not up to code.

"Did you put the skating rink up?"

"Mom, there's no room."

"Sure there is, right over in the corner."

"Then I have to move the church, and if I move the church, then the cottages wouldn't make sense."

"Why not put it on the table?"

"Because the table is full of carolers."

"Where's the wooden semitruck?"

"Mom! A semi?"

"Yes…you remember…your son made it in Cub Scouts."

Somehow I found room for an out-of-scale semitruck and a skating rink with magnetized skaters forever doing figure eights that buzzed when it was plugged in.

The Dickens' Village provided adequate housing and employment for its original inhabitants—Scrooge, Marley, Tiny Tim, the old lady, the Constabulary, et al.—but my mother kept adding to the population, so that by the time I had found spots for Snow White and the Seven Dwarfs, a Boy Scout troop, several springer spaniels, a golden retriever, corgis, a black Lab I put in front, a duck hunter, a Holstein, Mother Teresa, Ralphie from *A Christmas Story*, and a Brett Favre action figure, it looked more like the streets of Mumbai.

Would the Dickens' Village be kept in the dark, boarded up, underneath my dad's basement stairs, the bay window empty as the result of Ye Olde Walmarte being built on the outskirts of the village? My father called with some last-minute gift clarification, then...

"Um, yeah, I was thinking...you want that village?"

I'd had a funny feeling this would happen, that my dedication to helping my mother with staging would be misinterpreted as a desire for bequeathing. But if he wanted me to have it, I would take it. I'd make it work. As a tribute to Mom.

"On second thought...I don't know. Maybe I'll put it out, but not all of it, just a few houses... Maybe you could come over? You know? To put it up? Like you did for Mom?"

Of course I would.

If my father had allowed dogs inside his house, I would have taken Seamus with me. But my father doesn't allow dogs in the house. Never. Ever. A dog's place was outside the home and in the nicely appointed garage.

"I'm going over to Grandpa's to help him with the village." I wasn't sure, but I think I saw pity in his big, brown dog eyes.

I have to make a retraction. In the middle of my dad's kitchen was the largest dog crate I'd ever seen. Mugsy was comfortably caged, lying on a soft, padded piece of carpeting. My father *had* never ever allowed dogs in the house, but since Mom had died, old habits, rules, traditions had been up for discussion.

"Mugsy? In the kitchen?"

"Yeah. It was just too cold for him to be out, and well, he's got

225

a bad back, and I know what that's like, so I bring him inside for the night."

"But it's the afternoon."

"Oh. Yeah. Well, he's fine inside there. He and I talk."

My father. A dog in the house. What's next? Was he dating?

"The ladies at the kennel club are trying to talk me into a started dog. One of them offered to house break it for me."

"Started dog?"

"Yeah, a dog that's maybe one year old, somewhat trained but maybe not for field trials."

Dear God. Ladies? Offering their services? Oh hell no!

"Maybe in spring—maybe. I'll think about it."

Had he changed his mind about getting a dog post-Mugsy? The fact that he was entertaining the idea was enough to make me feel like life was correcting itself. That despite the loss of my mother, there would still be a dog in my dad's life.

He had already unwrapped, unboxed, and plywood platformed.

"This doesn't look like 'a few pieces,' Dad."

"I was only going to put out the police station, but it didn't look right all by itself, and your mother liked those thatchy things, and well, I had to put out the Counting House, because, where was Scrooge supposed to go? And you know she liked the skating rink, and—just make it look good."

I got to work recreating my mother's version of Department 56's version of Dickens's London. Scrooge, Tiny Tim, the duck hunters, the wooden semi, Brett Favre, Mother Teresa, etc., and four hours later, I called Dad up from the basement for the ceremonial first flick of the switch.

There was no oohing or aahing, no gleeful clapping of gnarled hands, no fanfare. All that he said was "Okay. Turn it off. All the bulbs work!"

CHAPTER TWENTY-SEVEN

TRIGGERS

My husband, Mark, is of the subspecies who craves the thrill ride of last-minute Christmas shopping and, consequently, last-minute wrapping. Twenty years ago, I worked in the gift wrap department for a large retail store on a Christmas Eve—panicked, desperate crowds pushed and shoved the counter like Parisians trying to board the last train out before the Nazis marched in. I only worked in gift wrap once, but by the time my eight hours were up, I could wrap the shit out of anything.

Mark was a poor judge of tape dispensing, and he did not understand the importance of accessories other than peel-and-stick gift tags. His methods were not up to my standards: the wrapping paper patterns were not properly aligned, the bottom seam wasn't centrally located, and the ends were not creased with military precision. I wouldn't have let my children leave the house looking like refugees dressed from the ragbag, so how could I allow these wrinkled and disheveled items to be seen by the public—even if by "public" I meant my family? Of course I would rewrap!

What made me think this year would be any different from his pitiful attempts of years past? Perhaps I thought he'd have learned by now? Hadn't he paid attention during my many tutorials? Or…wait. Had this been his plan all along?

I couldn't leave the house with all that wrapping shrapnel on the floor—pieces of ribbon and wire just long enough to tempt Seamus and wreak havoc on his internal organs. We had already reached our quota for emergency vet trips for the year, so I insisted on vacuuming. It wouldn't take long. We'd still make it to Dad's in time for Christmas Eve.

I expected a lot of emotional triggers during the holiday season, like when I opened the Christmas card from Dad with Mom's name still imprinted inside, the "too ra loo ra loo ra" parts in *Going My Way* (damn you, Father Fitzgibbon, and damn you, little old lady at the end!).

But not vacuuming.

Mom and her Electrolux canister took to the floor every Saturday morning. She and her stout, torpedo-shaped partner on wheels tangoed across the carpeting, sambaed on the linoleum, and waltzed over the hardwood. Sometimes my mother led the vacuum into chair legs and didn't (wouldn't?) compensate for its unwillingness to take a sharp pivot, so that the walls of our hallway looked like the first turn at the Indianapolis Motor Speedway. She had her way with the long cord like a dominatrix, tossing it left, right, then left, ending with a good yank.

They broke up after twenty years, not because of artistic differences, but because of bruised shins, bursitis, and small engine burnout. Her new partner, Hoover, stood upright. It lent itself to the back-and-forth motion of the carpet cha-cha, but never mastered the kitchen floor quickstep. She loved it for the excellent suction and great beater-bar action, but it was heavy, and as she got older, she could no longer take the lead. It was put into semiretirement behind the coats in the front closet.

And then, three Christmases ago, my father presented her with a sleek, lightweight new partner, Oreck. "I've died and gone to heaven!" she said as she sucked up all the tidbits of wrapping remnants. They had a good two years; then, it got to the point where she could no longer Paso Doble in the dining room, and they parted ways—she to the sofa and Oreck to the closet.

The car was packed with boxes that had been given a wrapping makeover—festive foils, proper ribbon ratio, and plump bows. Seamus was left at home to protect our worldly goods. We didn't have much to protect, unless somebody really, really needed a Sony Betamax machine or a stereo system that had once been the talk of the dorm…in 1975.

I put my emotional trigger on safety. On the short drive to my father's, I worried, *Would I go all Mafia-funeral mode and throw myself onto the Dickens' Village?* That was a possibility.

Christmas Eve was traditionally held at my parents'. My sister and I thought all the cooking, baking, and gifting would be too much for Dad, but he insisted. His driveway was full of cars—Linda's, Amanda's, the small subcompact my children rented (they're not really children, but calling them adult children just sounds weird), and my father's truck. We had to park on the street and negotiate the ice, heavy snow-pack, and alps of drifts.

My glasses weren't used to the dramatic temperature change from Arctic Circle to the rain forest of my father's kitchen, and they immediately fogged. I was temporarily flying blind again, just like those days coming in from shoveling with my mother. I did not well up, as I'd thought I would. The baked ham, polish sausages, cookies, and that undefinable Dad smell (Lifebuoy?) draped over me like the fringed, brown-and-gold ponchos Mom crocheted for me in 1971.

"Finally! What took you?!" he said.

I apologized for being on time.

As the fog lifted from my trifocals, things became clearer. Mugsy was in the house, inside his kennel. Was my father going soft? A dog in the house? Again? Mugsy, the outside dog? "Dad? What's with the dog?"

"It's ten degrees…too cold outside for the old guy, and besides, I needed a spot for the bar." The dog's crate had been pushed up against the kitchen wall, the top of it filled with vodka, gin, whiskey, brandy, and the ice bucket.

My daughter, Caitlin, sat in the spot that had been my mother's, next to the tabletop tree, with an unobstructed Dickens' Village view. I didn't expect to see her or anyone seated there. I thought maybe my father would have designated it as a sacred space, but he hadn't. A good thing? Yes. Roping off the spot would have been like opening our gifts in front of a garish, blinking neon sign—Mom Is Dead. Mom Is Dead. Mom Is Dead.

Who better to sit in Mom's spot than Caitlin? When she was little, she and Grandma would make up stories about the goings-on in Dickens' Village: Where did the lamplighter live? Did the children have parents? Was the policeman cold?

"You outdid yourself with the village this year, Mom. Brett Favre and Mother Teresa as a couple? Who knew?"

My son, Angus, sat a cushion away. He did his best to balance a plate piled with shrimp, coils of kielbasa, and slews of slaws. I kissed the tops of their heads. They still smelled like baby them. Apricots. Roses. Lily of the valley. This was one of those times that I wished they lived within a pop-in distance, instead of a two-hour bus ride away. Time had made those days with them at home and the no-hot-water-left-for-my-bath, no-sleep-until-I-heard-the-back-door-open, sleepover-"crime-scene"-cleanup memories warm and fuzzy.

When they were growing up, I'd thought that they would never become close. Their annoyance for each other would grow and expand like their feet. I remember a series of incidents:

A rant taped to the refrigerator door titled "I Hate My Brother. Why Does He Have To Live Here?"

A retaliatory amputation of an American Girl doll's leg that resulted in a two-week stay at the doll hospital—of course, we were underinsured.

A six-year-old brother being stuck inside Grandpa's garage with a headless deer carcass hung from the rafters, the heavy door held shut by a ten-year-old sister.

Now, they live two blocks apart and regularly cook each other dinner. I don't know what shocks me more—how much they like each other or that they cook.

"Jesus Christ, it's about time!" My sister came into the living room. She was forty proof, well on her way to eighty. She wore a very large, trendy-in-its-tackiness Christmas-themed sweater. Bedazzled reindeer flew across her lumpy chest, while sequined snowmen and embroidered candy canes brought up the rear. Her *I Love Lucy* hair was accented with streaks of green.

"I like the hair. Festive," I said, trying to sound sincere instead of sarcastic.

"Thanks!"

"And the sweater. Very ironic. Very kitsch."

"What do you mean, kitsch? I like this sweater!"

The mood wasn't what I had expected. No long faces. No requiem for a missing mother. It was happy and fun, and it carried me along with it. The entire family unit was there, minus three: my New York nephew, Adam, was currently somewhere in Asia. My sister had no specifics other than that, since he had unfriended her on Facebook due to her incessant commenting. Another family member who was not in attendance? My niece Amanda's husband. They had been married seven years, and I think he made it to only one of our loud, raucous family get-togethers, where he sat in the corner, stunned, unable to get a word in edgewise. No one noticed when he had gone out to smoke and then just never came back. And, of course, Mom.

There were two piles of wrapped gifts on the living room carpet. The organized heap closest to the tabletop tree was for the "legitimate" gifts. The other larger, higgledy-piggledy pile, wrapped mostly in brown-paper grocery bags was for a fairly recent tradition that my husband had brought to the marriage called Grab Bag—an alternative to the usual post-gift-opening food comas.

We had picked names at Thanksgiving due to the increasing numbers of the financially challenged—cash-strapped undergrads (and the now cash-strapped parents who had taken out loans for the cash-strapped undergrads), the limited-income grad schoolers, the underemployed, and the retirees. There was always hope that yours was the lucky name pulled by Adam. He worked at a well-known American multinational technology company, and every time I asked him what he did there, his answer was the same: "World domination." If he got your name, well, then you won the gift-getting lottery. This year? Angus was the lucky one. Word was sent via Skype that Adam would be bringing him something super-duper from Japan.

"Not a war bride, I hope!"

Oh, Dad.

I got a selection of all-occasion training dummies that came with an explanation.

"The black-and-white one is for water retrieves!" my father said. He could barely contain himself. "The blaze orange is so you can see it in high grass—"

"Yeah, Dad. I know."

"—and the other white one is guaranteed to break a hard mouth. Oh, by the way, in case you were wondering, I got your name."

No! I couldn't have guessed.

There were gifts of out-of-print books, clothes, framed photos of Mom from the family archives. There were no tears, not even when Dad opened the picture of Mom with his dog Whiskers. "I'm putting this on the wall by my computer!"

So far, I had guessed wrong about everything—the mood, my sister's sweater, and the use of Mom's spot. One thing I was certain I was going to be right about? Amanda's gift. From me.

In the gift-giving department, I am above average. Who was it that had found the long-lost photograph of my sister in her Davy Crockett cap that caused her to break with tradition and give me a hug? I did. Who compiled a DVD for Dad of the home movies not seen since he gave away the movie projector and screen? Yeah, that was me. Squeals of "Where did you find this?", a few tears, mouths agape were all guaranteed.

I had spotted the "Fighting Bob" Lafollette marionette dangling from a rod at the Wisconsin State Historical Society. He had been in good company. There was a Frank Lloyd Wright, a Gaylord Nelson (the father of Earth Day and the Environmental Movement), Les Paul, Harry Houdini, Liberace, John Muir, Hank Aaron, and Vince Lombardi, all hanging from a rod on the ceiling. In a way, it was Wisconsin's papier-mâché, cloth, and string Mount Rushmore.

Fighting Bob Lafollette was a Progressive who fought against railroad trusts and something called "bossism." He was opposed to the growing dominance of corporations over the government and is considered to be one of the ten greatest senators in US history. A big-time liberal, although he opposed the League of Nations and getting involved in World War I. But, overall, he was a Progressive liberal poster boy.

If Fighting Bob was the Progressive poster boy, Amanda was the Progressive poster girl. She went to the state capitol to protest with hundreds of thousands when the state legislature passed a bill to end collective bargaining. Had a degree in political science with a minor in rabble-rousing. As far as I was concerned, this handmade puppet had "best gift ever" written all over it.

I hadn't liked the box Fighting Bob came in. He had to be folded in half, and I wanted him to be presented face up. I'd found a cardboard box that was a little bit too long and wide, but when I centered the marionette and put something around it, it worked. Newspaper wasn't as festive as, say, red, plastic grocery bags from the upscale grocery store. It had come together so nicely!

I knew my niece had an irrational fear of elves and gnomes. Did I think it crossed over into the puppet realm? I did not. I had purposely told my father to hold hers back for the closing act in the gift-giving-getting frenzy. The big box was brought out from behind the sofa where I had hidden it. I presented it to my niece. "This…is from me."

Cue the chorus of "Oooh!"

"Wait! Don't open it yet!" My daughter had chosen the break in the action to restock her poinsettia-printed paper plate with more shrimp, dip, and a grouping of minimeatballs. She had no idea what I had purchased. Usually, if I have a doubt, I'll ask her advice, but this time, with this gift, I hadn't wavered. *Sold!*

"Are we taking a break, 'cause I need another G and T?" my sister said before she turned to my son. "Get your auntie a drink." He rolled his eyes before he relinquished his seat on the sofa. "Go light on the tonic!" she yelled.

"People! Come on!" Amanda was eager to open her gift. Could I blame her?

With plates and glasses refilled, we resumed where we had left off. "Can I open it now?"

It took some effort to undo the wrapping paper. I tended to over-tape. She lifted the lid, took one look, and quickly closed it.

"Well? What is it?" my father said.

"I—I can't." She was shaken. Was that because she was overcome with its perfection?

"Let us see!"

"N-no. It's… I—"

"Oh for Chrissake! Give it to me!" Linda grabbed the box from Amanda's shaky hands and opened it.

"What the—"

"It's Fighting Bob Lafollette!" I said.

"In a coffin?" Angus said, his mouth full of cheese and crackers.

Amanda had her face buried in her hands. "You know how I feel about—"

"But this isn't a gnome!"

"Gnomes. Elves. *Puppets!*"

I guess that this year, my gift-giving radar wasn't spot-on.

She got up from her chair. Was she going to leave? Had I ruined everyone's Christmas? "What made you—?"

"I thought it was perfect!"

I offered her one of my minimeatballs on a green toothpick as a peace offering. "I'm sorry," I said. She sat back down and took the meatball. "So we're good?" I said.

My sister leaned over to my cushion. "Next time, get her a clown doll. She'll *love* it!"

We cleared the floor of paper, boxes, and ribbons. Refilled our glasses—no one needed a drink more than a certain niece. Round two of eating commenced in conjunction with Grab Bag strategizing.

Grab Bag was our family's version of a white elephant gift exchange: We draw playing cards to see who picks a gift first. The first picker chooses a wrapped gift from the pile (you touch it, it's yours!) and opens it. It could be anything. In the past, we've unwrapped vintage TV trays, pub glasses, bottle openers with the likeness of the pope on the handle (a popener!), gloves, mittens, socks, bags of dog food, and cash.

The second person up picks another wrapped gift and either opens it or can steal the first person's gift. Someone might pick something awesome only to have it stolen later, which results in hurt feelings, pouting, and eventually, bribery. When the kids were smaller, we adopted a no-steal amendment because my son kept getting his Pokémon cards taken by his older cousins or sassy sister, and then spent the rest of the evening on the coat bed crying into other people's sleeves.

The optimum picking position is the person who is last, because he/she can survey the already-opened gifts and steal or gamble and go with the unknown. Once the round is over, then participants are free to negotiate a trade, but only from the gifts from that round. These are the rules, and every year, my sister tries to change them because she always ends up with her own crap—mildewed and musty stuff that she pulled from her basement.

My father always pulled rank and stole gifts for my mother. She always got the good stuff—kitchen towels from Crate and Barrel, the Williams-Sonoma aprons. I liked to put gifts in the Grab Bag that I knew would cause a skirmish. I thought the life-size Joe Biden cut-out or the "Keep Calm and Carry On" mug would have been the gifts that led to a collective bargaining session ending with a hissy fit. But, again, I was wrong. It was a pair of large plaster sheep separated from a Nativity and a collection of Frankie Yankovic polka LPs that caused quite the kerfuffle.

We ate too much, drank too much, laughed too much. Fighting Bob Lafollette became a punch line. Not seeing Mom sitting on her sofa cushion felt more like she was away, in the bathroom, or had gone into the basement to get something and would be right back.

We were packing our haul, getting ready to leave, when my father handed me an envelope. "Here, I kind of forgot to give you this."

It wasn't sealed shut. I pulled out a birthday card. My birthday was in August. The day had passed without a phone call from my mother, telling me the Story of Mel's Birth, how hot it had been, how the hospital had had no air-conditioning. I had searched through my drawers of old cards I had saved. I'd wanted to find one from her that I could put out, but I couldn't find any. I swore at myself. I knew I had saved some somewhere.

"Mom was always the card getter, and I forgot I bought it, and then I couldn't find the damn thing until yesterday…"

There was a picture of an old Lab lying on a sofa, and on the inside:

> *There comes a time in everyone's life when they have to switch to senior dog food.*

He had written in his neat printing underneath:

> You are a wonderful daughter.
> Thank you for EVERYTHING.

My emotional trigger had been pulled.

CHAPTER TWENTY-EIGHT

NO GIFTS, PLEASE

GONE WERE THE DAYS of kids padding down the hallway in their footie pajamas, bursting into our bedroom, and rousting us at 5:00 a.m. "*Santa came!*" Did I miss them? Yes. Back then, my mother was the baker of pies, go-to sitter of babies, and, when needed, dispenser of advice.

Christmas Day used to be a chaotic, dysfunctional bacchanalia back when my in-laws lived in the Chicago suburbs. We would open our gifts, allow Angus and Caitlin twenty minutes for Lego construction or American Girl–doll dressing while Mark packed the minivan with more gifts, and then it was time to drive two and a half hours through Chicago expressway traffic to partake in another round of holiday-ing. But now? We get to stay put because Mark's family has scattered all across the country, and to visit them would involve boarding the dog or hiring a dog sitter, buying four airplane tickets, and booking hotel rooms—in other words, too much work and too much money. Facebook, FaceTime, and those riveting family updates would have to suffice.

I liked our little Christmases with just the four of us, at home, opening gifts at a leisurely pace, not getting dressed up, napping, watching football, and making homemade pizzas. We had all slept in after the long night of marionette-induced psychosis. I was sleeping better due to a combination of prescription medication and the feeling of hibernating that overtakes us all when the days get shorter.

We found our way into the dining room in time for brunch. Mark, assisted by Angus, made quiche, and Caitlin poured the mimosas for the post–Christmas Eve debrief before we would be diving into the pile of presents under the tree. Seamus sniffed the boxes waiting to be unwrapped.

"There's nothing there for you!" I said. He looked back at me, then under the tree, then back at me. He knew Grandpa Santa had given him some dummies. *Where did they go?*

I had put them in the basement, thinking, *Out of sight, out of mind,* but to a Labrador, they were out of sight but not out of smell. Seamus parked himself by the basement door and wouldn't budge. We had to step over him, around him, nudge him to get past. He would not be moved. Not even for cheese. Or bacon. *I know they're down there! I want them! They cannot hide!*

"Seamus! Give it a rest!"

He looked at me. *I can't!*

I knew what had to be done. I had to put my sockless feet into a pair of cold boots, go outside, and put the three dummies in a plastic bin, on a high shelf, out in the garage. When I came back in, he was curled up in a dog ball, sleeping until a nanoparticle of food hit the floor.

Pictures were taken of the wrapped gifts stacked under the tree. Seamus refused to cooperate. The only parts of him in any photos were a blurry tail or his nose and one eye. He wasn't used to having two extra humans around, let alone two who had the gall to sit on his chairs and his sofa.

"Why is the dog looking at me like that?" Angus had just settled in with his coffee mug in optimum reachable range of the only end table that could fit in the front room after the tree had been set up. I gave Seamus a new, real bone full of gristle and sinew—not because it was Christmas. I'm not the type who gets her pets gifts—I just wanted him occupied and out of the way. He grabbed it, sat down, then dropped it on my foot without any cajoling or prompting, which was a first for him.

"Why can't you do that with a dummy?" He looked at me, gave me his I-have-to-go-out stare. "You realize it's ten degrees outside?"

He tilted his head. Barked. Picked up the bone and trotted toward the back door. The North Pole–like landscape did not faze him. He walked across the recently shoveled patio, then up and over the mountains of snow to his favorite winter getaway: underneath the steps that led up to our garage.

Coffee was rebrewed and cups were refilled. Seats were taken.

To Angus. From Caitlin.

"You'll like this book," she said. "It's about this guy who goes on a bicycle journey back in the 1890s and goes missing."

"Cool," he said.

To Caitlin. From Angus.

A pair of socks. "Those are engineered to keep your feet warm and dry when you run in the snow."

"Thanks!" she said.

The kids had pooled their money and bought Mark a cycling jersey from his alma mater, Marquette University. "Neat!" he said. He had just started cycling in the latter part of the summer, after his doctor had warned him that he needed some kind of physical activity, and since Mark hadn't taken up dog training, just like I knew he wouldn't, cycling seemed like a good alternative.

I gave Mark a handmade scarf I'd started knitting for him while I sat beside my sleeping mother in the hospital. It was two-thirds of the way done and still on the needles. "I promise, I'll have it finished before spring," I said.

"No hurry."

We took a break to reheat coffee and the leftover minimeatballs, polish sausage, Christmas cookies, and ham that my father had gladly Glad wrapped, Tupperwared, and plastic bagged. He was at home. Alone. I had invited him over to our house, to spend Christmas Day watching us open our gifts, but he'd declined. "No, you spend time with *your* family."

"But you're part of *my* family," I said.

"I know, I—I kind of just want to stay home."

I would have pressed him, insisted that he come over, but I took him at his word. Spending time with him, out with the dog, I was learning that he is the type of guy who, if he doesn't want to do something, won't do it. Back in the fall, my sister had insisted he accompany her on a tour of a tall ship, the *S/V Denis Sullivan*, a replica of a nineteenth-century Great Lakes cargo ship.

"No," he said.

"Dad, come on! It's really cool. You'll like it!"

"No," he said succinctly.

"Why not?!"

"'Cause I don't want to."

Case closed.

He didn't feel like coming over. If he had, he would have said so. He needed to be alone. I was okay with that.

I hadn't been given a box, an envelope, or a bag to open. Yet? I had told my daughter weeks ago, when she had called to reserve the car for her socializing, "I don't want any gifts. Just having you and your brother around is gift enough for me."

"Really, Mom? No gifts? Does that mean 'you better get me something or I'll be mad'? Or you seriously don't want a gift?"

"No, really. No gifts."

That was something my mother would have said—or, "You could make me something." Over the years, I made her boxes covered in macaroni spray-painted gold, broaches made from felt, and a kitchen witch from one of her old stockings, which my father hated because she had hung it from a string just low enough to be in his way. I had offered to move it when I came over to Dickens up the place, but he had barked, "Leave it where it is!"

Round two began as the sun was setting. Angus opened a box of bicycle parts he needed to finish the bike he was building. A vase and some artsy kitchen stuff for Caitlin, along with a photo of her and her grandmother I had enlarged and framed: "Awww!"

Pictures were taken and posted on Facebook.

"Well? That's it!" At 4:17 p.m., Mark declared Christmas 2013—present-opening phase—officially in the books. Caitlin started to clean up the papers and ribbons, and flattened the empty boxes for the recycling bin. Angus tidied his pile and went into the kitchen to scrounge for more food. Mark checked to see what football game was on. I remained seated in the chair.

"Thanks for everything, Mom," Caitlin said, making a tighter ball of the already-crumpled wrapping paper.

"Sure. You're welcome," I said, trying to make it sound like I wasn't disappointed. How had my mother done it? Been happy without getting a gift? When she opened the gilded and noodled creations, she'd seemed genuinely thrilled. I thought I could do it. Be like her. But...I wasn't her. I was me. I needed stuff.

"Do you want to save any of this ribbon?"

"Um, yeah...just put it..."

"Mom? You okay?" she asked.

"Uh. Sure."

"I know...you're thinking of Grandma, aren't you?"

No. I'm thinking about what an idiot I am for telling you not to get me anything!

"Yeah. Uh-huh. Grandma."

She offered to get me a glass of hot cider with some brandy. She was going in the kitchen anyway; it would be no problem. It had begun to snow, as if on cue. Just like in the movie *White Christmas*. I loved that movie. My sister and I used to watch it every year when it was on *NBC Saturday Night at the Movies*, then reenact the "Sisters" number, only with dish towels instead of the ostrich plumes that Rosemary Clooney and Vera-Ellen had used, while my mother laughed.

The cider tasted like an apple in a cup. The brandy added that extra zing.

"How about a movie?" Caitlin asked. "*White Christmas*?"

"Sure. Go ahead. Whatever."

"Mom, you said we shouldn't get you anything—"

"I know, but—"

"But you didn't mean it?"

"No. I meant it," I said, and muttered, "at the time."

My spirit was as flat as the cardboard shirt boxes.

Sheesh. Even the dog got a bone.

Speaking of the dog...where was he? "Have you seen the dog?" I said.

244

"Uh…is he under the table?" Caitlin went to look for him. Then she went to peek inside his kennel.

"Maybe he's upstairs, on my chair in my little office?" I went up, calling him. He wasn't there. He wasn't by the bed. Not in one of the kids' rooms. Not on a chair, watching football with Mark.

Oh. My. God. He was still outside! When had I let him out? Five hours ago?

I opened the frost-covered back door and called him. "Seamus!"

Nothing.

"Seamus!" His name vaporized from my frozen breath.

Nothing.

I grabbed a coat, didn't bother with boots. Or a hat. Or gloves. It was very quiet. There was no traffic noise. Nobody was out. I stood in the middle of the patio in slippered feet. The only sound came from behind a drift of snow, underneath the garage steps. Gnawing. I climbed over the snowbanks.

He was lying in his lair, gnawing the bone, surrounded by the three dummies. "How the hell—?" The lock on the side door of the garage had frozen, and when I thought I had shut it, I hadn't. He must have pushed it open, crawled up onto my gardening bench, pulled down the bin, got it open, and emptied of its cache. The fact that none of our cars were scratched or dented and he hadn't been made into a pupsicle were Christmas miracles.

I walked into a kitchen that seemed big most of the time, but was now very full of my little family—humans and dog. I wiped my glasses on whatever cloth I found first, the hem of my son's T-shirt. They had started the pizza-making procedure, Angus in charge of dough, Caitlin chopping vegetables, Mark browning the sausage meat. I walked into the dining room; the table had been set. Candles lit. There was a box where my dinner plate should have been. I could tell Mark had done the wrapping.

"What's this?"

"We know you said no gifts, but…" Caitlin used the chopping knife for emphasis and pointed the tip in my direction.

"Open it!" Angus's hands were full of flour. Seamus and his tongue were seeing to the floor. I undid a corner of the snowflake-themed paper.

It was a frame of something. The only way to find out was to slip it out of its cardboard sleeve. I saw the big green *G* first.

Gasp.

And then…the photo. Number twelve. Aaron Rodgers in action.

Autographed!

"You guys!" I said, five, six times. My eyes teared up, and not from the onions Caitlin was mincing. I hugged her. Got a floury hug from Angus. A hug and a kiss from Mark.

"We couldn't *not* get you anything!" Caitlin said, scraping the diced onions into a small bowl.

"How did you—? When? Did he really sign this?"

"Never mind. Never mind. And yes." Mark slid one pizza into the oven and pulled out another to cool, while Aaron, Seamus, and I sat there, supervising. It was the one time I was grateful that no one had listened to me.

CHAPTER TWENTY-NINE

HOME FOR SUPPER

Dᴀᴅ, ᴅᴏɢ, ᴀɴᴅ I hadn't been out training in over two months. Our regular Wednesdays had fallen off and become whenever Wednesdays. Then possible Thursdays. And it-depends Tuesdays. Back in November, Dad had been busy with deer hunting, and then came the holiday hubbub along with the evil north wind. Seamus and I would have done yard work, but the yard was covered by a six-inch-deep sheet of ice, and I didn't want to risk Seamus pulling a muscle or tearing a tendon this close to our retrieving Super Bowl.

The usually predictable mid-January thaw must have been postponed until…May? Even I, the lover of all things snow related, whose bucket list included a trip to Norway for a Lapland Christmas and skating on the frozen canals in Amsterdam, had had it with winter. The romantic nostalgia of shoveling had turned to dreaded drudgery. I was in my little office, ignoring the drifts and typing. My outfit for the day? Flannel sock monkey–printed pajamas, a wool Irish sweater, fingerless gloves, mukluks, and an afghan. Very Bob Cratchit.

I heard a Seamus whine coming from somewhere. The hallway? Downstairs? He was stair stuck.

Again.

"Come on!" I said cheerfully. I remembered what my father had said about tone: "You could be threatening the dog with impending doom, but if you say it in a nice way, he won't know the difference."

Seamus stood on the first landing of the stairs, unable to move. He'd put one paw on the next tread, pull it back, try again, pull it back, like a car rocking out of an icy pile of snow. Every time I saw him do this, his behavior baffled me. He'd be all fine and dandy, running up and down the steps, and then he was like a kid who had taken a running start, about to jump into the outstretched arms of a parent waiting in the swimming pool, but stopped at the edge, frozen with fear.

I had to go get the leash, clip it to his collar, and gently pull him up the first few stairs in order to get him started. Once he got going, he was fine. He was panting. And his eyes darted around the room, searching for something random to retrieve. He found nail clippers, which he released when I told him to "Give!" Then he disappeared and came back, coughed up a quarter without prompting, left again, returned with a Styx guitar pick he found I don't know where, wandered off and came back with the cable bill, and finally he sat down and stared at me. Into my soul.

Why do I feel so unfulfilled?

"Sorry, buddy. We can't do our thing today. Too cold." I unsnapped the leash.

The weather forecasters had the population on lockdown. The dangerous windchill and snowmaggedon risked turning anyone who stepped outside into a victim of Mr. Freeze. Seamus harrumphed and walked out. He had no problem going down the stairs.

"Oh, come on!" I yelled after him.

The thermometer outside my kitchen window registered twenty-five degrees below zero. Things around these parts were getting serious. Water mains erupted. Pavement heaved. I wore long underwear—*inside* my house.

He was curled up on one of his auxiliary sofas in the family room, pouting. When I made a move to chuck him under his chin, he hoisted himself up and went to check out his favorite corner for crumbs.

"So you're not speaking to me?" I pressed my nose to his. "Can I have a kiss?"

He turned his big, black face away. *No.*

"Oh, come on. Give us a kissy," I said through pursed lips.

He shook his head, flinging drool strands like a pinwheel in a lawn sprinkler. *No retrieving. No kiss.*

"I told you, it's too cold."

He had taken to his bed and was not receiving any visitors.

● ● ●

February brought the hope of spring, or something close enough to it. It also came with VD—Valentine's Day. It would be the first time Dad didn't have to buy the love of his life a box of fancy chocolates, flowers, or an outfit for her, like he used to do on his lunch break by going into Gimbels in his police uniform, pointing to a mannequin, and telling the salesperson, "I'll take all of that in a size four."

My mother worked during the day, and by the time we got home from school on Valentine's Day, he had already left for his shift, but not before he had set the table with fancy dishes, put roses in a vase and the heart-shaped box of fancy chocolate on her plate, and laid out the new outfit on her side of the bed.

This Valentine's Day, the universe's gift to us was the temperature. It was supposedly going to be forty degrees *above* zero! Dad called. We were on for kennel clubbing.

The days and weeks of not being able to go out seemed long even to me, but to Seamus? He'd press his nose on the window, I'm certain thinking, *I remember a time…decades ago? I used to be able to run into water that wasn't a solid.*

I couldn't wait to tell my mopey, pouty, out-of-sorts dog the news.

"I just talked to Grandpa. We're going to the kennel club!"

He perked up his ears. I got a little lick of approval. *Really? Now? Are we doing this now? Right now? Let's go!*

"After lunch."

After lunch! That's like years from now!

Mountain ranges of snow lined the parking lot's perimeter. This was shaping up to be one of those endless winters, with snow piles that would still be around in May. We set up our fastest-retriever course next to the foothills next to the snow-covered chain-link fence. For not having retrieved anything for almost three months except for shoes, the paper, and credit card bills, Seamus did okay. He messed up the first retrieve (to prove a point?) but one growl from Dad put him right.

"So when is this fastest-retrieve thing?" my father said.

"Um, like ten days."

"Well, he's about as ready as he's going to get."

"Dad? Um, I'm a little worried."

"About what? Just 'cause he had that one bad—"

"No, not that. He's got this…phobia."

"What do you mean 'phobia'?"

"Sometimes, he won't go upstairs."

"Hmm. Did he slip and fall?"

"No."

My father watched as Seamus lifted a leg; a stream of pee turned the snow yellow. "Can't be a toenail. He doesn't look lame."

"Dad, if he won't go up stairs, he won't get on the stage. You can't lift him. I can't lift him. What do we do if that happens?"

"Then we just go out for a fish fry."

How very Zen of him.

● ● ●

All the below-zero weather, along with menopause, had made that forty-degree day feel like the middle of July. I didn't need Seamus on the sofa next to me. I needed to de-layer one layer. I even turned the thermostat down. With his belly full of dog food and his retrieving needs met, Seamus was in his posttraining calmness. He plopped onto the floor and fell into a deep sleep. Occasionally, a paw would twitch; then he'd let out a little yip that caused him to wake and lift his head as if asking, *Was that me?*

I read through the "Important Things to Know" section on the website. Again.

> Dogs must be leashed at all times, until designated
> by an official to remove leash. Training equipment
> such as pinch collars, e-collars, etc., are not allowed.

Duly noted. We had prepped for a no-shock-collar performance by exchanging it with a similar-to-the-shock-collar collar but without the shock box. This impotent collar was tested on Seamus with limited success. After a couple runs, he had the ruse figured out and could get away with slight errors. My father was right; Seamus wasn't stupid.

I re-reread the rules:

> Each contestant will have two timed runs; official
> time will be the better of the two runs.
>
> This is a land retrieve—going after a retrieving

251

dummy. The retrieve is thirty-five to forty yards each way. Owners may bring their own retrieving dummy or use one provided.

Dog and handler will stand at starting line on one end of the main stage. The retrieving dummy must be dropped within the designated area at a distance point on the other end of the stage.

Contestants may bring someone with them to drop (toss) the retrieve to the designated spot, or the show will provide someone.

Handler will release their dog. The dog will be timed from the moment they cross the start line to when they cross the line back to the handler with the dummy. The dog will be disqualified for leaving the stage area, entering the water/pool located on stage, or not returning the retrieving dummy to the handler.

See? I must not have been the only person whose dog had decided to take the scenic route.

● ● ●

Mother Nature is a fickle bitch. Yeah, I said it. After our little one-day break from the cold, she decided that the hors d'oeuvre of spring was enough of a taste for now, and for the next two weeks, she knocked some sense back into us with more snow and colder cold. Seamus followed me around the house with an anticipatory look in his eyes. *Where are you going? Are you going out?* I couldn't go anywhere without him— laundry, kitchen, vacuuming. He even followed me into the bathroom, pushing the door open with his nose while I was on the toilet or in the tub, letting in all the drafts along with him.

I tried to do yard work, but Seamus slipped and couldn't get his footing, and after only one toss of the dummy, I called it. We would have to rely on his muscle memory, trust that the new wrinkles we hopefully made in his doggy brain were numerous and deep.

A couple of days before the contest, I had a dream. I dreamed that Seamus and I were at the bottom of a steep, Salvador Dalí–designed staircase. We were being chased by something evil, and if we didn't get up the steps, we'd be eviscerated. But Seamus wouldn't budge, and I kept pulling him and pulling him, and the more I pulled, the more he dug in. He screamed and screamed, and the thing that was going to rip us to shreds got closer and closer. I yelled at him to come on, but he wouldn't, and then all of a sudden, my mother was on the steps, calling him, making kissy noises. Mom? Why was she here? She was talking, but it was like one of our old home movies. No sound. And then I was back at the parking lot of the rehab place. I don't know where the dog went. The fire department truck was there with its lights on. I was at the door, waiting to get in, then they slid open and this girl, maybe twelve or thirteen, with long, wavy brown hair, walked past me. Her coat was unbuttoned. She wore an argyle sweater and a pleated skirt. Saddle shoes and bobby socks.

"I have to go. I'm late for supper!" she said to me.

"But it's raining! Where's your hat?" I said. And she just started running past the truck and down the street toward Cleveland Avenue.

• • •

I knew what the dog-on-the-stairs part of the dream meant. Surely it was my anxiety over the impending contest. But the girl part? As the day of the contest crept closer, I had to keep busy in order to stave off a panic attack. I decided that it would be a fine time to organize the family photos. I had purchased archival boxes a long time ago, with the plan of going through all the photos with Mom. I thought she'd be able to remember who was who and I would write something identifying on the back, but she and I never got around to it, and then one day, my father came over with the boxes plus a big grocery bag full of old pictures.

I was pulling out all the black-and-white snapshots that I had never seen. Picnics. My grandmother as a flapper. One of so many people in a basement, it had to have been a fire hazard. And then… It was taken in a backyard. A group shot. I recognized a young Aunt Ellen. Aunt Jane. A small boy…my uncle? And the girl. In my dream. Wearing an argyle sweater, a pleated skirt. My mother.

Could it have been—maybe it was—Mom? Trying to tell me…that night…when I had arrived at the rehab center and waited frantically, pounding on the glass doors…waiting to get buzzed in, there was nothing anyone could have done to save her. She *had* to go. Her mother was calling her. Back home. To eat supper.

CHAPTER THIRTY

D-DAY

MARCH 5 WAS JUST an average get-your-dog-on-a-stage-in-front-of-two-hundred-people, hope-nobody-screws-up kind of day. I took deep, cleansing breaths when I folded the laundry. I centered myself before I loaded the dishwasher, picked up poop, got the mail, and surfed the Internet. I tried to keep from thinking, dwelling, worrying. I do not say I succeeded.

We had been given the five-thirty time slot but had to arrive twenty minutes prior for check-in. I told my father I would pick him up at four thirty to allow for traffic, which meant I had to have the dog in the car by four, which meant I had to start getting ready to get the dog ready at three, but I was nervous, so why not two thirty? Seamus knew something was up when I picked up the crate and carried it out to the garage.

We're going somewhere? Now? You? Me?

"Listen," I said as I strapped the fake shock collar on him, "all I'm asking is, just, please, for the love of all that is holy, do what I tell you. Remember what we've been practicing? You wait. I say, 'Okay.' You get the dummy. Bring it back. To me. No trucks. No duck pond. No goofing around. Okay?" I cupped his head in my hands, but he wriggled out of my grip. He executed a perfect double axel. I wanted to grab him by his scruff and shake him, to show him I was the boss, but I had to remember what my father'd said about this behavior—it wasn't wildness; it was eagerness, and eagerness was good. Seamus, after all, came from field-trial and hunting stock. He only had two switches: on and go!

I made him sit inside the crate, in the car, in the cold for almost a half an hour (calming purposes) while I readied myself and ran through my checklist:

Whistle?

Check.

Heavily scented lucky training dummy?

Check.

Directions?

Check.

Fake shock collar?

Check.

Dog?

Check.

I locked the back door. Did I have everything?

Whistle?

Check.

Heavily scented lucky training dummy?

Check.

Directions?

Check.

Fake shock collar?

Check.

I got into the car, opened the garage door, made sure I had everything again. Did I have the dog?

"Seamus? Are you back there?"

I heard a thump of a tail.

Check.

I backed the car out and into the alley, called my father and told him I was on my way. I drove the familiar route to his house, half on autopilot because I was thinking, worrying, hoping. Had we done enough training? Would I remember how to blow the whistle? I had my whistle, right?

I didn't have to get out of the car and knock on his back door when I pulled up because my dad was already outside, waiting. Seamus wasn't the only one who was wired for eagerness.

"You got your whistle?" he asked, sliding onto the seat.

Did I? "Yes."

"The dummy?"

"Yes."

"The other dummy…the one in the crate?"

"Got him. I'm a little nervous. You?" I said.

"What for?"

"You know…what if he can't—won't… The stair thing?"

"All you can do is hope for the best."

Hope for the best. Like we had done with my mother, and look how that turned out. I'm not an overly religious person. I pray—sometimes to a specific saint (see: the dog-drowning episode)—but mostly I just make requests to the universe and see what happens. Sometimes my requests are answered in just the way I ordered, but sometimes not—wrong color, wrong size, wrong outcome—like in the case of my mother. I wanted her to live, but…maybe that wouldn't have been the best outcome…so…who knows? Sometimes, in some round-about way, the thing that I didn't want to happen happens, and it leads to something else, and that something else turns out to be better than what I had hoped for.

We pulled into Gate Two.

"Are you sure you know where you're going?"

"Dad, read the email. Southeast corner of the building. That's the building. That's the corner. That's south. That's east." I parked in a spot with good sight lines of the door. We sat there with the motor running, our two pairs of eyes fixed for any signs of movement.

"Should I get out and see what's going on?" I said.

"No. Just sit tight. We've got time. Wait until you see other people going over there with their dogs."

"Hey, Dad?"

"What?"

"Have you ever seen a winter like this?" Small talk. It's what I do when I get nervous.

"Oh yeah. When I first got on the job and walked a beat, it was cold like this… I didn't have down-filled nothin'. There was no Thinsulate. All I had was long underwear, a wool coat, and a wool dickey that your mother knit for me."

Ah. Yes. The dickey. It was a kind of bib with a turtleneck. He wore it under his shirts. Fishing. Camping. Hunting. It provided warmth without bulk. It had gone missing. His best guess was he'd left it in a cabin at deer camp somewhere. Mom resurrected the old knitting pattern and started to knit Dickey 2.0, but by that time, she couldn't remember how to do the decreases and she ripped it, started it over, ripped it, started over. She got so mad at it, she threw it—knitting needles and all—across the living room. It became her Moriarty. It tormented her from inside her knitting bag.

I decided that it would be good for her if I came over one day a week and knit with her. I thought it would help with her memory and keep her fingers nimble, and I could help her finish her maddening project.

"Mom, a lady at the yarn store told me I knit wrong."

"What? I taught you the way my mother taught me."

"She said I hold the yarn the wrong way."

"That's ridiculous! I hope you told her where she could stick her knitting needle."

It took her (me) almost a year. It was a little lopsided, and we used different yarns from different dye lots, but...

"Mom, look! It's finally finished."

"Did I knit that?"

"Yep."

"Sheesh. I did a bad job."

Dad and I sat in the car with the defogger running. Dad stared out the window. I thought about all we'd been through with Mom and now this stupid-yet-smart dog.

"Um...I had lunch with some buddies of mine."

Dad? Lunching?

"And out of the eight guys, six were widowers."

That's the first time I ever heard him use the word *widower*.

"Yeah, we had lunch at that place that I wanted Aunt Florence to move into, real nice place. It's got like apartments and condos, and if you need assistance, it's got a wing for that."

"So, Dad...like, how are you going to know when it's time for you to sell the house?" It seemed the natural next thing to say.

"I've been thinking about that."

"And?"

"Well, it would have to be...if...I couldn't drive. Like as of now? I can still drive my truck and go fishing and go grocery shopping and stuff."

"But…say you couldn't. Would you want to live there?"

"Oh sure! They got a pool, a weight room. I wouldn't have to shovel…"

All those magazine articles I had read about having the hard talk with aging parents… Oh, I just had it?

An official-type person with a clipboard and standard-issue ID on a lanyard poked her head out the southeast door and immediately attracted a trickle of people with leashed dogs from their warm, idling cars.

"I'm going out there," I said.

"Leave the dog!"

There was a sheltie, some sort of terrier, a corgi, and a goldendoodle. The rest were young, feisty, uncontrollable Labs who pulled and dragged their handlers along the icy parking lot. Should I warn them about the crabby Mr. No-Nonsense? Why should I? No one had warned me back when I had the wrong collar! One of the Labs had wrapped the leash around and around its handler. Six years ago, that would have been me. *Oh, honey, talk to me after the show. I could give you some pointers!*

The door opened. A guy in a blaze-orange deer hunting jacket and camo-printed baseball hat stepped outside. The downlight from the security light made a shadow across his face. Mr. No-Nonsense?

"Thanks for being patient! I have to apologize. We're trying to see if we can get you inside, instead of having you wait out here, in the cold or in your cars!"

Who was this apologizing? Had Mr. No-Nonsense gone to therapy?

He took roll.

He asked if we had questions.

He bent down and petted the sheltie, calmed the wired wirehair.

Maybe he was just a helper and Mr. No-Nonsense was inside,

building his rage, waiting to release his tirade in front of the audience? I walked back to the car. It felt good to sit inside something heated.

"Well?"

"We're all signed in and good to go!"

My father opened the door and had to grip the handle to pull himself out. I opened the back hatch but not the crate door, because I wanted to give Seamus time to calm down before I released him.

I opened the kennel door. "Wait!" I had to be ready to grab the leash or his scruff or whatever part I could before he bolted. But he didn't. He waited. I took his leash in my hand, told him to heel, and was I surprised that he did? I'm ashamed to say yes. I allowed him his eager whine, but when he started jumping, I had to rap him on his snout with the leftover leash end. My father gave me a that's-my-boy look of approval.

My father had always wanted sons. Perhaps that's why my sister and I tend to dress like lesbian lumberjacks. My mother felt like she had let my father down, that not giving him a son was her fault. "I was never able to give your father a son," she told me after Angus was born. It was as if she had put in an order in the outdoorsy catalog, but sons were temporarily out of stock.

The staging area was inside the loading dock. There were pallets filled with stuff wrapped in shrink-wrap, pieces of displays, portions of signs. Dad picked a spot far enough away from the other dogs but too close to the large, plastic soda-bottle-shaped recycling receptacles, as Seamus, in his controlled eagerness, managed to knock them over like pins in a bowling alley.

Dad and I stood with Seamus in between us, saying nothing to each other. My father kept crossing and uncrossing his arms. Putting his hands in his pockets, then taking them out. For a guy who said he wasn't nervous, he seemed nervous. I was something like nervous and excited and eager. I knew my lines. I had rehearsed. I was so much better trained this time. And I had my father with me. He had my back in case I was berated by the host/emcee. *Perhaps I should be more worried about my father making a scene, as opposed to the dog? Wasn't he kicked out of a competition for foul language and arguing with an official?*

First dog up was the wiry terrier, named Wally. Once the metal door to the exhibit hall had shut behind the contestant, we couldn't hear any crowd noise. All we heard was a distorted male voice coming from a bad sound system.

"Cup your hands when you blow the whistle, like a megaphone, so he'll hear it above the crowd noise," Dad said.

"Okay."

Seamus squealed and barked like he did at the front desk at the vet's. He started panting his nervous pant. It was accompanied by a little hopping thing he did from front legs to back, then back to front, like he does when I'm trying to get him onto the vet's scale. This is usually followed by Labrador insanity. *Oh shit.* Was that where this was going? Crazy town?

Seamus returned to a state of semicalm zeal. But the goldendoodle's person had a squeaky toy that kept squeaking. Seamus started to whine again. I was concerned that if we didn't get on the stage soon, our window of his controllability would shut and he'd start yapping and barking, and the other dog people would judge me a "dippy broad."

None of the contestants who had already finished came back the same way they had gone on. Was there another door? How would I know what to do once Seamus had completed his run? *If* he completed it. He sniffed at the hem of my father's L.L.Bean jacket like he was sniffing the yard in the morning to see via snout what had traipsed through in the night. To a dog, my father's jacket must have seemed like a loud patchwork of smells. Deer. Duck. Goose. Pheasant. Other dog. Trout. Walleye.

"And remember to stand a little bit behind the starting line, so he gets a good head of speed up."

"Uh-huh."

Goldendoodle with the squeaky toy was next.

Then the corgi.

A black Lab.

Another Lab.

And then Clipboard Lady pointed to us.

My stomach did the thing it does when I have to get up in front of strangers and say words that sound intelligent or witty and I don't remember what I'm supposed to say or do. There was a trickle of panic. I should have said something to my father about how much fun I'd had over the past few months, even though the circumstances surrounding my idea to do so were horrible. Why hadn't I told him when we were standing next to the pallets how much he meant to me? How glad I was that he had taken me under his bruised and wounded wing?

"Dad?"

"Just do it like we've been doing and he'll be fine."

I wanted Seamus to feel my alpha-ness. I remembered that I didn't want him to win. I just wanted him not to screw up. Right? I took a deep breath. I told Seamus to heel, and together, Dad, dog, and I walked toward the light.

CHAPTER THIRTY-ONE

FORTY YARDS DASHED

There.

Were.

No.

Stairs.

Not a ramp. Not a step. No incline. No decline. *Hallelujah! Praise Saint Rocco!* We would be doing the run on blue indoor-outdoor carpeting secured to the concrete exhibition hall floor with duct tape. Not a stage per se. We weren't on a platform. We were at street level, and therefore, the fake duck pond that had proved to be Seamus's undoing was now an aboveground pool. For the dog to give in to his water lust, he would have to climb up the sides and crawl in. Even for him, that seemed a stretch.

And...no more Mr. No-Nonsense! Camo-cap guy who had given us instructions had stepped into the role of MC. I could not believe my luck! This could only mean one thing in my glass-is-half-empty view of life: epic failure to come.

We were introduced to the audience as "a very handsome seven-year-old black Lab named Seamus." No mention of who I was or who was standing at the other end of the blue carpet with a dummy dangling from his hand. At least I wasn't referred to as the dog's mother.

Seamus and I walked past our pickup truck nemesis. We had to. There was no other route to take. He gave it a look, and I gave him a quick jerk. We took our positions a bit behind the white-taped starting line, just like Dad had said. I kept the lead short, to assure optimum heeling and sitting.

Camo-cap guy prattled on and on about the lumberjacks and something about ESPN and then made a joke with a punch line that was lost on me but not on the audience. I had time to think. The last time I'd done this, my mother had been in the crowd, and I had already been on my way to full-on embarrassment. This time, I was ready, and familial representation fell to my sister. Linda had offered to record the event, so she could show her Facebook friends either our sports show fail or our triumphant return to the stage.

The MC's little infomercial went long, and I had mental time to fill.

Well, this is it. Here we are. Back at the scene of the crime. It's make-or-break time. I just don't want to look stupid. I want to look like I know what I'm doing. And…what is that? I'm an expert? At what exactly? Dog stuff? Dad stuff? Death stuff? Well, I am…kind of? Expert? Maybe not expert. Better than I used to be. Yeah, that's better. I just… I don't… I wouldn't want to embarrass my father. He obviously knows people here.

But on the other hand, if Seamus bolts, I hope that he'll at least listen to my whistle commands and we won't go down in flames. Still though, say he blows it big-time. Was all that training a waste of time? No, not really. Seamus is better trained. And come on…time spent with Dad? How could that be a waste? And if we F up? Well then, Dad can tell the story of the Time My Daughter and Her Dog Screwed Up in Front of Two Hundred People forever. So, win-win-win.

The camo-cap guy reintroduced us and gave the audience a refresher on the rules.

Oh my God. Enough! Let's go! Stop talking!

I looked down at the dog. He was focused on my father.

Seamus panted heavily. I waited for camo-cap guy to shut up and give me the official signal…which hadn't really ever been discussed. A wink? A nod? A finger? All of the above?

"Whenever you're ready," he said.

I guessed I was ready. Enough. I slowly unhitched Seamus from the leash.

"Wait!" I felt Seamus shaking in anticipation. I used my left hand as a blinder, and as a communication device: *I want you to go straight ahead to Grandpa, not the truck, not the pool,* my hand said. I watched as my father threw the dummy in a nice, high arc. It hit the carpet with a dull, flat *thunk!* Seamus's nostrils went into overdrive. He fixed his gaze. He had the target locked.

"Okay!"

In the six years since our last stint on the sports show stage, he hadn't lost any acceleration. I had to stay focused on the task at hand and not play to the audience. They oohed and aahed as he tore down the carpeted runway. He slid a little bit, like a base runner stealing second, and overshot the dummy but regained his footing enough to grab it in his mouth before he turned. "Oh! He's got it folks!" said camo-cap guy.

Okay. So far, so good.

I cupped my hands to amplify the whistle and blew it like my father had told me to back in May—like I meant it. And I meant it.

"Here he comes! Here he comes!" camo-cap guy shouted into the mic. He obviously had never been to broadcasting school.

I fixed my eyes on Seamus's. His head remained level with each smooth stride.

Come on. Come on!

He had the dummy in an awkward position, not quite horizontal, not quite by the rope. It looked as if it could slip out at any moment.

Don't drop it! Yet!

I crouched. Held out my hand for a target. "Give him something to aim for," Dad told me in June. Back then I hadn't understood why. Couldn't the dog see me? Wasn't I a big enough target? Seamus got to the midpoint—where our misadventure had happened the last time—and I saw a flash of white in his eyes. He had averted his gaze and shifted his focus toward the aboveground pool. No!

"Heel!" I shouted in my best not-a-girl voice.

He turned his head to the right and veered off course.

Oh shit. Oh no. Oh f*ck!

"Heel!" I yelled.

Blow the damn whistle! my father screamed, telepathically.

Oh. Right. The whistle! Where is it? I had unzipped my down-filled jacket and it had fallen inside. My fingers tangled with the lanyard before I got it into my mouth. I blew it so hard, spit came out the airhole.

Still veering.

No! No! Not again!

I blew the whistle again. Harder. Causing my eardrums to pop. I added three short claps.

"Heel!"

Seamus refocused. On me.

Come on. Come on! A few more feet! Dear God. Come on!

He barreled across the finish line, dummy in mouth, and delivered it into my hand only because I intercepted him after he crossed, so he wouldn't keep running, over to the popcorn wagon.

"Good dog! Good dog!" I jumped. I woo-hooed. I did a little dance. You'd have thought I had just won the Showcase Showdown on

The Price Is Right. I scratched his ruff. He looked at me. *I got you with my little head fake, didn't I?*

Twelve seconds!

I had to be reminded, by camo-cap guy off mic, that we had a second run. *Oh, right. Right. Second run. Right.* We regrouped. The stagehand carried the dummy back to my father. We reset. This time, Seamus knew the drill. I looked at him, he at me. Dad repeated his flawless toss. Seamus's nostrils hit on it.

"Okay!"

On run number two, he knew when to apply his brakes and not overshoot. He picked it up and had the wherewithal to adjust his grip on the way back, but not in a hard-mouth-y way.

I blew my whistle with verve and gusto, and accompanied it with a very impressive "Heel!"

"Here he comes! Here he comes!"

Really? That was all camo-cap guy had in his play-by-play arsenal?

I had to refocus. I was still high from our last run. This? This was our victory lap.

"Look at him go, folks!"

And then, someone in the audience clapped. Three quick claps. And Seamus looked. *Do I keep running straight? Is the Woman over there? I thought she was straight ahead?*

I blew the whistle. Again.

He turned on the afterburners and came at me with such force I thought he'd crash into me and cause some serious femur damage. 9.86 seconds!

"Let's hear it for Seamus and his handler!" The audience clapped, and I heard a *woot, woot* from my sister. I reattached the lead to Seamus's collar. I took a bow. Gestured toward my father to let the audience know it was really all him, ladies and gentlemen. He's the one who deserved all the credit. I just did as I was told.

We were ushered off the carpet and out a different door that opened up into the parking lot. The blast of arctic air hit me like the first jump into a cold northern Wisconsin lake.

"Dad! Ohmygod! Ohmygod!" I jumped little jumps all the way back to the car. Seamus was a good dog and did not jump with me. "Nine. Point. Six. Eight. Effing seconds!"

"Yeah, that was pretty good."

"Pretty good?!"

"Come on, Dad! He knocked off three seconds from that first run!"

"Two point one four seconds."

"Shit he was fast!"

"Okay. Okay. Calm down." He used his nothing-to-see-here-folks police tone. *Calm down? Uh, no thank you.*

I opened the hatch of the car. It had been Seamus's cue to jump around, but he had a new cue: Hatch open. Butt on floor. I swung the metal kennel door open. "Kennel." He jumped in, happy to sit in his crate and frost up my car windows while we went back inside the exhibition hall to watch the remaining contestants and bask in our afterglow. Dad did the analysis and I did the color commentary.

We found my sister in the bleachers and sat next to her. "Did you get it on video?"

"Well…"

Wembly, a twelve-year-old, white-faced, swayback chocolate Labrador, sauntered across the stage, taking her own sweet time, picked up her squeaky toy, and dropped it back where she started four minutes and thirty-seven seconds earlier.

"Jesus! If that's the competition, we could win this!" my father said.

"Dad, we already won, remember?"

"Huh?"

"I just wanted to finish and not get kicked out?"

"Oh, yeah. That."

Wait. Was he all in to win this? I thought I had made my intentions clear back when you could see the grass.

I couldn't have cared less about the other contestants. I wanted to relive the glory. I needed to see the video. I grabbed my sister's coat sleeve. "Did you get it? Did you record it? Both runs? Or just the first one would be fine, 'cause that was the one—vindication!"

"I—I *tried* to get the first run…"

Tried?

She pulled out a fist-sized clump of lint, a charger for something electronic, followed by a sleek, chrome-y camera from her slouchy pocket. "It's a Sony digital camcorder. I just bought it…but I forgot to charge the battery."

No!

The black Lab did what rookie Seamus had done, but it went off course and was disqualified, which made my father laugh and the guy in front of him turn around and give him a dirty look.

"But…I managed to get the second run with my iPhone! Look!" She scrolled and tapped until she got the video up.

Was that me? I looked so professional!

There was only one dog left—a sleek, shiny, two-year-old black Lab who writhed at the end of a leather lead.

"I think I know that guy," my father said. It wouldn't have surprised me. We were always running into people he knew from his old childhood neighborhood or the police department or the kennel club. "I've seen that dog."

The person at the other end of the run tossed the dummy high and yelled, "Hey! Hey! Hey!"

"What's with the hey-heying?" I said.

"That's to get the dog's attention."

The guy my father knew, with the dog that looked fast just sitting at his side, let it go, and I knew from its first strides that Seamus's time wouldn't stand. Camo-cap guy didn't have time to do the play-by-play.

Eight seconds. Eight.

His second run? Seven.

My father nudged me. "If you had started this seven years ago—"

"Dad!"

"Training a puppy is a lot easier than retraining an old dog, and I should know, 'cause I'm an old dog."

He had trouble getting down the bleacher steps but didn't want any help from me or my sister. "Okay, let's go eat!"

Can a person be arrested for driving while under the influence of accomplishment?

On the way to the celebratory dinner, Dad and I debriefed. "I should have probably stepped back a little; maybe he wouldn't have overshot it that first time. When I saw him veer a little, I thought, *Oh shit!*" he said.

"Yeah! Me too!"

"And then, when that dippy broad in the front clapped—"

"Yeah! I know! Dippy broad!"

Was this the first time my father and I had worked together on a project? He and I never built anything together. He never asked me to help him do things around the house, other than to hold a board while he sawed it with a handsaw. He did the painting. The yard work. He taught us how to bait a hook and took my sister and me fishing with him, on the rare occasions in the summer that he was off during the day and didn't have to go to court. Other than that, this was our first ever Dad and Daughter and Dog with a dummy bonding.

Had we? Bonded?

We met my sister at a local diner for some postperformance greasy-spoon food. It's a classic diner, not a place trying to *be* a diner. There were chrome-and-vinyl seats that swiveled at the counter and booths near the window. A must-stop place for politicians. There's a special chair with a plaque on the back where Bill Clinton sat once, and another where Michelle Obama lunched. Betty, our server, hovered next to our booth, pen poised, ready to take our orders. Linda and Betty knew each other from their budding low, low, low-budget indie movie careers—my sister has played a drunken Girl Scout leader, a drunken zombie, and a drunken hairdresser.

"In my next role, I play a happy suburban mother who turns into a drunken harridan. It will be my most challenging role to date," she said. "I'll take a cheeseburger."

Linda showed Betty the video of the second run. Betty was impressed. She gave my father a pat on the shoulder with her pen.

"Way to go!"

We ate and drank while the star of the show sat inside his kennel in the car, warmed by my down-filled jacket and my father's zip-in, zip-out Thinsulate liner.

I was famished. Everything on the menu looked good to me. I ordered the double-decker hamburger with cheese, seasoned curly fries, and a chocolate malt.

Mark came in from work. I had texted him and had preordered him a bacon cheeseburger with homemade potato chips. He wanted to hear all the details: Did Seamus falter? What about the collar? What were his times? Linda showed him the video.

"I—I'm impressed!" he said.

"What? You thought we couldn't do it?" I said, making room on the table for Betty to place the plates of hot, greasy wonderfulness.

"Onion rings?" said my sister, holding the plate out to the table.

"No! No. I'm just impressed, that's all."

"And what about the different emcee?" Dad said. "Ketchup?"

"I've already got ten likes on the video!" my sister said. "Maybe it will go viral; it could be the start of my career as an award-winning director!"

An old man came over to the table and asked my father if he had lived near Saint Josaphat's Basilica. Of course he had! That neighborhood was ground zero for Ciesliks. The man was a friend of my father's older brother, Jerry. They traded a few stories. Dad told him that Jerry had died back in 1988. "This is my son-in-law, my daughter, and my other daughter, whose dog just ran in the Fastest Retriever Contest at the sports show!"

Oh man! My father was tickled pink. He was glowing. I was glowing. My little plan...all those months ago... Wait, had it been my plan?

"Dad?"

"What?"

"I think Mom had something to do with there not being any stairs," I said.

Betty brought us a few Styrofoam boxes for the leftovers. Seamus would be eating later than usual, but he'd be eating chopped sirloin. We had to wait for the defroster to clear the windows from Seamus's panting. We didn't talk too much on the way back to Dad's house. There wasn't much left to talk about. That's funny, how I refer to it now as his house. It didn't feel right to keep calling it my parents' house or my mom and dad's.

I noticed that he had started to speak about Mom in the past tense, instead of, "Your mom likes it that way." I never corrected him when he had done that. I'd figured he needed time to break old habits, like Seamus had done with his hard mouth, his goofing around, his lack of focus.

I pulled into the driveway. Dad fumbled a little with his seat belt as he unbuckled. Now would be a good time to say how much fun I'd had over the past few months, how much he meant to me, or how grateful I was that he had retrained the trainer. I noticed a grimace as he slid his leg out the door. Was it his back?

"Hey, I gotta ask you something," he said.

"What? Sure. Anything. Name it," I said.

"Do you…by any chance…have Mom's knitting?"

"Uh, yeah. I do. I have her bag."

"Could you look and see if you have that dickey?"

"The one I helped Mom with?"

"Yeah, that one. Do you have it?"

"I—I think so. Why?"

"Well…when I go…I'd really like for you to put it inside my coffin."

CHAPTER THIRTY-TWO

THE TAIL END

Easter Sunday and the one-year anniversary of my mother's death crash-landed on the same day. We would mark the 365th day since Mom had crossed over with ham, au gratin potatoes, asparagus wrapped in phyllo dough, lamb cake (cake not made *from* lamb, but cake made in the *shape* of a lamb), and drinking. I had everything under control. The food. The table setting. The dog. My father called on Palm Sunday to ask me if he could bring anything in the way of more food, more potatoes, more alcohol. "You know what Sunday is? Besides Easter, don't you?"

"Yeah, Dad. I know."

"One whole year."

"Yeah."

I spent Holy Week baking ham, even though I'm not a ham fan, and making side dishes and a herd of lamb cakes. Besides my mother's apple pie dish, I had inherited her cast-iron lamb-cake molds. The last time I had used them was at her house, while she and my father sat at the kitchen table and discussed end-of-life issues with their attorney. Fun! But not as much fun as watching my sister blow a gasket after that Easter's brunch, when she found out that I had been named the Decider. She went into filibuster mode, citing her vast experience in dealing with the elderly (she worked for the department on aging) and didn't we all know she had a PhD? Yes, we did, because she constantly reminded us. "Technically, you should all be referring to me as 'Doctor.'" It was done. All legal. Papers signed. Notarized. Slamming doors and burning rubber as she left my parents' driveway did not help her cause; it only reassured my father he had chosen well.

This year, it was a nice, sunny Sunday, very springlike, which is atypical for Easter in Wisconsin. Usually Easter hops in on the back of a low-pressure system, bringing high winds and sleet. Caitlin and Angus were in town. Amanda and Linda had driven over in the same car due to an issue of someone's license being revoked because of unpaid parking tickets. New York City nephew, Adam, was somewhere in the Mediterranean, according to rumor. Amanda's husband was at home with a house full of neurotic dogs.

We sat around the table, eating, drinking, and talking. No mention of the anniversary. Talk was about Seamus and his flawless—enough for him—performance.

"So, Mom, now that you've conquered this, what's next?" I felt like my daughter was interviewing me at a postgame press conference.

"I don't know. Ham?"

"Are you and Grandpa still taking him out to the kennel club?"

"Uh, no. Potatoes?"

"No? Why not?"

We hadn't been going because…something was going on. With Dad. Whenever I'd call and suggest we go out there, he was booked. A little part of me was glad. I had dipped my toe into the dog training world; I didn't know if I wanted to jump in and get soaked.

"If only you had started training him seven years ago!" Again with the *if only*!

"Geez, Dad! Okay. Enough. I get it. Let's just say I had. What then? Would he be some kind of big deal?"

"Maybe—pass me those spuds." I had expected my father to be a bit down today, being the day it was—one year.

"He's fine!" I said passing the bowl with the gooey, crusty potatoes. The potential Big Deal was under the table, licking the crumbs off the carpet.

"Of course he's fine. *Now.* He's a different dog!" My father was right. Seamus had a different look about him, a finally-somebody-gets-me look. When he refused to abide by the heel command (rare) or the toot, toot of the whistle (rarer), I followed through with a grab of his scruff and a firm shake with a guttural "No!" The shock collar, the stick, the empty bucket were in the garage, framework for the spiderwebs.

Plates of food were passed. The ham had completed one lap of the table before it was overtaken by the asparagus, and then the inevitable comment about stinky pee was made.

Dad got up and tink-tinked his empty wineglass with his butter knife. "Attention! I'd like to thank everyone…for…all—everything. The help…" His voice broke. My chronic dry eye was suddenly not. "I couldn't have gotten through…without you guys…and—and to Seamus, for not embarrassing the family!"

We clinked our glasses all around and wiped our eyes with our napkins.

"Speaking of dogs…a woman had the cutest dog in Petco," Amanda, the parking ticket scofflaw, said.

My family's conversation zigs and zags like Seamus had done all those months ago with a training dummy. No wonder gentlemen callers have a hard time keeping up.

"Why on earth do people take their dogs into the store?! What's the point? I can see it if they have a grooming appointment. I would never take Seamus into Petco."

"Come on, Mom, never?" Angus was on his third helping of everything.

"No! Never. Could you imagine what he'd do to that snack-bar thing?" Heads nodded.

"I had to turn in my resignation." My father handed the plate of asparagus to Linda.

"From the kennel club?" I asked. Oh no. Was this the old-man-walking-off-into-the-sunset time?

"From cutting the grass in the fields." Since his old dog had been semiretired, he had taken on the duties of kennel club groundskeeper. He loved riding on that big John Deere tractor. He treated those fields with respect. He wasn't just cutting the grass because someone told him to; he cut it for the dogs. They gave their all, unconditionally. The least he could do was make sure he repaid their loyalty and hard work with a nicely cut field, but the jostling of the tractor had aggravated his arthritic back. "I was getting off the seat, and I damn near fell!"

"Dad! When are you going to admit you are eighty-three?" Linda was warming up to give him the What Happens to Old People When They Fall lecture.

"I'm eighty-*four*!" he said.

"No, you're not!" she said. "If you're eighty-four…then how old am I?"

"Aren't you pushing seventy?" I could have told her her real age (sixty-two), but what fun would that have been?

"No!" I wasn't sure if she was telling me to shut up or if she was shocked. "Wait. I am not. Am I?" she said.

"So, Dad, if you aren't cutting the grass, who is?"

"Nobody. You should see it. That field we used to run Seamus in? The grass is as tall as you."

We were ready to tear into the herd of lamb cakes. I cut a big chunk off the butt end (Dad's favorite part) of the one with the creamy white frosting made from my mother's smudged recipe.

"Not bad. Not bad," he said. I hadn't expected to be graded on the frosting. It wasn't apple pie, for crying out loud.

"I think this whole dog training idea was Mom's," I said. "Who else would have put the thought into my head? The last thing I wanted to do was grab a dead duck out of a wet dog's mouth."

"Come on. You loved it," my sister said, her mouth full of lamb cake.

No I didn't. Maybe? When I would be out with the dog, and he'd do what I told him, yeah, it made me feel like I had it all under control. And Seamus? All he wanted to do was run through the fields, jump into the ponds, but with a purpose. He needed to know he had done a good job, and isn't that what we all wanted?

There's no football game on during Easter to keep everyone around, so after brunch, my father left. "I'm going to visit your mother," he said. On Sundays after Mass, he goes to the cemetery and sits there, on the cold, cast-concrete bench. Her name is on the right. His on the left, corresponding to the same sides of the bed they slept on.

My son and daughter had a bus to catch, and my sister and her daughter had their respective doggy disorders to tend to.

I hadn't been to the cemetery since Mother's Day. It brought me no peace. I didn't feel like she was there. And seeing my father's name on the granite slab next to hers was too surreal.

Instead, I took Seamus to a field near Miller Park to keep him in retrieving shape. I could have stayed in the yard, but it was still too soft and muddy, and having Seamus running back and forth on it would have worn too many ruts.

I brought my whistle and the one white training dummy.

No kennel in the back of the car. I parked. Opened the back hatch. Told Seamus to wait. He didn't move. He sat there, doing just as I had told him to. He waited. I clipped the lead to his collar and told him to heel. He got excited once he saw the dummy in my other hand and half jumped, but I intercepted him and gave him a healthy jerk and my very best growl.

I made him sit in the middle of the field, and then I threw the dummy farther than I had planned and it landed in a prairie grass area. There was a woman walking her little bichon. They were dressed in matching outfits. They stopped. I sent Seamus, and he raced into the tall grass. It took him longer than I had expected—fifteen seconds instead of five—to find the dummy. I whistled him back, and he ran to my side and didn't quite sit before he dropped the dummy. "Good enough!" I said and gave his ears a good scratch.

We must have done three or four more retrieves before I heard the woman yell, "Excuse me!"

"Yeah?" I said. Seamus was holding a sit, stay.

"Um...what kind of toy is that?"

Wait. Did she just say toy?

"This?" I held out the dummy.

"Yeah! I've never seen a toy like that!"

"*This* is *not* a *toy*. This is a *retrieving dummy!*"

"A what?"

"*Retrieving. Dummy!*"

She said something unintelligible. To which I said, under my breath, "Dippy. Broad."

The other day, I had to scold our mail carrier for making Seamus jump up to get a treat she had pulled out of her mailbag. I have deballed the dog bin, given all the tennis balls and the baseballs Seamus found on the Hank Aaron Trail near Miller Park to my sister and Amanda. I kept the Frisbee as a reminder of what never to do again. A year ago, I would have never considered removing temptations such as these from Seamus's retrieving (or what passed for it back then) repertoire. I would have tossed him a tennis ball, and he would have bounded after it, catching it on the bounce, then would have gummed it and gotten it all foamy with his spit, making me reach into his mouth to get it. I would have thrown him a stick and he would have brought it back, chewed it until it was the size of a toothpick that he'd spit at me, and bark until I flicked it into the grass. You may think that would have been when the game was over, but he would find it, and hold it in his mouth, proud of himself.

Easter Monday, my father called. He had some bad news. "I…uh, had to put Mugsy down."

"Oh no!" *Enough death!*

"Yep, the old guy just couldn't stand up anymore—his back legs, his spine…"

"Oh, Dad!"

"Yeah, yeah. I've got some of his dog food, if you want it."

"Sure, I'll come over and get it."

When I pulled into his driveway, I expected to see the black-and-white face poking out of the garage doggie door. For the first time in…forty years? There was no dog in the kennel. No Trooper. No Belle. Duke. Buddy. Shadow.

My father was at the kitchen table, sitting in what had been my mother's place. He gripped the edge and hoisted himself up and out of the chair. He walked stiffly to the sink and took a few pills. "For my back," he said.

I told him about Seamus when I had taken him to the field, how well he had done.

"Of course!" he said. Then about the lady, how she referred to the dummy as a "toy." "Dippy broad!" he said.

He drank a glass of water.

"Hey, Dad."

"What?"

"I think you've turned me into a dog-training snob."

"I wouldn't say snob...just somebody who knows what they're doing."

For him to say... I mean... I needed a drink of water to get the lump to go down my throat.

"I gotta sit down," he said. He walked back to the chair and eased himself onto the cranberry-colored quilted pad.

First my dad without my mom, and now Dad without a dog?

"So, no puppy, then?"

"No. I don't think so. I can't... Bending... It's hard. I wouldn't be able to give a dog what it deserves."

That was hard to hear. Dad's dog days had come to an end. He had known how many dogs? Steelie. Major. Whiskers. Cinnamon. Shadow. Belle. Duke. Buddy. Trooper. Mugsy. And Seamus, by proxy. He'll have quite the pack in the afterlife. He and Mom. I'll make sure when the time comes...the dickey *and* his whistle. He'll need it.

I sat in the chair across from him, with a view of the yard where my mother hung her laundry. A tree stood where we had once put up our aboveground pool, which we took down at the end of swimming season, leaving behind a twenty-foot oval area that Dad would flood with the garden hose, making a backyard skating rink for me to pretend that I was Peggy Fleming.

We both sat there, the kitchen witch floating above our heads. We looked out the window at the lifeless, dog-less kennel. It would have been the perfect time for me to tell him that the only thing that got me out of bed all those Wednesdays ago was knowing that he'd be waiting for me in the parking lot of the kennel club. How much he had taught me. How grateful I was for the time spent…how much I loved him.

"Dad? I—I just…" I couldn't get the words out. They were stuck inside the lump in my throat. I bit my lower lip to keep from crying.

He looked at me. I could see tears in his Paul Newman–blue eyes. He sniffed, then put his weatherworn hand on mine.

"Yeah…yeah, me too."

ACKNOWLEDGMENTS

I want to thank (not in any specific order of import) my husband, Mark, for his unwavering support; Mr. Lamb Free; the West Allis Training and Kennel Club; and Doug and Patti Kennedy of Waterdog Specialties, because without them and Linamia's Worth the Wait and Waterdog's Zoey, Seamus wouldn't be here.

I also have to thank Elmbrook Veterinary Clinic and Dr. Bob Marold, for his endless patience and intimate knowledge of Seamus's digestive tract; the Wisconsin Veterinary Referral Center; the hex-a-bumper designer; the inventor of the e-collar; my son, Angus, and my daughter Caitlin, for being the wonderful offspring any mother would want; my sister, Linda because if I didn't thank her, she'd hold it against me and I wouldn't get the cuckoo clock; Amanda Stys—hopefully she won't need therapy after the Fighting Bob Lafollette incident; Adam Deer; Robert Vaughan, my writing guru; all the Red Oak writers; my agent, Kathy Green; Nanette Varian; Mr. Wallace Grey; Shana Drehs, Grace Menary-Winefield, and the team at Sourcebooks; and, of course, I have to thank my father, the guy who had to put up with my girlish whistle technique, whose knowledge of a certain Labrador retriever's brain will never be forgotten, and I can't forget my mother—I swear, she was the one who gave me the idea to get Dad and me and dog together. I'd say I love you all, but we're not a big "I love you" family.

ABOUT THE AUTHOR

Mel C. Miskimen is a contributor to *Huff/Post50* and the Moth story-telling events. She's had essays published in the *Irish American Post*, *Rosebud* literary magazine, and *FETCH Magazine,* and she was a 2014 cast member of the "Listen to Your Mother" live show. She has won the Wisconsin Regional Writers Association Florence Lindemann award and the WRWA's Jade Ring. She is a frequent guest essayist on Wisconsin Public Radio.